Mountain Biking North America's Best 100 Ski Resorts

TOM STILLO PHOTO COURTESY CRESTED BUTTE MOUNTAIN RESORT

MOUNTAIN BIKING

North America's
BEST 100 SKI RESORTS

by

Delaine Fragnoli

Fine Edge Productions

ACKNOWLEDGEMENTS

I would like to thank all the ski resort, bike park, and lodge personnel who took the time to answer my questions, respond to my questionnaire, and provide slides and media kits. Thanks also to Don Douglass for believing in this project, Sue Irwin for her design work, and Tim Blumenthal for his comprehensive foreword. As always, my biggest thank you goes to Jim MacIntyre for his love and support, even when it seemed this project would never end.

Delaine Fragnoli
Altadena, California
June 1996

COVER DESIGN: Laura Patterson Design, Mammoth Lakes, CA
BOOK DESIGN, LAYOUT, AND MAPS: Eastside Desktop Publishing, Carpinteria, CA

IMPORTANT LEGAL NOTICE AND DISCLAIMER

Mountain biking is a potentially dangerous sport, and the rider or user of this book accepts a number of unavoidable risks. Trails by nature have numerous natural and man-made hazards; they are generally not signed or patrolled and they change with time and conditions.

While substantial effort has been made to provide accurate information, this guidebook may inadvertently contain errors and omissions. Any maps in this book are for locator reference only. They are not to be used for navigation. Your mileages will vary from those given in this book. Contact resort or lodge personnel before attempting routes to check for suitability and trail conditions.

The editors, authors, contributors, publishers and distributors accept no liability for any errors or omissions in this book or for any injuries or losses incurred from using this book.

LIBRARY OF CONGRESS CATALOGING-IN-PUBLICATION DATA

Fragnoli, Delaine, 1962–
Mountain biking North America's best 100 ski resorts / by Delaine Fragnoli.
p. cm.
Includes index.
ISBN 0-938665-46-4
1. All terrain cycling–United States. 2. All terrain cycling—Canada.
3. Ski resorts—United States. 4. Ski resorts—Canada.
I. Title.
GV1045.F73 1996
796.6'4'097–dc20 96-15086
CIP

ISBN 0-938665-46-4

Fine Edge Productions, Route 2, Box 303, Bishop, CA 93514

Table of Contents

Foreword, *by Tim Blumenthal* 9
Ski Resort Mountain Biking: A Little History, *by Bill Cockroft* 11
Introduction 12
About This Book 12
Special Considerations 14

CHAPTER 1: THE PACIFIC NORTHWEST

Alaska
Alyeska Resort 17

Washington
Crystal Mountain 18
MAP: Washington 19
Mountain Home Lodge 20
Mt. Spokane State Park 21
Ski Acres Mountain Bike and Hiking Center 23
Sun Mountain Lodge/Methow Valley Sport Trails Association 24

Oregon
MAP: Oregon 26
Mt. Bachelor Ski and Summer Resort 27
Mt. Hood Ski Bowl Winter and Summer Resort 28

Idaho
Brundage Mountain 31
MAP: Idaho 32
Galena Lodge 33
Hill's Resort 35
Schweitzer Mountain Resort 36
Silver Mountain Ski and Summer Resort 38
Sun Valley Resort 38

CHAPTER 2: THE WEST

California
Bear Valley Cross-Country Ski and Adventure Company 39
Donner Ski Ranch 40
Mammoth Mountain Ski Area/Mammoth Mountain Bike Park 41
MAP: California and Western Nevada 44
Mt. Shasta Ski Park 46
Mt. Waterman Ski Resort 47
Northstar-At-Tahoe 49
North Tahoe Regional Park Trail System 51
Ski Homewood 51
Snow Summit Mountain Resort 53
Squaw Valley, USA 55

Nevada
Diamond Peak Ski Resort at Incline Village/Crystal Bay 57

CHAPTER 3: THE ROCKIES

Montana
The Big Mountain Ski and Summer Resort ... 59
MAP: Montana and Wyoming ... 60
Maverick Mountain ... 61

Wyoming
Grand Targhee Ski and Summer Resort ... 63

Colorado
Aspen ... 65
Beaver Creek ... 67
MAP: Colorado ... 68
Breckenridge Ski Resort ... 69
Copper Mountain Resort ... 71
Crested Butte Mountain Resort ... 72
Keystone Resort ... 74
Latigo Ranch ... 77
Monarch Ski Resort ... 77
Purgatory Resort ... 79
SilverCreek Ski Area ... 81
Snowmass ... 83
Steamboat ... 84
Telluride and the San Juan Hut System ... 87
10th Mountain Division Hut Association ... 90
Vail ... 90
Vista Verde ... 92
Winter Park Resort ... 93

CHAPTER 4: THE SOUTHWEST

Utah
Brian Head Resort ... 95
Deer Valley Resort ... 98
Elk Meadows Ski and Summer Resort ... 99
The Homestead ... 100
MAP: Utah ... 100
Park City Ski Area ... 101
Snowbird Ski and Summer Resort ... 102
Solitude Ski Resort ... 103

Arizona
Flagstaff Nordic Center ... 105
MAP: Arizona ... 106
Sunrise Park Resort ... 106

New Mexico
Angel Fire Resort ... 108
Sandia Peak Ski Company ... 110
MAP: New Mexico ... 110
Sipapu Lodge and Ski Area ... 112
Ski Rio ... 113

CHAPTER 5: THE SOUTH

North Carolina
- Sugar Mountain Resort ... 115
- MAP: The South ... 116

Virginia
- Wintergreen Resort ... 117

West Virginia
- Snowshoe Mountain Resort ... 119

Kentucky
- Ski Butler/Bike Butler ... 121

Florida
- Hardrock Mountain Bike Park/Gone Riding! ... 123
- MAP: Northeastern Florida ... 123

CHAPTER 6: THE MIDWEST

Minnesota
- Buck Hill Ski Area ... 125
- Giants Ridge Resort ... 126
- MAP: Minnesota ... 127
- Golden Eagle Lodge, Inc. ... 128
- Lutsen Mountain Bike Park ... 129

Wisconsin
- Chequamegon Area Mountain Bike Association (CAMBA) Trail System ... 131
- MAP: Wisconsin, Michigan, and Ontario ... 132
- Levis Mounds/Bruce Mound ... 133
- Paust's Woods Lake Resort, Inc. ... 134
- Pines and Mines Mountain Bike Trail System ... 135

Michigan
- Shanty Creek ... 136
- Vasa Trail ... 138

CHAPTER 7: MID-ATLANTIC STATES

Pennsylvania
- Hidden Valley ... 141
- MAP: Mid-Atlantic States ... 142
- The Inn at Starlight Lake ... 143
- Whitetail Ski Resort and Mountain Bike Center ... 144

Maryland
- Wisp Four Seasons Resort ... 146

New York
- The Bark Eater Inn ... 148
- Garnet Hill Lodge and Cross-Country Ski Center ... 148
- Holiday Valley Resort ... 150
- Ski Plattekill Mountain Biking Center ... 152

Connecticut
- Woodbury Ski and Racquet ... 154

CHAPTER 8: THE NORTHEAST

Vermont
Bolton Valley Resort/Mountain Bike and Adventure Center 155
MAP: The Northeast 156
The Outdoor Experience at Catamount Family Center 157
Craftsbury Nordic Ski Center 158
Killington Resort 160
Mount Snow Resort 162
Stratton Mountain Resort 164

New Hampshire
Attitash Bear Peak Cranmore Resort 166
Gunstock 168
Mt. Sunapee Ski Area and State Park 169
Waterville Valley Ski Area Ltd./Base Camp Adventure Center 170

Maine
Back Country Excursions 172
Lost Valley Mountain Bike Center 173
Sunday River Mountain Bike Park 175
Troll Valley Cross-Country Ski and Fitness Center 177

CHAPTER 9: CANADA

British Columbia
Silver Star Mountain Resort 179
MAP: British Columbia and Alberta 180
Whistler Resort/Blackcomb Ski Resort 181

Alberta
Canmore Nordic Center 182

Ontario
Searchmont Resort 183

Quebec
Mont-Sainte-Anne 185
MAP: Quebec 186

APPENDIX

IMBA Rules of the Trail 190
Resorts Offering Lift-Served Mountain Biking 191
Unconfirmed Programs 192
Upcoming Programs 197
Discontinued Programs 199
The Care and Feeding of a Mountain Bike, *by R. W. Miskimins* 200
Basic Skills for Mountain Biking, *by R. W. Miskimins* 202
Resources 205
Resort Index 206
Map Index 207
Outdoor Publications from Fine Edge Productions 208

Foreword

BY TIM BLUMENTHAL

If you wanted to create the perfect mountain biking resort, here's what might appear on your shopping list:

- a large parcel of land with woods, meadows, and hills;
- a relatively flat, central base area for lodging, restaurants, and bike rental/repair facilities;
- trail-building machinery and trail maintenance tools;
- an outdoors-minded staff skilled in marketing, hospitality, trail construction, emergency medical care, and search and rescue procedures;
- a scenic location within easy driving distance of a major city.

Most of North America's 400-plus ski resorts already boast every one of these attributes. While nearly all were designed for winter sports, many are practically perfect for mountain biking. As off-road cycling has boomed, more than 150 resorts have initiated mountain biking programs, and most have found the fat-tire business to be the ideal warm-weather complement to skiing.

What powers these off-road cycling programs is mountain biking's continued growth. Nearly five million mountain bikes are sold to U.S. adults each year, and the number of off-road cycling enthusiasts has climbed from 200,000 in '83 to more than 10 million today.

Earlier I said that ski areas are *practically* perfect for mountain biking. Why the qualifier? Nearly all ski areas are fairly steep, with anywhere from 150 to 5,000 feet of sharp elevation relief between base and summit. In the West, many ski resorts are situated high in the mountains with base elevations a mile or more above sea level. Mix steeps with high altitude and the result is tough cycling.

Ski areas answer this concern in three ways. First, they offer lift-serviced mountain biking that allows you to skip the heavy-breathing uphills and move directly to the thrills of gravity-assisted downhill riding. (Mountain biking purists may cringe, but this is how thousands of people first experience our sport.) Second, resorts construct new trails that meander through the base area, creating easy loops with minimal elevation gain. Third, new trails are built that climb the mountain, but do so gradually, thanks to the use of gentle switchbacks that take some of the sting out of the ascent.

Nearly all ski areas charge a fee for mountain biking on their land. This is true whether you use their lifts or not. You're paying for regular maintenance, accurate signage, a reliable map, and often the work of a bike patrol. This fee is usually reasonable and appropriate.

As the executive director of the International Mountain Bicycling Association (IMBA), I represent a broad-based group that is committed to improving mountain biking opportunities *everywhere* it makes sense—city, county, and state parks, state and national forests and parks, Bureau of Land Management (BLM) territory, and ski resorts. We are enthusiastic about ski area cycling, but certainly don't want fee-paying mountain biking to be the *only* option for off-road cyclists. Our commitment includes preserving and improving trail access for cyclists closer to home.

TOM STILLO PHOTO COURTESY CRESTED BUTTE MOUNTAIN RESORT

Don't misunderstand me, though. Mountain biking at ski areas has added so much to our sport and seems certain only to improve. After all, people are always looking for new scenic, exciting, and varied places to ride. Ski area trails provide this...and the creature comforts at the base are usually superb.

It's true that ski areas can and do provide mountain bikers precisely this type of opportunity, and it's one that is much appreciated by riders all over our continent. But for convenience and, most important, for variety of experience, mountain biking access must continue on narrow riverside trails, on desert loops lined by cacti, in city parks beneath the shadows of old hardwoods, and on the rolling trails of grass-hilled watersheds.

IMBA is also committed to a shared-trails philosophy. We want mountain bikers, hikers, and horseback riders to share trails wherever possible. This strategy disperses use and impact, improves communication among different trail user groups, and unifies the groups of people who are committed to trails and open space preservation.

Delaine is a highly skilled cyclist and best-selling author. With this useful, timely guidebook, she'll help you savor your next ski area ride. Take a deep breath of pure mountain air.... How lucky we are to have so many fantastic places to ride. Have fun!

Tim Blumenthal
Executive Director, IMBA

Tim Blumenthal is executive director of IMBA. Previously an editor for Mountain Bike Magazine *and* Bicycling Magazine, *he serves as consultant to NBC Sports for their Olympic cycling coverage.*

Ski Resort Mountain Biking: A Little History

BY BILL COCKROFT

In the summer of 1985, I met Don Douglass at the Main Lodge sun deck of Mammoth Mountain Ski Area. An avid skinny-tire cyclist at the time, I was taken aback as Don challenged me to create a race that would be held on the ski slopes before us. Little did we know this meeting would also lead the transformation of dormant summertime ski areas into active recreation centers called mountain bike parks.

Don was asking me to add a mountain biking venue to the Whiskey Creek Stage Race in Mammoth Lakes—a road cycling event that I and others had already been promoting for a couple of years. He knew that Mammoth Mountain was a natural location for downhill racing. The result? One of the most famous mountain bike legends to this day—the Mammoth Mountain Kamikaze. Before that first meeting was over, we had established the name, the race, and a piece of mountain biking history. We joined forces that summer and combined road, mountain, and BMX bicycling into a one-weekend event, with Don as the race director and sponsor of the Kamikaze. It was the first-ever mountain biking event to use ski lifts.

With the birth of the Kamikaze, we knew that riding on knobby tires was going to be a revolution. We had caught the beginning of a huge mountain bike wave that wouldn't begin to crest for another decade. The 1985 inaugural Kamikaze was successful, but it was the growth of the event the following year that overwhelmed us. We realized then the untapped potential of recreational mountain biking as a summer alternative for ski resorts. Don went on to help found the International Mountain Bicycling Association (IMBA), serving as its first president, and by 1988 Mammoth Mountain was able to boast one of the first formal mountain bike parks at a ski area, including uphill lift service and singletrack trails specifically designed for recreational mountain bike use. Today, well over a hundred ski areas utilize their facilities during summer months for mountain biking.

I have continued to work on a volunteer basis with USA Cycling to promote cycling and races, and the acceptance of mountain biking as an Olympic event is my reward. I am pleased with the growth this great sport has enjoyed. The Mammoth Mountain event has become the largest in the country, mountain bike parks at ski areas are now more the norm than the exception, and best of all, mountain biking has become the sport of millions of enthusiasts.

Bill Cockroft is the Director of Mountain Operations at Mammoth Mountain Ski Area. He has promoted and produced many major cycling events, including World Cups and World Championships. Don Douglass and his wife Réanne own Fine Edge Productions, the publisher of this and other fine outdoor guides and maps (see page 208). Both Don and Bill have been inducted into the Mountain Biking Hall of Fame as pioneers of the sport.

Introduction

Back in 1985 when mountain bike racers first hurtled themselves down Mammoth Mountain's "Kamikaze," they unknowingly launched a trend that is still accelerating today—ski resort mountain biking. Ski resorts quickly became popular race venues, but it took a bit longer for them to begin catering to the recreational off-road cyclist.

By 1991, *Mountain Bike Action* estimated that out of 596 ski resorts in the United States, roughly 10% to 15% were offering mountain biking programs in the summer. A survey by *Bicycling* magazine in the same year recorded fewer than 20 ski resort-based mountain bike parks. But four years later, *Bicycling* profiled 122 resorts with some kind of mountain biking services.

As Tim Blumenthal points out in the Foreword, ski resorts should not become the only places open to mountain bicyclists, but they are certainly ideal locations for racing and learning to ride. Ski resort terrain is uniquely suitable for downhill racing, and many of the West's top resorts caught onto lift-served riding very quickly. In recent years, the trend has moved eastward, and many smaller areas and cross-country ski lodges have realized that mountain bikers are the perfect summer users for their trail systems.

The rocketing popularity of mountain biking brings with it a staggering variety of mountain biking services. Enterprising resorts have realized that their ski shops and ski schools can be converted into bike shops and off-road cycling schools in the summer. Now the neophyte cyclist can rent a bike, take a lesson, and learn about the sport within the relative safety and comfort of a resort area.

Adding to the appeal of ski resort mountain biking are the off-season rates offered by most ski areas. Lodging is considerably cheaper in summer than in winter, and many resorts have lodging and lift or rental packages for cyclists.

About This Book

This guide is the first attempt to detail these programs and services in book format. Where can the downhill fanatic find the most lift-served vertical? Where can families find the best package deals? Where can a beginner rent a bike and take lessons? Inside these pages you will find the most comprehensive listing to date of the mountain biking services available at over 150 ski areas, lodges, resorts, and mountain biking parks and centers, along with supplemental information about the areas' other amenities, attractions and activities.

In preparing this book, we contacted over 200 U.S. and Canadian resorts that were known or rumored to have mountain biking services. Then we sent each resort a standardized questionnaire, along with a request for their logo and photographs of the area. Entry length and thoroughness of information is solely based on what was provided to us by the resorts.

Resorts that did not respond or that responded with incomplete information are listed in an appendix, "Unconfirmed Programs." Other appendices list programs that are in the development stage, programs that have been discontinued, resorts offering lift-served biking, and an alphabetical index of the resorts.

For the purposes of this book, we have defined "ski resort" rather loosely. In addition to full fledged downhill resorts, we have included cross-country lodges, inns, and Nordic centers that cater to mountain bicyclists, several trail networks and hut systems, and a few mountain bike parks/centers—even one in Florida that has no skiing at all in winter. The litmus test for inclusion was whether or not the "resort" in question had a trail network of some kind, provided facilities for mountain bikers, and would make a good weekend or week-long mountain bike vacation destination. This variety provides more options for meeting your particular needs and tastes, and it reflects the tremendous diversity of mountain biking experiences available today.

The chapters represent geographic regions, and each chapter is divided into sections for each state or province. Resorts are listed alphabetically under each state/province heading.

Within each listing, an introductory paragraph gives a brief overview of the resort. Next, the "Location, Hours, and Prices" section provides nuts-and-bolts information about the resort and includes travel directions, biking season, elevation, and regulations. This is followed by "The Rides," a section describing the terrain and giving statistics about trail mileage, vertical drop, trail ratings, etc.—everything you need to decide if a resort's cycling terrain is right for you. (Please see "Special Considerations" in the front portion of the book for important safety information.) The final section, "Local Services," provides information on lodging, dining, and other services, and gives you additional sources for planning your trip.

Throughout the text, we have used certain abbreviations:

IMBA—International Mountain Bicycling Association

K—kilometer

NORBA—National Off-Road Bicycling Association (America's race-sanctioning body)

TBA—to be announced

TBD—to be determined

A note about prices and dates: We have included 1996 prices and dates, and these are likely to change before we print a second edition of this book. After 1996, use price and date information as guidelines to give you an idea of the events held at each resort and the resort's general pricing structure. Please call the resorts if you need more specific information.

Since ski resort mountain biking is a fast-growing and fast-changing recreation trend, we urge you to contact the resorts you are interested in for the latest information on their facilities. While we have made every effort to ensure that the information contained here is accurate and up-to-date, please be aware that services and prices may change. In particular, construction and maintenance programs may temporarily alter a resort's services.

Whether you are a downhill fiend in search of the ultimate gravity fix or a stop-and-smell-the-roses bike tourist, you can find fun and affordable adventure within these pages. And if we've missed your favorite resort, drop us a note and tell us about it. At the rate mountain biking is growing, there's sure to be more ski resort programs opening in the near future. That can only mean more fun and adventure for you.

Special Considerations

Although ski resort mountain biking provides a certain sense of security (trails are usually marked and rated, guides are available, and first aid and bicycle repair is often nearby), that does not relieve you of your responsibility to ride in a safe and courteous manner. To enhance your pleasure and safety, we ask that you observe the following special considerations:

1. **Courtesy.** Many areas have multi-use trails, and in addition to hikers and horseback riders, you may encounter ski resort maintenance vehicles on some roads. Extend courtesy to all other trail users and follow the golden rule. Please observe the IMBA Rules of the Trail.

2. **Preparation.** Plan your trip carefully; develop and use a checklist. Know your equipment, your ability, and the area in which you are riding, and prepare accordingly. If you are new to off-road cycling, consider hiring a guide and renting the necessary equipment. Aim for self-sufficiency, wear a helmet (helmets are mandatory at most resorts, and can usually be rented), keep your bike in good repair, and carry necessary gear for changes in weather or other conditions.

3. **Mountain Conditions.** Many ski resorts, particularly in the West, provide extremes in elevation, climate, and terrain. While many resorts have first-aid facilities and even bike patrols, you should still be prepared to deal with dehydration, hypothermia, altitude sickness, sunburn, and heatstroke. Watch for the following conditions:

Intense Sun: Protect your skin against the sun's harmful rays by wearing light-colored, long-sleeved shirts or jerseys. Some of the rides in this book are at relatively high altitude, and the higher you go, the more damaging the sun becomes. Use sunscreen with a sufficient rating. Wear sunglasses that offer adequate protection. Guard against heatstroke by riding in the early morning or late afternoon when the sun's rays are least intense.

Low Humidity: East-facing slopes and high elevation usually have low humidity. To avoid headaches or cramps, start each trip with a minimum of two or more full quart water bottles. (*Gallons* of water may not be sufficient for *really* hot weather or hard rides.) Force yourself to drink before you feel thirsty. Carry water from a known source or treat water gathered from springs, streams, and lakes. Untreated drinking water may cause giardiasis or other diseases.

Variations in Temperature and Weather Conditions: Carry extra clothing—a windbreaker, gloves, stocking cap—and use the multi-layer system so you can quickly adapt to different weather conditions. Afternoon thundershowers occur frequently in the high country, so keep an eye on changing cloud and wind conditions and prepare accordingly.

Fatigue: Sluggish or cramping muscles and fatigue indicate the need for calories and liquids. Although many ski resorts have snack bars, it's wise to carry high-energy snack foods such as granola bars, dried fruits, and nuts with you to maintain strength and warmth. To conserve energy, add clothing layers as the temperature drops or the wind increases.

Closures: At ski resorts, trails may be closed periodically for maintenance, special events, or other reasons. Please check ahead of time with ski resort personnel, and observe any such closures. Mountain and foothill areas may also be closed to the public during times of high fire danger, during hunting season, or because of logging activity.

4. **Navigation.** Any maps in this book are not intended for navigation but as guides. Most resorts publish trail maps, which we recommend you carry and use. Make sure you understand the map before you take off. If you're confused, ask resort personnel, or consider taking a guided tour. Some resorts require that you sign in before you use their trail system. Even if a resort doesn't, it's wise to tell someone where you're going, when you expect to return, and what to do in case you don't return on time.

5. **Horses and Pack Animals.** Some of the trails described in this book are open to recreational horse riders as well as cyclists and hikers. Some horses spook easily, so make them aware of your presence with a friendly greeting or bell *well in advance of the encounter.* A startled horse can cause serious injuries both to an inexperienced rider and to itself.

If you come upon horses moving *toward* you, yield the right-of-way, even when it seems inconvenient. Carry your bike to the downhill side and stand quietly, well off the trail in a spot where the animals can see you clearly. If you come upon horses *moving ahead of you in the same direction,* stop well behind them. Do not attempt to pass until you have alerted the riders and asked for permission. Then, pass on the downhill side of the trail, talking to the horse and rider as you do. It is your responsibility to ensure that such encounters are safe for everyone. Do not disturb grazing sheep or cattle.

6. **Respect the Environment.** Many ski resorts go out of their way to meet and exceed environmental and Forest Service regulations. Help them by minimizing your impact on the natural environment. Remember, *mountain bikes are not allowed in Wilderness Areas* (some ski areas in this book border on Wilderness Areas) *and in certain other restricted areas.* Leave plants and animals alone; historic and cultural sites untouched. Stay on established roads and trails, do not create any new ones, and do not enter private property. Follow posted instructions and use good common sense. Resorts may close some trails because of trail and weather conditions. Respect these closures.

7. **Control and Safety.** Crashes usually don't cause serious injury, but they occasionally can and do. Stay under control and slow down for the unexpected. Wear protective gear—helmets, gloves, and glasses—to protect yourself from scrapes and impacts with rocks, dirt, and brush. Guard against excessive speed. Avoid overheated rims and brakes on long or steep downhill rides. Lower your center of gravity by lowering your seat on downhills. Lower your tire pressure on rough or sandy stretches.

Most ski areas rate their trails and slopes (easiest, more difficult, most difficult), but some do not. Please note that these ratings are relative to that particular area. A "more difficult" trail at one area might be harder than a "most difficult" trail at another area. Some of these difficulty ratings are based on the skiing difficulty of the trail, which is not always a good measure of the mountain biking difficulty. Ask resort personnel for guidance, and be conser-

PHOTO COURTESY INCLINE VILLAGE/CRYSTAL BAY V'CB

vative until you get a feel for the difficulty of a particular resort. Study the trail map and read any other safety material before selecting a route.

Quite a few ski resorts now offer lift-served or gondola-served mountain biking. Many areas only allow resort personnel to load and unload bikes. Follow the lift operator's safety instructions for loading and unloading yourself and your bike. Obey all posted instructions as well.

Unfortunately, some would-be downhill racers see lift-served mountain biking as an invitation to "shred." Remember, you are likely to encounter other mountain bikers and trail users, so please behave accordingly. At ski resorts, the easiest trails are often at the bottom of the mountain. Thus, if you are an advanced rider, be aware when you enter easier terrain, and watch out for slower, less-skilled riders. As in skiing, it is the rider coming up from behind who is responsible for avoiding a collision. Also, although some resorts designate one-way trails, you may encounter two-way traffic on some trails.

8. **Trailside Bike Repair.** While many resorts now have bike shops with repair facilities, you will still want to carry some basic tools for minor trailside repair: pump, spare tube, patches, 2 tubes of patch glue, 6" adjustable wrench, Allen wrenches, chain tool, and spoke wrench. Correct tire inflation, wide tires, and avoiding rocks and other trail hazards will prevent most flats. Grease, lube, and proper adjustment prevent most technical failures. Frequent stream crossings wash out chain lube, so carry extra if you are in a wet area.

9. **First Aid.** Although many resorts have emergency facilities, you still need to carry basic first-aid items. If you have allergies, be sure to bring your medicine. Sunscreen and insect repellent will increase your comfort. Bring bandages and ointments for cuts and scrapes, and aspirin for aches that won't go away. Additional first-aid items you might carry in your kit are antiseptic swabs, moleskin, a single-edged razor blade, a needle, elastic bandage, Tums or other stomach remedy, and waterproof matches.

CHAPTER 1

THE PACIFIC NORTHWEST

Alaska

Alyeska Resort

1000 Arlberg Avenue, P.O. Box 249
Girdwood, AK 99587
(800) 775-6656
(907) 754-1111

While Alyeska Resort does not consider itself a mountain biking resort, it does make a good base for exploring the surrounding area. Just 40 miles south of Anchorage via the scenic Seward Highway, Alyeska is on the way to the Portage Glacier and the Kenai Peninsula, where there are quite a few good trails for mountain biking. Within one hour of the resort there are several mountain biking trails, with 5 to 50 miles of singletrack for all levels of riders (and without high altitude— the summit is just 3,939').

Recommended rides includes Bird Trail, Resurrection Trail, Resurrection Pass (upper intermediate), Johnson Trail (some technical sections), and Powerline Pass. Two miles from the resort is Crow Creek Road, a 7-mile gravel road with a steady grade that offers a good workout without technical terrain. It ends at Crow Pass Trail, where you can access more technical terrain. Biking season is mid-May through mid-September. The resort rents cruiser bikes, and other rentals are available in the nearby town of Girdwood. The tram operates year-round, but does not allow bikes. Lodging and dining are available at the 307-room chateau-style Westin Alyeska Prince Hotel.

PHOTO COURTESY ALYESKA RESORT

Washington

Crystal Mountain

One Crystal Mountain Road
Crystal Mountain, WA 98022
(360) 663-2265

Located in the shadow of Mt. Rainier, Crystal Mountain offers a wealth of summer activities: beginner to expert mountain biking, romantic sunset dinners at the Summit House, hiking, fishing, and scenic chairlift rides.

Location, Hours, Prices

General Location: In the Mount Baker/Snoqualmie National Forest on the northeast boundary of Mt. Rainier National Park, 76 miles southeast of Seattle

Getting There: From Seattle, take I-5 south to Exit 142A (Route 18) to Enumclaw/Auburn exit (Route 164). Follow Route 164 to Enumclaw and Route 410 east for 33 miles to the Crystal Mountain turnoff, just before entering Rainier National Park. Drive 6 miles up Crystal Mountain Boulevard to the resort.

Biking Season: Late June–early Sept.

Elevation: Base 4,400′; summit 7,012′

Hours: Weekdays 10–8; weekends 10–9

Prices: $10/adult one ride, $7/senior and junior one ride; $18/adult all day, $12/senior and junior all day; $60/adult summer season pass, $40/senior and junior summer season pass; children 6 and under free

Regulations/Restrictions: Helmets required; mandatory dismount to yield to horses. Chairlifts provide access to upper intermediate and advanced terrain, but Rainier Express does not upload bikes.

The Rides

Mountain bikers will find beginning and intermediate terrain in the base area and in the valley below the base. For more skilled riders, chairlifts provide access to upper intermediate and advanced terrain.

Terrain Description: Combination

Mileage/Number of Trails: 35 miles of singletrack, doubletrack, and access roads

Difficulty: Approximately 15% easiest, 40% more difficult, 45% most difficult

Trails Under Development: No new trails are under development at this time, but a chairlift (Chair 5 Campbell Basin) has been opened for the first time, taking bikers to 6,100′.

Recommended Trails: Singletrack Silver Creek Trail (intermediate/advanced); Circuit Course is ideal training for any bike race, featuring steeps and a 1,900′ rise in 1.5 miles.

Mountain Bike Lifts: 3

Trails Accessible from Lifts: Not indicated

Biggest Vertical Drop: 1,900′ from lift; 3,200′ possible without lift ride

Longest Trail: Possible to ride from top of highest chair to bottom of valley, 8 miles

Other Local Trails: Crystal Mountain trails access others on the Mt. Baker/Snoqualmie National Forest.

Trail Map: Available in summer

Local Services

Crystal Mountain offers plenty of services for cyclists and other vacationers, and its proximity to Seattle is a bonus for travelers who enjoy the excitement, events, and activities of an upbeat urban center.

Mountain Bike Services: Equipment rentals at main lodge; prices TBD

Special Events: None at this time

Emergency Facilities: On-site heli-pad and patrol room; EMT on call

Accommodations: Call 360/663-2558 for lodging information.

Dining: Beautiful sunset dinners in the Summit House (6,872') at the top of Rainier Express Chairlift offer a breathtaking view of Mt. Rainier. Breakfast and dinner is served in the main lodge.

Off-the-Bike Activities: Horseshoe tournament, July 20–21, 1996; golf tournament; tennis; basketball; volleyball; horseback riding permitted; hiking; scenic chairlift rides; sunset dining

Other Services and Features: Crystal Mountain claims the most terrain and vertical of any ski area in the state of Washington.

PHOTO COURTESY TEAM BIG BEAR/SNOW SUMMIT MOUNTAIN RESORT

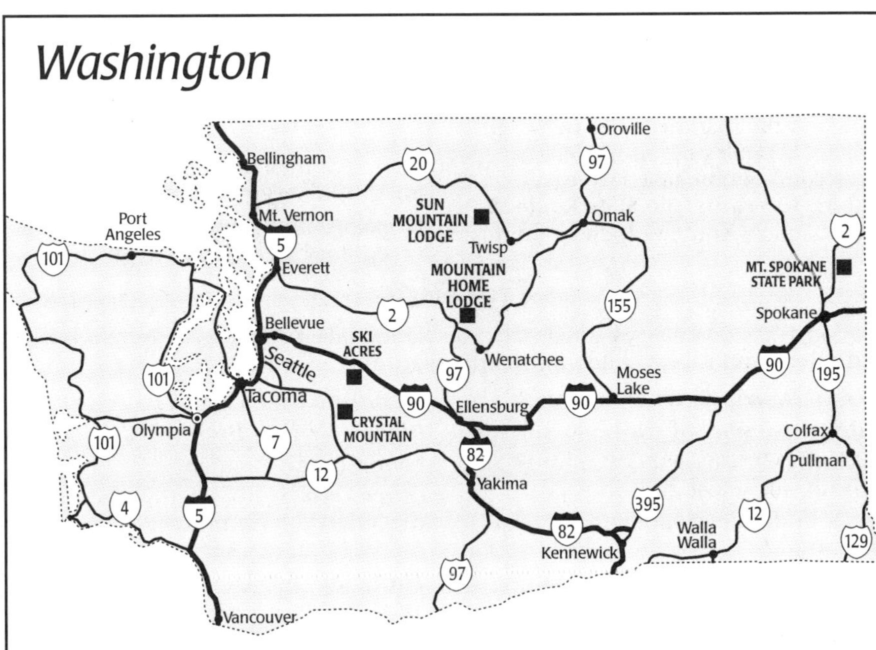

Mountain Home Lodge

P.O. Box 687
Leavenworth, WA 98826
(800) 414-2378
(509) 548-7077
(509) 548-5008 (fax)

Secluded in its own alpine valley above the village of Leavenworth, Mountain Home Lodge boasts a spectacular setting, including views of the Stuart Range of the Cascades. Often hailed as one of the Northwest's most romantic getaways, the lodge offers an array of outdoor activities, from mountain biking to tennis. Wildlife, including elk, deer, bear, and eagles, is plentiful. After a day in the saddle, try the hot tub and first-class cuisine.

Location, Hours, and Prices

General Location: 2½ hours due east of Seattle on the east slope of the Cascades

Getting There: From Seattle, you can get to the Lodge via Stevens Pass or Snoqualmie Pass/Blewett Pass. For the first option, pass through Leavenworth on Highway 2 to the bridge over the Wenatchee River. Turn right on East Leavenworth Road, then left on Mountain Home Road. The pavement ends and the road becomes rustic. The lodge is 2.5 miles up on the left. For the second option, take I–90 east to Exit 85. This turns into State Route 97 North. Follow Route 97 to State Route 2 West. Turn left toward Leavenworth. Just before crossing the bridge across the Wenatchee River, turn left onto East Leavenworth Road. Turn left on Mountain Home Road and follow it 2.5 miles to the lodge.

Biking Season: Late April–end of October

Elevation: Base 1,000′; resort 2,000′; summit 5,800′

Hours: Daily, 7:00 a.m.–10:00 p.m.

Prices: No charge for mountain bikers staying at the lodge; nominal charge for shuttle service

Regulations/Restrictions: None except for Forest Service regulations

The Rides

The lodge sits on 20 acres surrounded by National Forest land. The terrain is fairly steep and is best suited for intermediate and advanced cyclists.

Terrain Description: Combination

Mileage/Number of Trails: 40 miles

Difficulty: 10% easiest, 50% more difficult, 40% most difficult

Trails Under Development: All trails are complete.

Recommended Trails: Mountain Home Road (beginner); Boundary Butte (intermediate); Helicopter Pad (advanced)

Mountain Bike Lifts: None

Biggest Vertical Drop: 3,100′

Longest Trail: 16 miles

Other Local Trails: All trails begin at the lodge and connect with the Wenatchee National Forest trail system.

Trail Map: Available from the two local ranger districts. The lodge provides these maps and a trail map of lodge trails to registered guests.

Local Services

Lodging and dining are on-site at the lodge, while rental bikes, equipment, and guided adventure tours are available in the town of Leavenworth.

Mountain Bike Services: Full equipment rental is available nearby. Call the lodge for current price list.

Special Events: None at this time

Emergency Facilities: Helicopter service to Wenatchee and Leavenworth hospitals

Accommodations: At the lodge

Dining: Room rates include breakfast. Gourmet lunch and 4-course dinner (not included in room rates) are served daily in the lodge.

Off-the-Bike Activities: Hiking, whitewater rafting, horseback riding, fishing, swimming, and tennis.

Other Services and Features: In winter, guests arrive by snowcat and can enjoy a 1,700′ sledding hill, cross-country skiing, and snowmobiling.

WENDY CRAGG PHOTO

Mt. Spokane State Park

N. 26107 Mt. Spokane Park Drive
Mead, WA 99021
(509) 456-4169

The first Washington State Park established east of the Cascades, Mt. Spokane State Park attracts winter enthusiasts who come to cross-country ski, downhill ski, snowmobile, and sled. In the summer, this same terrain beckons to hikers, cyclists, and horseback riders. A trip to the top of Mt. Spokane rewards you with views into Washington, Idaho, Montana, and Canada.

Location, Hours, and Prices

General Location: Northeast of Spokane, 1 hour from airport

Getting There: From the Spokane airport, go east on I-90. Take the Division Street exit and go north on Division to Highway 2. Follow Highway 2 to Highway 206 (approximately 15 miles) and go right to Mt. Spokane

Biking Season: Park is open year round, but June–September is best for biking.

Elevation: Base 3,200′; summit 5,883′

Hours: Open daily; summer hours 6:30–dusk (about 10 p.m.); winter hours 8:00 a.m.–10:00 p.m.

Prices: No fee to use trails

Regulations/Restrictions: All rules of the road apply; speed limits enforced. Trails are multi-use; bikes yield to all other recreational users. Camp only in designated campgrounds.

The Rides

Mt. Spokane offers every type of terrain the mountain bike enthusiast seeks. Most trails, except for the main roadway, have no vehicular traffic.

Terrain Description: Combination

Mileage/Number of Trails: 50 miles

Difficulty: 30% easiest, 50% more difficult, 20% most difficult

Trails Under Development: Ongoing maintenance, but no new trails under development

Recommended Trails: Beginners should try the trails in the Nordic area, while intermediate and advanced riders should head more toward the summit. Trails are undergoing new classification, so they are not named at this time.

Mountain Bike Lifts: None

Biggest Vertical Drop: 1,621′ from summit to bottom of ski lodge

Longest Trail: Trails interconnect, so many options are possible.

Other Local Trails: Mt. Spokane encompasses just under 14,000 acres and adjoins 40,000 acres of Inland Empire Paper Company land, which has many logging and access roads that are open to public recreation.

Trail Map: Rough map available from the State Park. The Inland Empire Nordic Club produces a map of the trails in the Nordic ski area, and it is also available from the park.

PHOTO COURTESY TEAM BIG BEAR/SNOW SUMMIT MOUNTAIN RESORT

Local Services

While not heavily developed, Mt. Spokane State Park has some facilities, and others are located nearby. It's a popular place for races and events. In 1994 and 1995 it hosted an event in the NORBA National Championship Series.

Mountain Bike Services: None

Special Events: Mountain bike events are continuously happening, but are not known until about 6 months prior to the event. Check with the park.

Emergency Facilities: All hospitals and clinics are located 25 miles away in Spokane.

Accommodations: Camping in the park is $10/campsite (maximum 8 occupants); $5/extra vehicle price; $25/group camp; $1/per person reservation fee. Located just outside the park, The Resort at Mt. Spokane, 509/238-9114, provides overnight lodging.

Dining: Gussies Restaurant on the mountain, 509/238-9550; The Resort at Mt. Spokane has a restaurant and lounge.

Off-the-Bike Activities: Hiking, horseback riding, camping, picking huckleberries, picnicking. Check with the resort for a schedule of their upcoming summer events.

Other Services and Features: The Resort at Mt. Spokane has a small store and Kwik Fix maintenance shop.

Ski Acres Mountain Bike and Hiking Center

7900 S.E. 28th St. #200
Mercer Island, WA 98040

(206) 236-6141 (office)
(206) 434-7664 (mountain)

Conveniently located just east of Seattle, Ski Acres Mountain Bike and Hiking Center offers chairlift service, access to great terrain, rental bikes, riding instruction, guided tours, a deli-cafe, and facilities for picnics, parties, special events, and races.

Location, Hours, and Prices

General Location: On Snoqualmie Pass, 47 miles east of Seattle

Getting There: From Seattle, take Interstate 90 east to Exit 52. Follow the signs to the mountain bike center at the east end of Ski Acres.

Biking Season: Late May through early September

Elevation: 3,000′–4,000′

Hours: 9:30–4:30 Friday–Sunday and holidays

KELLY O'NEILL PHOTO COURTESY SKI ACRES

Prices: $8/unlimited lift rides; $6.50/lift with rental bike; children 5 and under ride free; hikers $5/1 lift ride

Regulations/Restrictions: Helmets required

The Rides

Most trails are Forest Service roads, but several challenging singletracks are available as well. Two of the roads are open to vehicles, so keep alert. Trail surface is generally smooth hardpack or gravel.

Terrain Description: Combination

Mileage/Number of Trails: 30 miles

Difficulty: 8% easiest, 52% more difficult, 40% most difficult

Trails Under Development: More single- and doubletracks being added.

Recommended Trails: Powersurge (beginner); Rockdale Loop (intermediate); Cut-Off (advanced)

Mountain Bike Lift: 1

Trails Accessible from Lift: 17

Biggest Vertical Drop: 1,000′

Longest Trail: 5 miles (Cold Creek)

Other Local Trails: Easy access to John Wayne Trail (a.k.a Iron Horse Trail)

Trail Map: Yes

Local Services

In addition to its full range of bicycling services, Ski Acres caters to the multisport athlete with hiking, fishing, and rafting trips. The center is also popular for special events, from NORBA races to company picnics.

Mountain Bike Services: Rental bikes by Scott and Specialized run $24/day, $15/half day (including helmet); mountain bike school lesson costs $34/1½ hours, $49/4 hours; helmet rental is $5. With Mountain Outfitters (206/409-0459), Ski Acres runs a weekend shuttle that allows cyclists to pedal downhill and catch a ride back up to the pass; call for reservations.

Special Events: Ski Acres hosts the Pacific Crest Cup, part of the American Mountain Bike Challenge, a NORBA race series for top regional racers; date for 1996 event is August 10–11.

Emergency Facilities: Complete first aid room, with qualified personnel

Accommodations: Summit Inn, 206/434-6300; Wardholm West Bed and Breakfast, 206/434-6540

Dining: The center has a deli-cafe. Two miles away is Webb's Bar & Grill at Snoqualmie Ski Area.

Off-the-Bike Activities: The center works with Mountain Outfitters (206/409-0459) to plan hikes, fishing trips, and river-rafting trips for guests.

Other Services and Features: The center hosts company picnics featuring volleyball, horseshoes, horse riding, Frisbee, golf, and, of course, biking and hiking.

Sun Mountain Lodge

(in conjunction with the
Methow Valley Sport Trails Association)
P.O. Box 1000
Winthrop, WA 98862
(800) 572-0493
(509) 996-2211

The Methow Valley may very well be mountain biking heaven. A private, nonprofit organization, the Methow Valley Sport Trails Association (MVSTA) develops, maintains, and promotes 175 kilometers of groomed trails—the Northwest's premier community trail system and one of the best such systems in all of North America. The area is also graced with a fine destination resort, Sun Mountain Lodge. This beautiful, full-service, four-star, mountaintop resort also has a 40-mile network of trails that is maintained through a cooperative effort of the MVSTA, the lodge, the Okanogan National Forest, and the Wolf Creek Reclamation District. Local residents strongly support trails and recreation—and just as strongly oppose what they consider to be inappropriate development (plans for an alpine ski resort were defeated by citizens), helping to preserve the character and beauty of the area.

Location, Hours, and Prices

General Location: North-central Washington, on the east slope of the North Cascades—2 hours north of Wenatchee and 4 hours east of Seattle on the scenic North Cascades Highway (Highway 20); 3½ hours west of Spokane

Getting There: From Wenatchee, in the center of the state, take Highway 97 north to Highway 153, HIghway 153 north to Highway 20, and Highway 20 northwest to Twisp. The resort is 8 miles beyond Twisp. Charter service is also available to Twisp.

Biking Season: Mid-April to Nov.

Elevation: Base 2,600′; resort 2,900′; summit 4,100′

Hours: Shop hours are 9–5; trails are open all the time

Prices: No charge to access trails in summer

Regulations/Restrictions: Rental bikes have a mandatory helmet requirement.

The Rides

Trails at Sun Mountain range from easy to difficult, with a combination of fire roads, doubletrack, and singletrack. Trail surface varies from smooth to rocky. Two of the trails are Forest Service roads, which are open to vehicles. The rest of the trails are mainly singletrack, some of which are fairly technical.

Terrain Description: Cross-country

Mileage/Number of Trails: 40 miles

Difficulty: 25% easiest, 50% more difficult, 25% most difficult

Trails Under Development: None

Recommended Trails: Sunnyside/ Short Cut/Beaver Pond loop (beginner); Rodeo/Yellowjacket (intermediate); Patterson Lake/ Radar Creek or Thompson Ridge/ Meadowlark (advanced)

Mountain Bike Lifts: None (all Nordic trails)

Biggest Vertical Drop: 2,000′ possible

Longest Trail: 4 miles

Other Local Trails: Networked with Forest Service roads and trails and National Park and National Wilderness Area trails. Contact MVSTA at 509/996-3287 and Okanogan National Forest at 509/826-3275 for information.

Trail Map: Free trail maps are available in the lodge's Activities Shop and are strategically placed along the trails. Maps are also available by calling 509/996-3287. The Methow Valley Ranger District sells copies of *Mountain Bike Routes,* which details 14 rides in the Methow Valley: P.O. Box 579, Winthrop, WA 98862, 509/996-2266.

DON PORTMAN PHOTO COURTESY SUN MOUNTAIN LODGE

Local Services

The lodge can help arrange just about any outdoor activity you might want, from badminton to fly fishing to whitewater rafting.

Mountain Bike Services: Rentals cost $6/hour, $18/4 hours, $25/day (with helmet). From June through September midweek, lodge guests can bike to the town of Winthrop and shuttle back to Sun Mountain for $5; check for shuttle availability on weekends.

Special Events: Annual mountain bike festival the first weekend of October

Emergency Facilities: Aero Methow Rescue, Methow Valley Family Practice; nearest hospital approximately 50 miles away

Accommodations: Sun Mountain Lodge has 91 rooms and cabins, and is rated 4-star/diamond by AAA and Mobil; call for rates and special packages. Additional lodging is available in Winthrop, Mazama, and Twisp; call Central Reservations at 800/422-3048, outside Washington call 509/996-2148, Monday-Friday, 9-5.

Dining: The lodge features a 4-star dining room, serving breakfast, lunch, dinner, and box lunches. Additional dining is available in nearby towns.

Off-the-Bike Activities: Horseback trails; Buckaroo Breakfast; Cowboy Camp Dinner with hay wagon or horseback ride and BBQ; whitewater rafting on Black Canyon or Gold Creek; scenic rafting; Sun Mountaineers program; Tiny Tots program; boat rentals at Patterson Lake; fly fishing; golf; reflexology; exercise room; outdoor swimming pool and 2 year-round hot tubs; tennis; playgrounds; games and equipment—volleyball, badminton, horseshoes, croquet, and board games.

Other Features: The beautiful lodge has been featured in *Interiors* magazine. Say Methow correctly; Met-how, not Meth-ow. The lodge is owned by man who invented Gummy Bears!

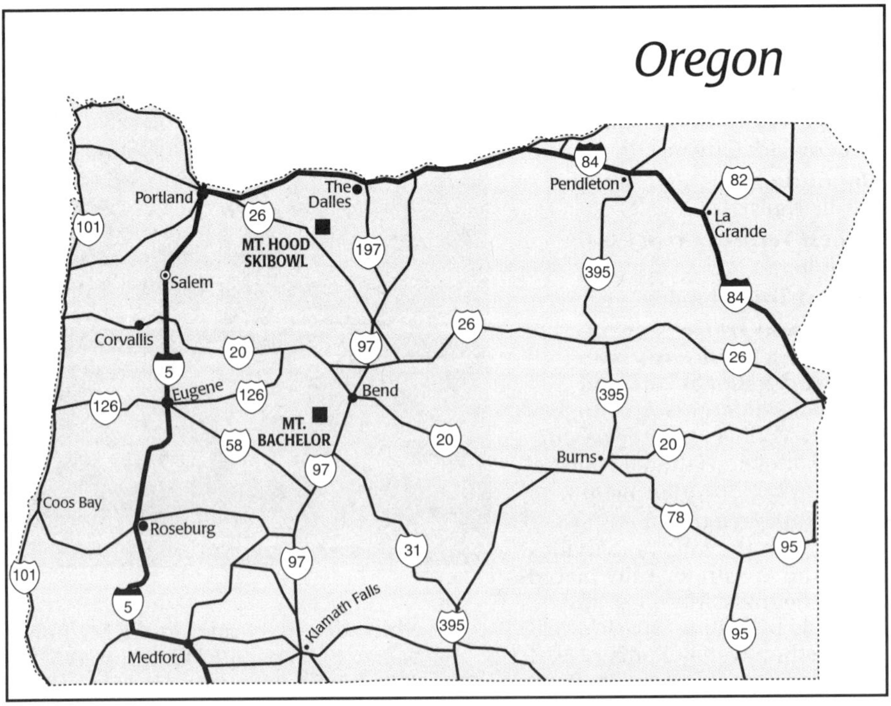

Oregon

Mt. Bachelor Ski and Summer Resort

P.O. Box 1031
Bend, OR 97709-1031
(503) 382-2442
(503) 382-7888 (recorded information)

Easily accessible from Bend, Mt. Bachelor is known for its friendly, family atmosphere and great views of the Cascade Mountains, especially the Three Sisters peaks. Bend is the recreational center of the region, providing great opportunities for a wide range of outdoor activities.

Location, Hours, and Prices

General Location: 160 miles from Portland; 20 miles west of Bend, 20 miles northeast of Sunriver

Getting There: From Portland take Highway 26 east to Highway 97 south. In Bend, head west on Century Drive Highway/Cascade Lakes Highway to Mt. Bachelor. Nearest airports are in Redmond and Portland.

Biking Season: May–October/November

Elevation: Base 6,000′; summit 9,050′

Hours: Daily, 10–4

Prices: No charge to use the trails

Regulations/Restrictions: Helmets mandatory with bike rental

The Rides

Although Mt. Bachelor's trail system is somewhat limited with just 12 kilometers of marked routes, you can find plentiful riding in the surrounding National Forest. This area was formed by volcanic activity, and you will find volcanic ash and pumice on the trails. The best riding is in spring and early summer before dry conditions turn the pumice into a fine powder.

Terrain Description: Cross-country

Mileage/Number of Trails: 12 kilometers of marked routes

Difficulty: Not rated

Trails Under Development: None indicated

Mountain Bike Lift: None

Other Local Trails: The surrounding Deschutes National Forest offers mountain bikers miles of roads and trails. The local ranger district in Bend has developed signed mountain bike routes, maps, and brochures. Contact them at Bend Ranger District, 1230 N.E. 3rd St., Bend, OR 97701, 503/388-5664. Deschutes County also produces a bicycling guide available from the Deschutes County Public Works Department, 61150 Southeast 27th St., Bend, OR 97702, 503/388-6581.

Trail Map: Yes; see address above

Local Services

While Mt. Bachelor offers bike rentals and tours, most lodging and dining opportunities are in the nearby city of Bend.

Mountain Bike Services: Sunrise Lodge rents mountain bikes for $4/hour or $15/day, helmet included. Guided mountain bike tours, including rental bikes, leave Sunrise Lodge at 10:30 a.m.; a 2-hour tour to Sparks Lake costs $39.50 (including sightseeing and lunch), while a 1-hour tour to Todd Creek runs $15.

Special Events: Pole/Pedal/Paddle from Bend to Mt. Bachelor takes place the third weekend in May.

Emergency Facilities: First aid stations at the lodges, medical facilities in Bend

Accommodations: In Bend or Sunriver; contact the Bend Chamber of Commerce at 63085 N. Highway 97, Bend, OR 97701, 503/382-3221.

Dining: Sunrise Lodge has a complete deli, outdoor BBQ, ice cream fountain, and beer and wine service. Mt. Bachelor also offers a professional catering service.

Off-the-Bike Activities: The Summit Express Chairlift is open Memorial Weekend through Labor Day, 10-4, and costs $9/adult, $4.50/children 7-12 years, children 6 and under ride free, seniors (65 and older) ride for $6.50. Two daily natural history presentations are scheduled for 11:30 a.m. and 2:30 p.m. at the Summit. Over Labor Day weekend, Mt. Bachelor offers special Twilight Dinners. Ride the Pine Marten Express lift to the Skier's Palate restaurant in the Pine Marten Lodge, where a gourmet 4-course dinner is served amid 270-degree sunset views.

Other Services and Features: Mt. Bachelor is the gateway to the Cascade Lakes Highway, a National Scenic Byway. Other attractions in the area include the High Desert Museum, Newberry Crater National Monument, and the Lava Lands Visitor Center. Contact the Central Oregon Visitors Association at 800/800-8334 or 503/382-8334 for more information.

Mt. Hood Skibowl Winter and Summer Resort

87000 E. Highway 26
P.O. Box 280
Government Camp, OR 97028
(503) 272-3206, x 244
(503) 272-3554 (fax)

MT. HOOD SKIBOWL Mt. Bike Racing

Mt. Hood Skibowl is the closest ski area to Portland and is the largest night ski area in the United States, with 34 lit runs at night and 65 runs during the day. In summer, the Skibowl turns into an interpretive nature and action park, featuring over 20 attractions, including a dual alpine slide, bungee tower, and 40-mile, lift-served mountain bike park.

Location, Hours, and Prices

STEVE BLY PHOTO COURTESY BRUNDAGE MOUNTAIN

General Location: 52 miles southeast of Portland on Highway 26

Getting There: From the Portland airport, take I-205 South to I-84 East to Exit 16A (Woodvillage) South to Highway 26 in Gresham. Continue east for 39 miles. Total distance is 50 miles.

Biking Season: Memorial Day to mid-October

Elevation: Base 3,600'; village of Government Camp 3,800'; summit 5,029

Hours: Weekends only Memorial Day to mid-June and mid-September to end of season; open daily mid-June to mid-September, Monday–Friday 11–6, Saturday–Sunday 10–7

Prices: Trail use permits $3/day, $12/2 weeks, $20/season; $5 for 1 ride on Sky Chair to Midway and trail permit, $2 each additional ride; $6 for 1 ride to top of Lower Bowl, $3 each additional ride; $6 for 1 ride to top of Multorpor Chair (July and August, Saturdays and Sundays) and trail permit, $3 each additional ride; $8 for Sky Chair to top of mountain and trail permit (Saturdays, Sundays, and holidays, 12–4), $5 each additional ride; $15 for unlimited 8-hour ticket and trail permit; $20 for unlimited mountain bike and alpine slide pass and trail permit

Regulations/Restrictions: Trail permit ($3), helmet, and registration and release forms required

The Rides

The trails at Mt. Hood Skibowl vary from access roads (closed to motor vehicles) to singletrack and doubletrack. Trail surface varies from smooth hardpack to technical rock.

Terrain Description: Combination

Mileage/Number of Trails: 40+ miles

Difficulty: 30% easiest, 40% more difficult, 30% most difficult

Trails Under Development: Plans call for 2 new trails in 1996—a 1.5-mile beginner trail in the Lower Bowl area, and a 2.5-mile trail on Multorpor Mountain connecting Cascade Climb with Rhododendron Trail.

Recommended Trails: Low/Lake Road to Summit Trail to Summit Meadow to Trillium Lake (beginner); Skyline, Rhododendron, Horse, and South trails (intermediate); Upper Bowl Downhill and Fire Hydrant (advanced)

Mountain Bike Lifts: From 1–3, depending on season

Trails Accessible from Lift: 9

Biggest Vertical Drop: 1,600' to Still Creek Road; 1,400' to Skibowl base

Longest Trail: 3 miles (Skyline, High Road, Low Road, Lake Road)

Other Local Trails: The surrounding Mt. Hood National Forest has become very popular with Portland area mountain bikers for its technical singletrack. Trails you may want to try include the East Fork Trail #650, Surveyors Ridge Trail #688, and the Gunsight Trail. For information on these trails, contact the Hood River Ranger Station, 6730 Highway 35, Parkdale, OR 97041, 503/352-6002.

Trail Map: Available at the Mountain Bike Park

Local Services

Besides offering a full range of mountain bike services, from rentals to lessons, the Skibowl sits in one of Oregon's hottest areas for recreation. On- and off-the-bike activities are plentiful and varied.

Mountain Bike Services: Over 20 bikes are available for rental and include helmet and trail permit—$7/hour, $19/4 hours, $27/8 hours; call for multi-day packages. Bike rental and Sky Chair packages are also available: $9/1-hour bike rental and 1 ride to Midway; $10/1-hour bike rental and 1 ride to the top of Lower Bowl; $12/1-hour bike rental and 1 ride to Upper Bowl; $29/bike rental and unlimited use of chairlifts (4 hours); $40/bike rental and unlimited use of chairlifts (8 hours). The bike shop also has high-performance, full-suspension demo bikes. The Mountain Bike School is open Saturdays and Sundays, 10–7 (reservations required on Sundays). Lesson prices include bike rental, helmet, Sky Chair, and instruction: $34/1½-hour lesson; $49/4-hour session (each additional person is $30, minimum of 3 people per session); $89/2-day (8 hours total) session (each additional person $45, minimum of 3 people per session). A bike patrol operates on weekends and holidays.

Special Events: The Skibowl has hosted NORBA races since 1989, including a National Championship Series event in 1990 and the yearly Oregon State Championship. In 1996 it will host the AMBC Western Regional Final, October 4–6. Pro racer Paul Thomasberg will lead a training camp/downhill training camp, May 24–27, 1996.

Emergency Facilities: The ski area has a first aid room and EMTs on staff. The Hoodland Fire Department is 12 miles away, and the Mt. Hood Medical Center is 39 miles away.

Accommodations: For information on nearby lodging, contact the Mt. Hood Visitors Information Center at 503/622-4822.

Dining: Starlight Lodge and Beers-tubbe at the ski area; additional dining in Government Camp, a half-mile into the business loop of Highway 26

Off-the-Bike Activities: The Skibowl Action Park has inverted spaceball, 18-hole miniature golf, CAN AM carts, inflatable bowling pin park, inflatable ball pond bouncer, inflatable human Velcro fly trap, inverted spaceball gyroscope, rapid riser, bungee bouncer, horseback riding, Frisbee golf, volleyball, horseshoes, and a half-mile dual alpine slide. The Columbia River Gorge is a windsurfing hotspot. Contact the Columbia River Gorge National Scenic Area at 503/386-2333. Summer skiing is available on Mt. Hood at Timberline. The Resort at Mt. Hood (800/669-7666, 503/622-3101) offers golf, tennis, swimming, horseback riding, hiking, fishing, and sightseeing. For hiking and backpacking information, contact the U.S. Forest Service at 503/352-6002.

Other Services and Features: The Skibowl specializes in large company picnics from 20 to 3,000 people.

STEVE BLY PHOTO COURTESY BRUNDAGE MOUNTAIN

Idaho

Brundage Mountain

P.O. Box 1062
McCall, ID 83638
(800) 888-7544
(208) 634-4151
(208) 634-7462

Brundage has light, dry powder and wide, groomed runs in winter. In summer, it's a beautiful peak in the Central Mountains of Idaho. From Brundage, you can see the Salmon River Mountains, Payette Lakes, Oregon's Eagle Cap Wilderness, and the Seven Devils overlooking Hell's Canyon.

Location, Hours, and Prices

General Location: Near the mountain village of McCall in central Idaho on Highway 55

Getting There: From Boise, drive north on Highway 55 for 110 miles. Brundage is 8 miles outside of McCall. Plenty of parking is available.

Biking Season: July 4–Labor Day

Elevation: Base 5,840′; resort 6,000′; summit 7,640′

Hours: Weekends and holidays, 11–6

Prices: $17/daily chairlift pass, $8 for a single ride with bike, $5 for a single ride without bike

Regulations/Restrictions: Helmets are required. No smoking on the lift.

The Rides

Over 15 miles of dedicated trails and roads within the ski area connect with Forest Service roads. Lift service gives riders access to nearly 2,000′ of vertical.

Terrain Description: Combination

Mileage/Number of Trails: 10 miles of dedicated singletrack mountain bike trails, 5–6 miles of established roads

Difficulty: 35% easiest, 40% more difficult, 25% most difficult

Trails Under Development: A re-route or alternate route is to be developed for the last half-mile of Elk Trail.

Recommended Trails: Elk Trail is the best first ride for everybody since it gives a good overview of the mountain and other trails.

Mountain Bike Lift: 1

Trails Accessible from Lift: All

Biggest Vertical Drop: 1,800′

Longest Trail: 6.5 miles

Other Local Trails: Brundage Mountain operates under permit on the Payette National Forest. Forest Service roads are accessible from Brundage Mountain trails. For more information, contact the Payette National Forest at 106 West Park St., Box 1026, McCall, ID 83638, 208/634-0700.

Trail Map: Availability not indicated

Local Services

You can find most day-use services at Brundage, with overnight lodging and dining nearby. Mountain bike services include rentals, repairs, and races.

Mountain Bike Services: Bike patrol of EMTs always on hand; bikes and helmets are available in the rental shop; rental shop offers accessories, minor repairs, and souvenirs; fast food items, and energy snacks are also available; lodge facilities are available for special events through the Brundage Mountain Catering Service.

Special Events: 1996 dates and events include the McCall Mountain Bikefest, July 13–14. This NORBA-sanctioned state championship event includes a hill climb, cross-country and circuit races. Contact race organizer, Ron Dillon, 208/342-3910, for more information.

Emergency Facilities: First aid room with EMTs; McCall Memorial Hospital in McCall, 8 miles away; Life Flight to Boise, Idaho

Accommodations: Lodging available in McCall or New Meadows. For lodging assistance, call 800/888-7544.

Dining: Fast food at Brundage; wide variety of dining in McCall.

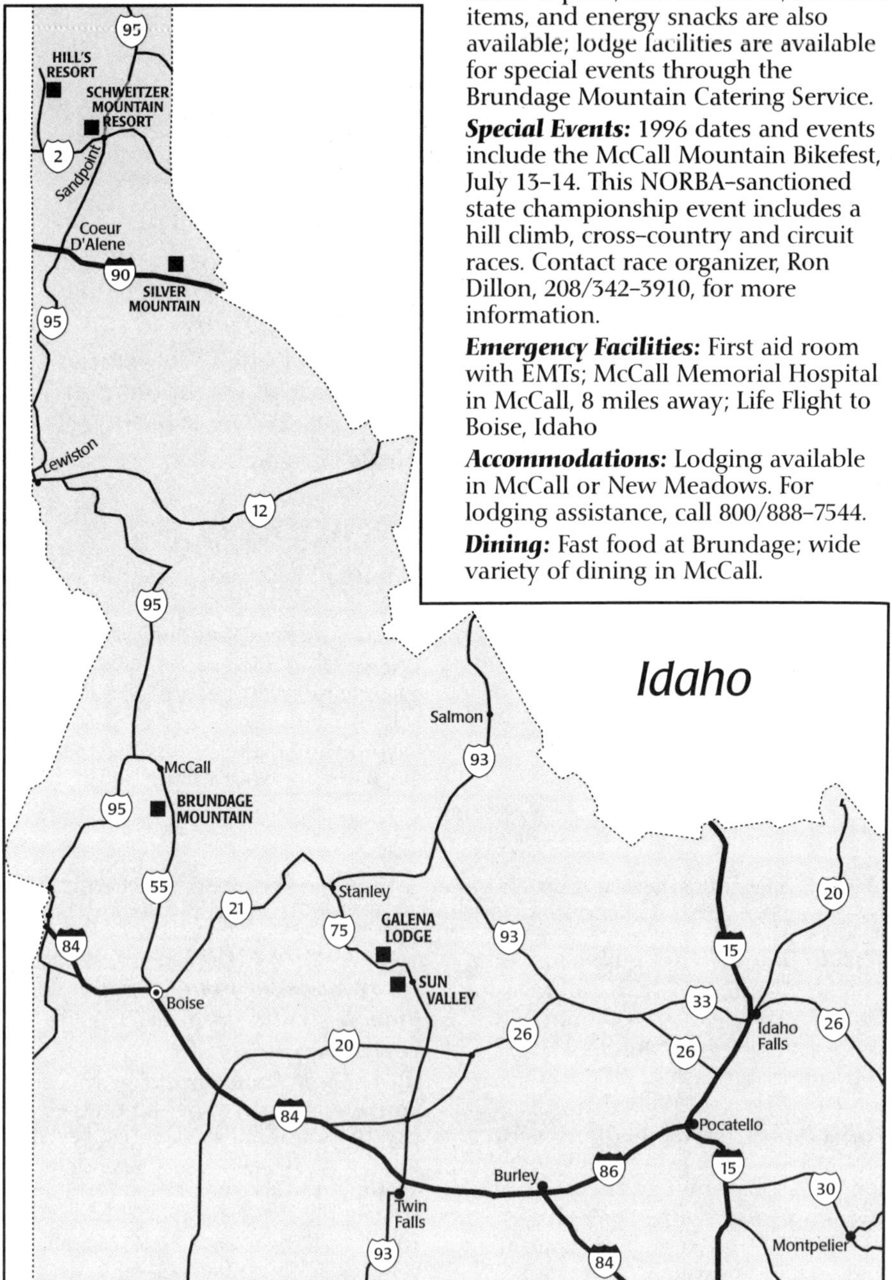

Off-the-Bike Activities: Hiking, rafting, horseback riding, swimming, canoeing, sailing, hot springs, golf. Brundage will host the 3rd Annual Blues Concert, July 8, 1996. Summerfest, a musical event, takes place August 2–4, 1996. Last concert is September 1.

Other Services and Features: Brundage has a large grass amphitheater with marvelous acoustics—a perfect venue for summer concerts and other events.

Galena Lodge

HC64, Box 8326
Ketchum, ID 83340
(208) 726-4010

Galena Lodge is a winter and summer resort in the Sawtooth National Forest offering cross-country skiing and snowshoeing, mountain bike and hiking trails, natural history programs, horseback rides, dining, and private parties. Galena can thank a rich history of mining, sheep herding, and logging for much of its trail system. The town of Galena flourished briefly as a mining community in the late 1880s when Galena ore was mined for silver and other minerals. Later the Galena Store was a stopover for travelers making the arduous journey over Galena Summit on the old toll road. Since 1974, Galena Lodge has been a center for cross-country skiing and outdoor recreation.

Location, Hours, and Prices

General Location: 24 miles north of Ketchum/Sun Valley in central Idaho

Getting There: Drive 24 miles north of Ketchum/Sun Valley on State Highway 75. Connecting flights from Salt Lake, Twin Falls, and Boise serve the Sun Valley airport.

Biking Season: Mid-June to late Sept.

Elevation: 7,300′

Hours: Trails open all the time. During summer, the lodge serves lunch Monday–Friday, 10–4, and brunch on Sunday, 9:30–4

Prices: No charge to use trails

Regulations/Restrictions: None

The Rides

Mountain bike trails at Galena Lodge include dirt roads, singletrack, and cross-country ski trails. Trails are marked with colored 4-inch diamonds, a different color for each trail. Trails are used by sheep, horses, and wildlife, as well as bikers and hikers, so please be courteous. Some routes are open to motorized vehicles.

Terrain Description: Cross-country

Mileage/Number of Trails: 4 trails, ranging from 4–10 miles

Difficulty: 25% easiest, 25% more difficult, 50% most difficult

Trails Under Development: Hariman Bike Path, a 20-mile route from the Sawtooth National Recreation Area

(SNRA) just north of Ketchum to Galena Lodge. The SNRA is also working on the old toll road, up and over Galena Summit and into the Salmon River Basin.

Recommended Trails: Pioneer Cemetery Loop/Galena Loop (beginner); Psycho or Rip and Tear (intermediate); Grinder (advanced)

Mountain Bike Lifts: None

Longest Trail: 10 miles (Grinder)

Other Local Trails: Trails connect with 4WD roads in the Sawtooth National Recreation Area. Contact the SNRA for more information and maps, 208/726-7672.

Trail Map: Available from Galena Lodge or the U.S. Forest Service

Local Services

Galena Lodge provides basic food, bike, and emergency services.

Mountain Bike Services: Bike rentals during lodge hours, daily from 11-5

Special Events: Annual NORBA race, the Galena Grinder, held in mid-July; 1996 dates are July 20-21.

Emergency Facilities: In direct contact with Ketchum Medical Services, 3 EMTs on staff respond to emergencies with their own basic emergency equipment. Nearest medical facilities are in Ketchum. Phone and water are conveniently located; a toilet is across the highway at the horse corrals.

Accommodations: In Ketchum; call the Ketchum/Sun Valley Chamber of Commerce at 800/634-3347.

Dining: On-site, lunch and apres bike, Monday-Friday, 11-4; Sunday brunch, with music by Sagebrush Reunion, 9:30-3; Saturday the lodge is available for private parties

Off-the-Bike Activities: Hiking and horseback riding. The lodge is affiliated with the Sawtooth Science Institute, which offers natural history classes throughout the summer, and the Sun Valley Center for the Arts and Humanities, which conducts cultural workshops.

Other Services and Features: Galena is a community-owned resource. After the property was nearly destroyed earlier in the '90s, the Blaine County Recreation District purchased the lodge with funds raised by locals. The area is now run in cooperation with the U.S. Forest Service, Sawtooth National Recreation Area, Blaine County Recreation District, and local citizens.

CRAIG HILL PHOTO COURTESY HILL'S RESORT

Hill's Resort

HCR5, Box 162A
Priest Lake, ID 83856
(208) 443-2551

Situated in the majesty of the Selkirk range in northern Idaho, Hill's is a year-round resort offering chalets, condominium units, and individual cabins. The main lodge has an award-winning restaurant, lounge, store, and gift shop. The resort has been owned and operated by the Hill family since 1946 and has been chosen by Better Homes and Gardens *and* Family Circle Magazine *as an outstanding family resort.*

Location, Hours, and Prices

General Location: In the Selkirk mountain range of northern Idaho on the shore of Priest Lake

Getting There: Hill's is 60 miles north of Spokane, Washington, and its international airport. Take the I-90 East to State Route 41 North to Highway 2/195 East to State Route 57 North. Hill's is on the south shore of Priest Lake. From Coeur d'Alene it's about 65 miles:, go west on I-90 to State Route 41 North and follow the directions above.

Biking Season: May-November

Elevation: Resort at lake level 2,500'; surrounding peaks reach 7,000'

Hours: Full time from mid-May to mid-October; restaurant and lodge open on weekends the rest of the year; accommodations year round

Prices: Trail use is free; cabins run $57-$255/night; dinners are $10-$18; lunch/breakfast about $6

Regulations/Restrictions: Some restricted trails

The Rides

Hill's is a cross-country ski resort and most of its trails are on Forest Service land. Many are singletrack, some technical. There are hundreds of miles of fire roads.

Terrain Description: Combination

Mileage/Number of Trails: About 200 miles of singletrack and 400 miles of fire roads

Difficulty: Singletrack—20% beginner, 40% intermediate, 40% advanced; fire roads—40% beginner, 40% intermediate, 20% advanced

Trails Under Development: None at this time

Recommended Trails: Lakeshore Trail (beginner); Woodrat Trail (intermediate); Upper Priest Falls Trail (advanced)

Mountain Bike Lift: No

Longest Trail: Multiple long-distance loops possible

Other Local Trails: Contact the Priest Lake Ranger District, Route 5, Box 207, Priest River, ID 83856, 208/443-2512, and Priest Lake State Park, Indian Creek Bay #423, Coolin, ID 83821, 208/443-2200, for more trail information.

Trail Map: The resort has a hand drawn map; the Priest Lake Ridgerunners Snowmobile Club, Priest Lake Chamber of Commerce, U.S. Forest Service, and Priest Lake Park jointly produce a map of snowmobile trails.

Local Services

You will find lodging, dining, and bike rentals on-site. The area offers plenty of outdoor activities, particularly water sports on nearby Priest Lake.

Mountain Bike Services: Bike rentals run $12.50/hour, $19/half day, $27.50/ day, $165/week. There is also a small retail bike shop at the resort.

Special Events: A mountain bike race every May

Emergency Facilities: EMT and ambulance service; closest hospital is 30 miles away

Accommodations: Hill's has a variety of chalets, cabins, and condominiums.

Dining: Available at Hill's award-winning lodge

Off-the-Bike Activities: Full service marina, public golf course, tennis courts, volleyball, groomed cross-country and snowmobile trails, hiking, fishing

Other Services and Features: Rowboat, canoe, Pak Yak, Duckling row boat, and motor boat rentals. Launch service and boat slips also available.

Schweitzer Mountain Resort

P.O. Box 815
Sandpoint, ID 83864
(800) 831-8810
(208) 263-9555

Schweitzer MOUNTAIN RESORT

Tucked in the panhandle of northern Idaho and surrounded by the Selkirk and Cabinet Mountains, Schweitzer Mountain sits 14 miles from the town of Sandpoint and gorgeous Lake Pend Oreille, Idaho's longest and deepest lake.

Location, Hours, and Prices

General Location: 45 miles north of Coeur d'Alene, 80 miles northeast of Spokane, Washington

Getting There: From Spokane International Airport, take U.S. 90 East to Coeur d'Alene. Then head north on Highway 95 to Sandpoint. Pick up Schweitzer Mountain Road 2 miles north of Sandpoint on Highway 95 North.

Biking Season: The biking season starts as soon as the snow melts, usually mid-May. The lift begins operating July 1, and runs daily until Labor Day.

Elevation: Base 4,000′; summit 6,400′

Hours: Lift-assisted riding 10–5 daily; trails open daily during daylight hours

Prices: No charge for trail use

Regulations/Restrictions: Mandatory helmets; no dogs beyond village area; leash law for dogs

DICK O'NEILL PHOTO COURTESY SCHWEITZER MOUNTAIN RESORT

The Rides

In its 2,350 rideable acres, Schweitzer has a little bit of everything and not too much of anything: doubletrack, singletrack, downhill, technical, easy, off-road, paved. Plans call for development of more trails and continued lift service.

Terrain Description: Combination

Mileage/Number of Trails: 16 miles

Difficulty: 30% beginner, 40% intermediate, 30% advanced

Trails Under Development: Lots of possibilities being examined and in the works. A new downhill trail from the top of the lift is planned for the summer of 1996. Additional miles of cross-country trails are slated to open in late summer 1996.

Recommended Trails: Overland (beginner); Grrr Trail (intermediate); Kamikaze From Top (advanced)

Mountain Bike Lift: 1

Trails Accessible from Lift: 4

Biggest Vertical Drop: 1,800′

Longest Trail: 4.7 miles (Overland Loop)

Other Local Trails: The area is surrounded by Forest Service and state lands, all with trails.

Trail Map: Not indicated

Local Services

Schweitzer is back in the mountain biking scene in a big way after a lull of year or two. In 1995, it hosted one event in the Washington-Idaho-Montana race series, and in 1996 it will host an American Mountain Bike Challenge event. Schweitzer may even snag a national event in the next few years.

Mountain Bike Services: Bike rentals available through Alpine Shop, $20/half day, $28/full day. Day lodge is open.

Special Events: Events for 1996 include the Schweitzer Hill Climb and Bike Fair, July 20—an 8.6-mile race up 2,574 vertical feet of paved road; AMBC event, August 16-18—downhill, cross-country, and children's races.

Emergency Facilities: Trained medical personnel on mountain, fire department, first aid room

Accommodations: Resort has 82-room

hotel and condos with pool and hot tubs. For on-mountain lodging, call 800/831-8810; for lodging in town, call 208/263-2161.

Dining: Cafe and restaurant/bar on the mountain; many restaurants in town (call 208/263-2161)

Off-the-Bike Activities: Icelandic horseback rides, guided hikes, elderhostel, swimming, hot tubs, huckleberry picking, Labor Day festival, children's day camp, residential teen camp

Other Services and Features: Gorgeous views of Lake Pend Oreille, 3 states, and Canada

Silver Mountain Ski and Summer Resort

610 Bunker Avenue
Kellogg, ID 83837
(208) 783-1111

A 3-mile, 19-minute gondola ride (the world's longest single-stage gondola) takes mountain bikers to the Mountain Haus, where they can access over 14 multi-use trails. There are routes for all abilities, ranging from 2 to 22 miles, with a longest drop of 3,400'. Rates for 1995 were $10/ride or $13/day with bike rentals available nearby. The biking season is May-October: May 27-June 15, weekends only; June 15-September 27, open daily; October 1-11, weekends only. The resort is located at Exit 49 off Interstate 90, about 68 freeway miles east of Spokane, Washington. Plentiful dining and lodging opportunities are available in the area.

Sun Valley Resort

Sun Valley, ID 83353
(800) 786-8259

Sun Valley's ald Mountain is not officially open to mountain biking, but there is trail access from the River Run side of Bald Mountain. Sun Valley is working toward eventually having the mountain and a few lifts open for mountain biking. Meanwhile, there is virtually unlimited singletrack and doubletrack riding at this world-class destination resort area. You can rent mountain bikes from Pete Lanes in the village or visit Sun Valley Sports Center in the village for more cycling information.

CHAPTER 2

THE WEST

California

Bear Valley Cross-Country Ski and Adventure Company

P.O. Box 5120
Bear Valley, CA 95223
(209) 753-2834

Nestled in a quiet corner of the central Sierra, this year-round adventure resort features skiing (downhill and cross-country), biking, kayaking, hiking, fishing, and camping. Full of rustic appeal, Bear Valley is a great destination in its own right, or can be a pleasant, relaxing stop on a trip to Lake Tahoe or Yosemite.

Location, Hours, and Prices

General Location: Between Lake Tahoe and Yosemite on Highway 4

Getting There: From San Francisco or San Jose, drive east on Highway 580 to Highway 120. Take 120 east to Highway 99, then head north. Exit at Highway 4 in Stockton, and go east on Highway 4 for 90 miles. From Sacramento, take Highway 16 to Highway 49 South to Highway 4. Plenty of free parking is available.

Biking Season: Late May to mid-November

Elevation: Base 5,800′; resort 7,000′; summit 8,500′

Hours: Daily, 9–5 (sometimes longer)

Prices: No charge to use trails

Regulations/Restrictions: Helmets included with and required for rentals, tours, races, and special events

PAUL PETERSEN PHOTO COURTESY BEAR VALLEY

The Rides

Here in the beautiful central Sierra, you will find mostly singletrack and rugged jeep roads, with little jeep or hiking use. Expect to encounter a little bit of everything in terms of terrain.

Terrain Description: Combination

Mileage/Number of Trails: 150 miles

Difficulty: 20% easiest, 50% more difficult, 30% most difficult

Trails Under Development: Several new trails for 1996, including a graded dirt bike path to Lake Alpine. New singletrack also being developed.

Recommended Trails: Lake Alpine Loop (beginner); Bear Trap Basin (intermediate); Slickrock Road (adv.)

Mountain Bike Lift: Perhaps in 1997

Trails Accessible from Lift: Tons when lift becomes available

Biggest Vertical Drop: 2,500′

Longest Trail: 17 miles

Other Local Trails: The area is surrounded by Forest Service land, with potentially hundreds of miles of interconnected trails.

Trail Map: 100 miles of trails described in Trail Guidebook, available from the center for $3.50.

Local Services

Bear Valley offers quite a few bike services along with day-use facilities. Although this is sparsely populated country, there's plenty of lodging, dining, and outdoor activities to be found in the surrounding area. But don't count on finding anything fancy—this is primarily camping country.

Mountain Bike Services: Rental bikes with front suspension, including helmet and water bottle, run $18/half day, $28/full day; demo and full-suspension bikes are $26/half day, $40/full day; child seat available at no charge. Full bike shop offering sales and repairs at the resort.

Special Events: Fat Tire Festival every August with tours, bike polo, videos, and party

Emergency Facilities: Excellent EMT team on duty 24 hours a day

Accommodations: Call the main number for all the different options, including lodges, condos, cabins, and campgrounds.

Dining: Cafe/mini-mart on-site. Several restaurants within riding distance serve breakfast, lunch, and dinner.

Off-the-Bike Activities: Kayaking, rock climbing, rollerblading, fishing, swimming, hiking, camping, river rafting

Other Services and Features: Bear Valley is in Alpine County, the least populated county in California. Resort folks say, "It's gorgeous. If you want crowds, go to Mammoth or Tahoe."

Donner Ski Ranch

P.O. Box 66
Norden, CA 95724

916) 426-3635

Donner offers lift-served mountain biking with access to 50 miles of trails for $5 a day (daily, 9-4, late June-early September). Rentals are available through the Sport Shop. Located less than 90 miles east of Sacramento, Donner also hosts the Rage'n At The Ranch mountain bike race series.

Mammoth Mountain Ski Area/ Mammoth Mountain Bike Park

P.O. Box 24
Mammoth Lakes, CA 93546
(619) 934-0606

Since the first Kamikaze mountain bike racer plunged down Mammoth's summit over 10 years ago, Mammoth Mountain has been at the forefront of ski resort mountain biking. Among the first resorts to host racing events, Mammoth has gone on to develop one of the best and most comprehensive mountain bike parks in the world. Mammoth Mountain Bike Park provides an extensive trail system, professional and amateur racing, and a chance to test yourself on the famed Kamikaze course. And, Mammoth Mountain is situated in the heart of the Eastern High Sierra, surrounded by magnificent peaks and close to hot springs, Bodie ghost town, Mono Lake, and the Tioga Pass entrance to Yosemite National Park.

Location, Hours, and Prices

General Location: Mammoth is 6 hours north of Los Angeles, 6 hours east of San Francisco, 3½ hours south of Reno, Nevada

Getting There: From Highway 395 in east-central California, take Highway 203 west to the town of Mammoth Lakes. The Mammoth Mountain Inn (Mammoth's only ride-in/ride-out hotel) offers free shuttles to and from

PHOTO COURTESY MAMMOTH MOUNTAIN BIKE PARK

Mammoth Lakes airport. Mountain Air Express, out of Long Beach, California, is currently the only airline flying to Mammoth. Mammoth Shuttle (cab service) is also available for transport.

Biking Season: Mammoth Mountain Bike Park usually opens by July 4 and operates daily through the end of September, then on weekends only for the first two weeks of October. Closing date for 1996 is October 13.

Elevation: Base 9,000′; Canyon Lodge 7,500′; summit 11,053′

Hours: Daily, 9–6

Prices: 1-day park pass is $23/adult, $12/child age 12 and under; 2-day park pass is $40/adult, $20/child age 12 and under; trail access pass is $12/adult, $6/child age 12 and under. Note that the park pass provides unlimited access to the gondola, trail system, and other park facilities; the trail access pass gets you on the trails, but not on the gondola.

Regulations/Restrictions: Helmets mandatory

CHRIS LOMBARDO PHOTO

The Rides

Mammoth Mountain boasts 65 miles of singletrack trails created for all riding ability levels. All trails are singletrack (excluding a small portion of the Kamikaze Downhill) and are exclusively for mountain bike use. The resort also offers a full-service mountain bike shop with rentals, repairs, accessories, snacks, and more. Park orientation rides, instructional clinics, guided tours, and lodging packages are also available.

Terrain Description: Combination

Mileage/Number of Trails: 65 miles of networked singletrack for all abilities

Difficulty: 20% easiest, 60% more difficult, 20% most difficult

Trails Under Development: Possible (not definite) 1996 construction of "The Gorge," a singletrack with a suspension bridge

Recommended Trails: Paper Route (beginner) provides gentle, rolling hills within a forested area; Off The Top (intermediate) is an alternative to the Kamikaze Downhill; Skid Marks (advanced) features technical singletrack beginning at the 11,053′ summit of Mammoth Mountain.

Mountain Bike Lift: 1 gondola stops mid-mountain and at the summit

Trails Accessible from Lift: Entire park

Biggest Vertical Drop: 2,053′ from Main Lodge; 3,553′ from Canyon Lodge

Longest Trail: All kinds of loops possible

Other Local Trails: Mammoth Mountain Bike Park is a self-contained singletrack network. The Downtown trail allows access into the town of Mammoth Lakes, which, in turn, opens up onto miles of dirt roads in the surrounding Inyo National Forest.

Trail Map: Available at the bike park

Local Services

Mammoth Mountain offers a full range of services: a complete bike shop, bike rentals, guided tours, lessons, camps, even picnic lunches. Throughout the summer, you can find special events, races, and lodging packages as well. In the town of Mammoth Lakes, you'll find everything from restaurants and lodging to movie theaters, art festivals, and coffee houses.

Mountain Bike Services: Bike rentals at "the Mountain" (for 1996) are fully suspended Schwinn F9Six.40; $35/full day, $25/half day, $15/hour. Demo bikes are available for $15 more than the above rates. Tours/instructional clinics available for 2 hours, half day or full day; price depends on the number of people participating. Two- and 3-night mountain bike lodging packages are available; price varies according to the number of people. Lil' Rider Fun Zone, a small self-contained area designed as a BMX-style course for beginning riders, is available for children. The bike patrol is on duty at all times. Picnic tables and water stops are located throughout the park. Free shuttle from specified locations in town (4 miles from the bike park) to the park is available for park pass holders.

Special Events: Home to the Kamikaze, perhaps the most famous mountain bike race course in the world, Mammoth is a regular stop on both the World Cup and National Championship Series race circuits. It hosts the 1996 NORBA Jeep National Championship Series Finals and the Reebok Eliminator (high speed, side-by-side downhill racing), August 28–September 1, 1996. Over 50,000 competitors and spectators and 225 exhibitors are expected, making it the largest mountain bike race/expo in history. Free to the public; competitor prices not available at press time.

Emergency Facilities: Full-service bike patrol/first aid room available for injuries; short distance to Mammoth Hospital

Accommodations: Mammoth Mountain Inn is located directly across the street from Mammoth Mountain Bike Park. Two- and 3-night mountain bike lodging packages available, May 1–October 31—call 800/228-4947 for information/reservations. The town of Mammoth Lakes has hotels, motels, and condos for a variety of different budgets—call 800/367-6572. Camping opportunities abound in the surrounding area—call the Mammoth District of the Inyo National Forest at 619/924-5500.

Dining: Mountainside Grill, located at Mammoth Mountain Inn, is open daily for breakfast, lunch, and dinner; Yodler Restaurant & Bar is open seasonally for lunch and dinner; Dry Creek Bar is open daily. Mountain Munchies Cafeteria at Mammoth's Main Lodge is open daily for breakfast and lunch. The Inn's Fireplace Coffee & Wine Bar is open daily for snacks, cappuccino, pastries. Numerous and varied restaurants are available in Mammoth Lakes, 4 miles away.

Off-the-Bike Activities: Events/activities at Mammoth Mountain include 32' climbing wall, full-service ropes course, junior ropes course, orienteering course, scenic gondola rides, hiking trails, shuttle to Reds Meadow (Devils Postpile National Monument, Rainbow Falls); 3-day WestFest western festival, August 16–18, 1996; live concerts at the ski area's Yodler Pavilion, July 4–Labor Day weekend. In-town activities include fishing, hiking, horseback riding, kayaking, golf, Dixieland Jazz Jubilee, Sierra Summer Festival, arts and crafts festivals throughout the summer, July 4 fireworks and parade, Mammoth Open tennis tournament, and more.

Other Services and Features: Mammoth Lakes and Mammoth Mountain Ski Resort/Bike Park is a true summer destination resort with activities and events for the whole family. Yosemite National Park, Mono Lake, June Lake resort area, and the Western town of Bishop (home of Mule Days) are all within 45 minutes of Mammoth.

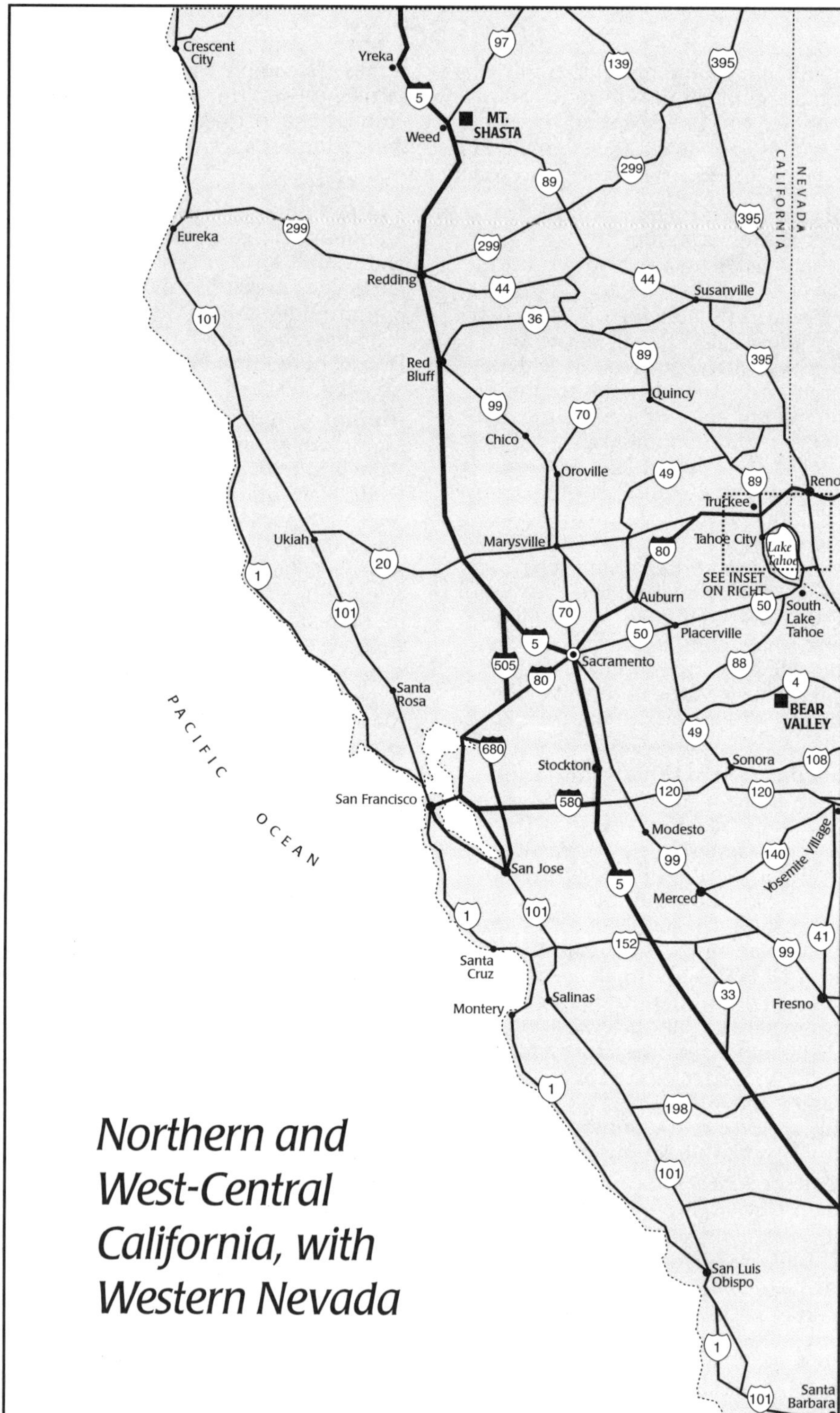

Northern and West-Central California, with Western Nevada

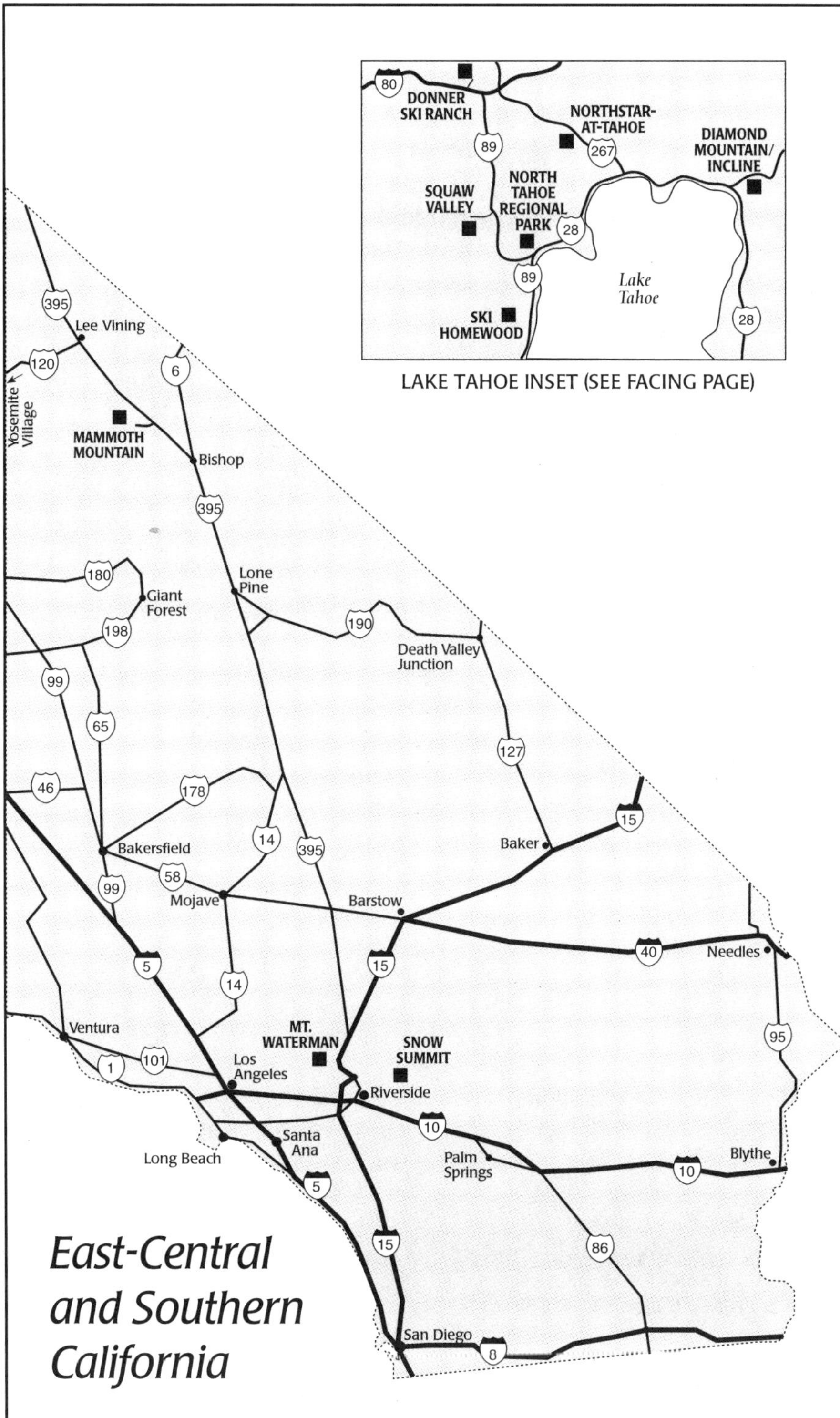
DONNER SKI RANCH
NORTHSTAR-AT-TAHOE
DIAMOND MOUNTAIN/ INCLINE
SQUAW VALLEY
NORTH TAHOE REGIONAL PARK
SKI HOMEWOOD
Lake Tahoe
80
89
267
28
LAKE TAHOE INSET (SEE FACING PAGE)
Lee Vining
Yosemite Village
MAMMOTH MOUNTAIN
Bishop
Lone Pine
Giant Forest
Death Valley Junction
Baker
Bakersfield
Mojave
Barstow
Needles
Ventura
Los Angeles
MT. WATERMAN
SNOW SUMMIT
Riverside
Long Beach
Santa Ana
Palm Springs
Blythe
San Diego
395
120
6
180
198
190
99
65
127
46
178
14
15
58
5
40
95
1
101
10
86
8
East-Central and Southern California

Mt. Shasta Ski Park

104 Siskiyou Avenue
Mt. Shasta, CA 96067
(916) 926-8610
(916) 926-8686
(Summer Information Line, 24-hour recorded message)

In winter, Mt. Shasta provides full-service snowboarding, downhill and cross-country skiing, complete with night skiing and snowmaking facilities. For mountain biking, Mt. Shasta is rapidly gaining a reputation for some of the most varied and exhilarating rides in Northern California. You can find bike tours, rentals, chairlift access, organized events, and lots of other services—all in the shadow of spectacular 14,162′ Mt. Shasta, one of California's most beautiful natural landmarks.

Location, Hours, and Prices

General Location: In north-central California, 10 miles east of Mt. Shasta City and Interstate 5 via Highway 89—about a $4\frac{1}{2}$-hour drive north of the San Francisco Bay Area

Getting There: Access is easy via Interstate 5, 65 miles north of Redding, or 100 miles south of Medford, Oregon. From I-5, go east 6 miles on Highway 89 to Ski Park Highway, then turn left.

Biking Season: Mid-June to Labor Day

Elevation: Base 5,500′; summit 6,600′

Hours: Daily, 10–4

Prices: Daily unlimited mountain bike/chairlift passes are $9/adult, $6/juniors 12 and under, $8/seniors 62 and over.

Regulations/Restrictions: Helmets mandatory at all times

The Rides

Trails range from wide, semi-improved gravel and dirt roads, such as the thrilling 1,100′ Coyote Road downhill trail, to 6 miles of singletrack.

Terrain Description: Combination

Mileage/Number of Trails: 6 trails

Difficulty: 20% easiest, 40% more difficult, 40% most difficult

Trails Under Development: 1–2 miles of additional singletrack

Recommended Trails: Coyote Road, any singletrack

Mountain Bike Lift: 1

Trails Accessible from Lift: 6

Biggest Vertical Drop: 1,100′ (Coyote)

Longest Trail: 5 miles

Other Local Trails: Hundreds of miles of trails throughout the nearby Shasta-Trinity National Forest, Whiskeytown-Shasta-Trinity National Recreation Area, and Klamath National Forest. It is possible to ride around Mt. Shasta in one long day or as a 2-day outing—check with local bike shop, The Fifth Season, at 916/926-3606.

Trail Map: Map includes new trails being developed

Local Services

You can find most bicycling services at the park along with other recreational activities. Lodging and dining are available in the nearby towns of Mt. Shasta City, McCloud, and Dunsmuir.

Mountain Bike Services: Tours, bike rentals, helmet rentals, accessories are available in retail store; call for rates.

Special Events: For 1996, Bike Shop Day, June 23; Dual Slalom Gate Race, June 30; cross-country race, July 28; Mad Dog Downhill Race, August 25

Emergency Facilities: National Ski Patrol-trained bike patrol on duty everyday

Accommodations: In Mt. Shasta City, call the Visitors Bureau at 916/926-4865; for McCloud, call the Chamber of Commerce at 916/964-2471; for Dunsmuir, call the Chamber of Commerce at 916/235-2171.

Dining: Outdoor Coyote Cafe on-site; numerous restaurants 10-12 miles away in Mt. Shasta City, McCloud, and Dunsmuir.

Off-the-Bike Activities: 2 summer concerts, a micro-brewery festival, 2 climbing wall competitions, and a vintage Datsun Roadster Rally. The town of Mt. Shasta hosts a huge 4th of July Festival. The Ski Park also offers scenic chairlift rides for non-cyclists, a free volcanic exhibit, and a recreational climbing structure.

KEVEN LAHEY PHOTO COURTESY MT. SHASTA SKI PARK

Other Services and Features: The Ski Park Lodge is available for receptions, anniversaries, reunions, and other special events.

Mt. Waterman Ski Resort

Star Route, La Canada, CA 91011
Business Office: 919 W. Sierra Madre Ave.
Azusa, CA 91702

(818) 440-1041 (information)
(818) 969-1727 (business)

Located only 55 minutes from downtown Los Angeles in the heart of Angeles National Forest, Mt. Waterman Ski Resort is the closest ski area to the urban hub of southern California. The area contains approximately 250 acres of terrain served by three double chairlifts in winter, one in summer.

Location, Hours, and Prices

General Location: Northeast of Los Angeles in the Angeles National Forest

Getting There: From Los Angeles International Airport, drive north on Interstate 405, east on Highway 134/101, north on I-210 and north on Angeles Crest Highway (Highway 2).

Biking Season: April to November

Elevation: Base 7,000'; summit 8,000'

Hours: Weekends and holidays, 9–4:30

Prices: Trail/lift passes are $15/all day adult, $10/children 12 and under (accompanied by paid adult)

Regulations/Restrictions: Helmets mandatory, stay on marked trails, no out-of-bounds biking

The Rides

Trails are access roads for grooming and maintenance equipment. They are fairly smooth, but have some rocky sections. There are some singletracks as well.

Terrain Description: Combination

Mileage/Number of Trails: 10 trails, 8 miles

Difficulty: 20% easiest, 40% more difficult, 40% most difficult

Trails Under Development: None

Recommended Trails: Warming Hut Trail (beginner); Fire Road (intermediate); Ridge Run (advanced)

Mountain Bike Lift: 1

Trails Accessible from Lift: All

Biggest Vertical Drop: 1,000'

Longest Trail: 2.5 miles

Other Local Trails: Ski area adjoins wilderness area, which is closed to bikes. Lots of other riding opportunities available elsewhere in Angeles National Forest.

Trail Map: Free with purchase of lift ticket

Local Services

Mt. Waterman offers mostly day-use services. For dining and lodging options, head down to one of the foothill communities, such as La Canada or Pasadena.

Mountain Bike Services: Bike patrol, helmet rental

Special Events: Events pending, no dates available

Emergency Facilities: EMT bike patrol

Accommodations: Lodging available 35 miles away in Pasadena. Call the Pasadena Convention and Visitors Bureau, 818/795-9311.

Dining: Newcomb's Ranch, a full-service restaurant, is 6 miles away. Lots of dining options available in La Canada at the junction of I-210 and Angeles Crest Highway.

Off-the-Bike Activities: Hiking, backpacking, fishing, camping, picnicking in Angeles National Forest

Other Services and Features: Mt. Waterman sits very near the Pacific Crest Trail (off limits to bikes) for those interested in backpacking or hiking.

PHOTO COURTESY NORTHSTAR-AT-TAHOE

Northstar-at-Tahoe

P.O. Box 129
Truckee, CA 96160
(916) 562-1010

The back roads and forested trails on Northstar's Mount Pluto and Lookout Mountain offer some of the best riding in the area, with spectacular views of Lake Tahoe and the Martis Valley. Three chairlifts offer access to over 100 miles of biking trails on 2,000 acres. A full-service resort, Northstar offers everything from guided tours to lodging packages to complimentary on-site transportation.

Location, Hours, and Prices

General Location: On the north shore of Lake Tahoe, 40 miles west of Reno, Nevada

Getting There: By car from Reno, take Interstate 80 West to the first Truckee exit, Highway 267. Turn left, and then left again at stop sign. Drive 6 miles south. From Sacramento or San Francisco, take I-80 East to the central Truckee exit. Turn right on Donner Pass Road and right at the stop sign; then continue 6 miles south. It's 96 miles from Sacramento and 196 miles from San Francisco. Major carriers fly into the Reno/Tahoe International Airport, or you can charter a flight into the Truckee/Tahoe airport. Call 800/GO-NORTH at least 24 hours in advance to arrange for a free shuttle from the Truckee/Tahoe Airport or the Amtrak and Greyhound bus depots in Truckee. To arrange ground transportation from the Reno airport, call Aero Trans at 702/786-2376.

Biking Season: Mid-June to October

Elevation: Base 6,330'; mid-mountain 7,040'; summit 8,610'

Hours: Daily, mid-June through Labor Day; weekends, early September through early October

Prices: Lift tickets are valid on Echo and Vista Express or Lookout lifts. Cost for bicyclists are $13/single ride, $10/children 5-12; $19/multi-ride, $14/children 5-12. Cost for hikers is $9/single ride, $7/children 5-12.

Regulations/Restrictions: Helmets mandatory for cyclists

The Rides

Riding at North Tahoe can be rigorous thanks to the rugged terrain and high elevation. Your efforts, however, are rewarded with views of Lake Tahoe, meadows, pine forests, and aspen groves. The terrain varies from smooth, beginner-friendly cross-country ski trails to rocky, technical singletrack. Access roads are open to vehicles, while bicyclists, hikers, and horseback riders share cross-country trails. Added bonuses: a technical singletrack course and a dual slalom.

Terrain Description: Combination

Mileage/Number of Trails: 100 miles

Difficulty: 20% easiest, 60% more difficult, 20% most difficult

Trails Under Development: Singletrack is added and upgraded continually

Recommended Trails: Crossover, Try-Umph (beginner); ride to Watson Lake from top of Lookout (intermediate); Buzzsaw to White Fir to Outland to Competition (advanced)

Mountain Bike Lifts: 3

Trails Accessible from Lifts: All
Biggest Vertical Drop: 2,280′
Longest Trail: 10+ miles
Other Local Trails: Northstar's trails connect with the surrounding Tahoe National Forest, which houses some of the best riding in California.
Trail Map: Free trail maps are available in the Mountain Adventure Shop in Northstar Village.

Local Services

Northstar has lodging, restaurants, and shops to suit a variety of tastes and budgets. Mountain bike services include guided tours, lessons, bike rentals, accessories, and minor bike repairs at the Mountain Adventure Shop. A fully-appointed resort, Northstar offers golf, tennis, and horseback riding. Check with the resort for special lodging and activity packages, as well as special events.

Mountain Bike Services: Part-time bike patrol. State-of-the-art Giant mountain bikes with front suspension are available for rent—$26/adult 4 hours, $18/junior 4 hours, $10/child 4 hours; $31/adult all day, $24 junior all day, $15/child all day; helmet, free souvenir water bottle, and trail map available with rentals. Guided tours, available Monday-Friday, $25; Intro to Mountain Biking Level I, 2-hour lesson for never-ever riders, available daily, $20; Intro to Mountain Biking Level II, 2-hour lesson for beginner to low intermediate riders, includes multi-ride lift ticket, available daily, $35; 2-Day Clinic and Guided Tour, 3-hour lesson, tech talk, guided tour with lunch and return transportation, 2-day lift ticket, for intermediate to advanced riders, available Saturday-Sunday, $99. Call the Mountain Bike Park for latest details at 916/562-2248. The 2-Day Clinic and Guided Tour can be combined with lodging for a weekend package, $188/per person, available from July-early October. Mountain Bike Getaway Package, $121, includes lodging and 2 days of multi-ride bike lift tickets, available daily, mid-June to early September, weekends from early September to early October.

BART BANKS PHOTO COURTESY NORTHSTAR-AT-TAHOE

Special Events: 5th Annual Sawtooth Ridge Challenge, July 28, 1996
Emergency Facilities: Fire station on-site; nearest hospital 6 miles away in Truckee
Accommodations: Call 800/GO-NORTH (466-6784) for on-site lodging. Other lodging options available in nearby Truckee.
Dining: Two restaurants serve breakfast, lunch, and dinner. A deli serves lunches and snacks. More dining is available in Truckee.
Off-the-Bike Activities: 18-hole golf course, tennis, horseback riding, hiking, swimming pool and recreation center, kids' programs, live music concerts, ropes course, climbing wall, orienteering course
Other Services and Features: Meeting rooms and conference center, romantic getaways, weddings/reunions, easy access to casinos and water sports at Lake Tahoe

North Tahoe Regional Park Trail System

North Tahoe Recreation and Parks
Box 139
Tahoe Vista, CA 96148
(916) 546-7248

Not a resort per se, but a winter ski and summer bike trail system, North Tahoe Regional Park trails are open for cyclists, and the park has been a mountain bike race venue in the past. The Tahoe North Visitors Bureau actively promotes mountain biking in the area, and publishes a free brochure outlining local mountain bike parks, describing recommended rides, and listing local bike shops and races. Contact the Visitors Bureau at Box 5578, Tahoe City, CA 96145, 800/824-6348 or 916/583-3494. For information on the Tahoe Fat Tire Festival, contact Cyclepaths Mountain Bikes at Box 887, Tahoe City, CA 96145, 916/581-1800, 800/780-BIKE.

Ski Homewood

5145 West Lake Blvd.
P.O. Box 165
Homewood, CA 96141
(916) 525-2992
(916) 525-0417 (fax)

Internet: http://www.aminews.com/homewood

On Lake Tahoe's west shore, Ski Homewood is literally across the street from the lake. The resort is a local favorite, known for excellent tree skiing and stunning lake views.

Location, Hours, and Prices

General Location: 6 miles south of Tahoe City on the west shore of Lake Tahoe

Getting There: From Reno, Nevada, take I-80 West toward Sacramento for 30 miles to Truckee. Then take Highway 89 south to Tahoe City, about 20 miles, and continue south on 89 to Homewood, another 10 miles. From Sacramento, take I-80 East about 90 miles to Truckee. Then head south on Highway 89 to Tahoe City and Homewood.

Biking Season: April–October

Elevation: Base 6,230'; summit 7,880'

Hours: Daily, 9–4

Prices: No charge to use trails, but you must check in at the front office (North Side Lodge) and sign a liability form.

Regulations/Restrictions: Helmets mandatory

The Rides

Riding is rigorous because of the Tahoe area's rugged terrain and elevation. Be aware that Ski Homewood's trails are not maintained specifically for bike use.

Terrain Description: Downhill

Mileage/Number of Trails: 57 trails

Difficulty: 15% easiest, 50% more difficult, 35% most difficult

Trails Under Development: None

Recommended Trails: Rainbow Ridge (beginner); Bonanza, Miners Delight (intermediate); Jimmy's Run (advanced)

Mountain Bike Lift: No

Biggest Vertical Drop: 1,650'

Longest Trail: 2 miles

Other Local Trails: No

Trail Map: Free when you check in

Local Services

Bike rentals, lodging, and dining are available in the Lake Tahoe communities near Ski Homewood. In summer, the lake is a big attraction for swimming, waterskiing, and just relaxing.

Mountain Bike Services: Equipment may be rented from Tahoe Gear, adjacent to Ski Homewood.

Special Events: TBA. The area has hosted the Homewood Hillclimb. Part of the Lake Tahoe Mountain Bike Series (LTMBS), the event is a 1,650', 3-mile ascent to the summit of Ski Homewood. Call 916/583-3753 for more information on the LTMBS.

Emergency Facilities: Urgent care facilities available in Tahoe City; Tahoe Forest Hospital in Truckee

Accommodations: Homeside Motel, adjacent to Ski Homewood, 916/525-9990; Homewood Marina, across the street from Ski Homewood, 916/525-6728.

Dining: Great breakfasts and lunches at Stony Ridge Cafe in Tahoma, 916/525-0905; lots of dining options in Tahoe City

Off-the-Bike Activities: The entire Tahoe area offers great hiking, backpacking, horseback riding, water sports, and other outdoor activities.

Snow Summit Mountain Resort

880 Summit Blvd.
Big Bear Lake, CA 92315
(909) 866-4565 **(Team Big Bear Mountain Bikes)**

The premier Southern California ski resort for mountain biking, Snow Summit attracts over 500,000 skiers in winter and over 30,000 cyclists in summer. Besides offering a full range of recreational cycling services, the resort is a perennial stop on the NORBA National Championship Series circuit and has hosted World Cup races. Tom Spiegel and Pat Follett of Team Big Bear are among the nation's top race promoters. In addition to the national races, they organize the southland's most popular amateur race series, the Snow Summit Amateur Cup.

Location, Hours, and Prices

General Location: 80 miles east of Los Angeles (about 2 hours) in the San Bernardino mountains

Getting There: From Los Angeles, take Interstate 10 East to Highway 30 North. Continue on Highway 30 to Highway 330 (Mountain Resorts exit). Take Highway 330 to Running Springs where you catch Highway 18 to Big Bear. It's about 2 hours from Los Angeles

Biking Season: Mid-May to the end of October

Elevation: Base 7,000′; summit 8,200′

Hours: Daily, late June through early September; weekends only from May through June and early September through the end of October

Prices: $7/one-way lift ticket with bike, $18/all day lift ticket with bike

Regulations/Restrictions: Helmets are mandatory. Riders must sign a waiver.

The Rides

Rugged terrain, a steep vertical rise, and high elevation make most of Snow Summit's trails suitable for advanced riders. Trails on the surrounding San Bernardino National Forest vary in difficulty; many of them are open to vehicular traffic, particularly motorcycles, so be alert.

Terrain Description: Combination

Mileage/Number of Trails: 60+ miles

Difficulty: 35% easiest, 45% more difficult, 20% most difficult

Trails Under Development: None

Recommended Trails: Skyline Drive (beginner); Skyline Drive (intermediate); Lodgepole Pine (advanced)

Mountain Bike Lift: 1

Trails Accessible from Lift: 4

Biggest Vertical Drop: 1,200′

Longest Trail: 2.5 miles

Other Local Trails: From the ski area, you can access the San Bernardino National Forest for over 60 miles of roads and trails.

Trail Map: Purchase at local bike shops; free map for all riders at Snow Summit

Local Services

Team Big Bear provides most bicycling services at the resort and organizes a full schedule of racing events. Other visitor services can be found in the small communities surrounding Big Bear Lake.

Mountain Bike Services: Full bike shop with bike and helmet rentals, expert mechanical repairs, commemorative T-shirts and hats, clothing and accessories located at the base area. Bikes rent for $6.50/hour, $22/half day (4 hours), $32/all day; $3/hour for Burley child's trailer and helmet. Full-suspension bikes go for $8.50/hour, $28/half day (4 hours), $40/full day. Bike rental includes helmets; helmets can be rented separately for $6.50/day.

Special Events: Events scheduled for 1996 are the Amateur Cup Series, May 17-19, June 14-16, July 26-28, September 13-15; Gotta Thunder Downhill Weekend, May 31-June 2; Women's Only Weekend, June 7-9; 12 Hours at the Summit, June 21-22; U.S. Mountain Challenge Downhill Mania, July 5-7; Fall Classic, October 11-13.

Emergency Facilities: Hospital 1 mile from ski area

Accommodations: Nearby lodging includes Northwoods Resort, 800/866-3121 and Mountain Lodging, 800/487-3168. Contact the Big Bear Chamber of Commerce at 909/866-4608 for more lodging options.

SHARON MCNEILL PHOTO COURTESY SUNDAY RIVER

Dining: BBQ at both the base area and the top of the mountain. Many restaurants 2-3 miles from ski area in the town of Big Bear.

Off-the-Bike Activities: Chairlift is open for non-bikers; Big Bear Lake offers lots of water activities. The Pacific Crest Trail passes through the area, so there are plentiful hiking and backpacking opportunities in the National Forest.

Other Services and Features: Snow Summit boasts plenty of sun—with clear-blue skies 90% of the time year-round.

TOM MORAN PHOTO COURTESY TEAM BIG BEAR/SNOW SUMMIT MOUNTAIN RESORT

Squaw Valley, USA

1960 Squaw Valley Road
Olympic Village, CA 96146
(800) 545-4350
(916) 583-5585
(916) 583-6955 **(24-hour information)**

Surrounded by 40 square miles of wilderness, Squaw Valley is an 8,000-acre residential and recreational preserve in California's High Sierra. Seventeen dirt trails and 7 miles of paved trail provide scenic excursions for cyclists.

Location, Hours, and Prices

General Location: 45 miles from Reno/Tahoe International Airport; 200 miles east of San Francisco; 100 miles east of Sacramento via Interstate 80 and Highway 89

Getting There: From Reno/Tahoe airport, take Highway 80 West to Truckee and then Highway 89 toward Tahoe City. Go right on Squaw Valley Road where signs will lead you to the mountain. Parking is at the base.

Biking Season: June–October

Elevation: Base 6,200′; High Camp 8,200′; Granite Peak (highest peak) 9,050′

Hours: Daily, 9:40–5

Prices: $19/1 cable car ride and park usage, $26/unlimited rides

Regulations/Restrictions: Helmets mandatory, gloves are recommended

NATHAN KENDALL PHOTO COURTESY SQUAW VALLEY, USA

The Rides

Riders not used to Tahoe's high elevation will appreciate the lift-served access to Squaw Valley's dedicated mountain bike terrain, while acclimated riders may choose to bike up the mountain. The area's rocky terrain includes singletrack, long straight-aways, and technical steeps.

Terrain Description: Downhill

Mileage/Number of Trails: 17 trails, 7 miles

Difficulty: 15% easiest, 50% more difficult, 35% most difficult

Trails Under Development: None

Recommended Trails: Not indicated

Mountain Bike Lift: 1 cable car

Trails Accessible from Lift: 17

Biggest Vertical Drop: 2,850′

Longest Trail: 3.5-mile mountain run

Other Local Trails: You can climb Squaw Peak for additional vertical drop. Entire Lake Tahoe area has hundreds of miles of riding.

Trail Map: Free at base of mountain

Local Services

Squaw Valley is a self-contained resort. You'll find lodging, dining, and recreational opportunities on-site. In recent years, the resort has become a popular stop for racers, most notably as host of a Downhill Mania event.

Mountain Bike Services: Rentals available. Prices TBD.

Special Events: (1996) Fat Tire Festival, August 15–18—races, tours, demos; Downhill Mania, September 6 & 7—head-to-head downhill and dual slalom racing; American Mountain Bike Challenge, Sept. 13, 14, 15—cross-country, dual slalom, downhill races.

Emergency Facilities: Dispatch facilities to call for emergency services

Accommodations: Contact Central Reservations at 800/545-4350.

Dining: 3 restaurants at High Camp; Grahams at the base of the mountain; Glissandi, Bullwhackers, and Montagnes at the Resort at Squaw Creek; more dining in Truckee/Tahoe City.

Off-the-Bike Activities: High Camp has a swimming pool and lagoon, restaurants, bungee jumping, tennis courts, soccer camp.

Other Services and Features: Just 10 minutes to Lake Tahoe

PHOTO COURTESY MAMMOTH MOUNTAIN BIKE PARK

Nevada

Diamond Peak Ski Resort at Incline Village/Crystal Bay

IV/CB Visitors & Convention Bureau
969 Tahoe Blvd.
Incline Village, NV 89451
(702) 832-1177

Although Diamond Peak Ski Resort is largely out of operation in summer months, adjacent Incline Village/Crystal Bay offers immediate access to a variety of mountain bike terrain on U.S. Forest Service land and in the Lake Tahoe/Nevada State Park. Among the local trails is the world-famous Flume Trail.

Location, Hours, and Prices

General Location: Northeast shore of Lake Tahoe

Getting There: 35 miles from Reno/Tahoe International Airport via Highway 431; 25 miles from Truckee, California (I-80) via Highways 267 and 28

Biking Season: May–October

Elevation: Incline Village is at 6,350′; elevations range to 9,000′

Hours: No limits except for State Park land, 8 a.m.–9 p.m.

Prices: $2 ride-in or parking/trail fee at State Park entrance at Spooner Lake

The Rides

The area offers a mix of singletrack and access roads with trail surfaces from smooth to very rocky. Singletrack riding includes the spectacular Flume Trail. You can also ride part of the Tahoe Rim Trail, a route that circles Lake Tahoe.

Terrain Description: Cross-country

Mileage/Number of Trails: 22 miles of roads; 4.5 miles of singletrack (Flume Trail); 4 of 16 miles of the Tahoe Rim Trail are now open to bikes

Difficulty: Not rated

Trails Under Development: None

Recommended Trails: Flume Trail (intermediate); Red House Loop (intermediate/advanced)

Mountain Bike Lift: No

Biggest Vertical Drop: 1,750′

Longest Trail: 22 miles

Other Local Trails: Lake Tahoe State Park trails are adjacent to USFS land in the Carson Range on the south and the Mt. Rose area on the north. For more trail information, contact the following land management agencies: Tahoe National Forest, 916/265-4531; Toiyabe National Forest, 702/882-2766; Lake Tahoe Basin Management Unit, 916/573-2600.

Trail Map: A free trail map is available at the Spooner Lake entrance to the State Park or at Sand Harbor.

Local Services

Most services can be found in Incline Village/Crystal Bay, or in the nearby communities surrounding Lake Tahoe. Once you're out on the trails, however, you are pretty much on your own.

Mountain Bike Services: While there are no services in the State Park, Incline Village has 3 rental locations and a full-service bike shop.

Special Events: No mountain bike events are planned at this time.

Emergency Facilities: Sheriff and fire department plus 2 emergency medical centers in Incline Village/Crystal Bay

Accommodations: Over 2,500 hotel, motel, and condo rooms are available in Incline Village/Crystal Bay; call 800/GO-TAHOE.

Dining: More than 50 restaurants in the area and in Incline Village/Crystal Bay

Off-the-Bike Activities: Annual Shakespeare at Sand Harbor Festival, August 2–September 1, 1996; Native American Snow Dance, October 11–12, 1996

Other Services and Features: Lake Tahoe is the largest alpine lake in North America; the surrounding area features wonderful beaches, swimming, camping, golf, and just about any outdoor activity you can imagine.

PHOTO COURTESY INCLINE VILLAGE/CRYSTAL BAY VCB

CHAPTER 3

THE ROCKIES

Montana

The Big Mountain Ski and Summer Resort

P.O. Box 1400
Whitefish, MT 59937
(406) 862-2900

Rising out of the surrounding plains, Big Mountain is just that: one huge peak. Located just west of Glacier National Park, Big Mountain covers over 4,000 acres. Besides the spectacular scenery, the full-service resort offers lodging, dining, groceries, gondola rides, hiking, tennis, and horseback riding in the summer months.

Location, Hours, and Prices

General Location: 8 miles north of Whitefish and 23 miles north of Kalispell in the northwest corner of Montana, west of Glacier National Park

Getting There: Northwest, Delta, and Horizon fly into Kalispell's Glacier International Airport, just 19 miles from Big Mountain. By rail, Amtrak's Superliner goes to Whitefish. By car, take U.S. Highway 2 or Interstate 90 to Highway 93, and then head north to Whitefish. From Whitefish, follow signs to Big Mountain, 8 miles from downtown Whitefish.

Biking Season: May–September

Elevation: Nordic area 4,000′; base and resort 4,700′; summit 7,000′

Hours: May–June and Sept., 10–5; July to early Sept., 10–7

Prices: $5/single ride, $10/all day lift

Regulations/Restrictions: Helmets mandatory; stay on trails and in designated areas

The Rides

Big Mountain's 20-mile trail network consists mostly of singletrack with pull-out areas and a small amount of access road. Most trails are rated intermediate, with limited rocky, technical areas. The area plans to add several trails and lift service in 1996; check with the resort for the latest developments.

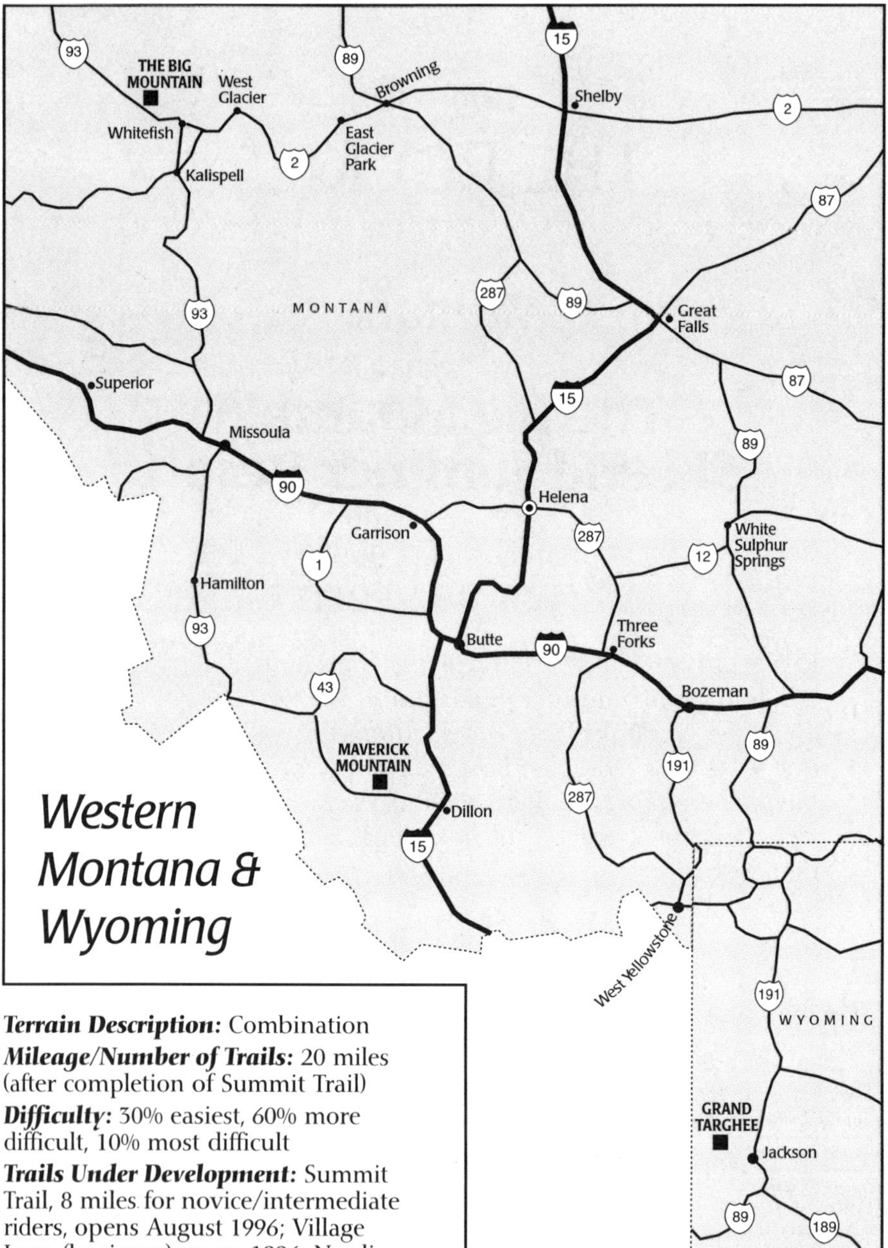

Terrain Description: Combination

Mileage/Number of Trails: 20 miles (after completion of Summit Trail)

Difficulty: 30% easiest, 60% more difficult, 10% most difficult

Trails Under Development: Summit Trail, 8 miles for novice/intermediate riders, opens August 1996; Village Loop (beginner) opens 1996; Nordic area (int.) some trails open 1996

Recommended Trails: Village Loop (beginner); Huckleberry, new Summit Trail (intermediate)

Mountain Bike Lift: 1 (opens mid-August 1996)

Trails Accessible from Lift: 1

Biggest Vertical Drop: Summit Trail

Longest Trail: 8 miles (new Summit Trail)

Other Local Trails: Ski resort trail connects with Haskil Basin Road to Whitefish, a 10-mile dirt road, 6 miles of which are closed to vehicle traffic.

Trail Map: New map being developed; check with resort at time of visit.

Local Services

A destination resort, Big Mountain offers everything you need for a mountain bike vacation, from plentiful lodging and dining options to bike rentals and classes. For a change of pace, check out the Wild West flavor of nearby Whitefish, or take a trip to Glacier National Park.

Mountain Bike Services: Bike rentals include suspension bikes $17/half day, $25/full day; recreation bikes $15/half day, $20/full day; child bike $10/half day, $15/full day. Two-hour guided tours run $25/person. Two-hour Intro to Mountain Biking classes offered at Level I for never-ever riders and Level II for beginner to low intermediate riders, $25/person.

Special Events: 1996 events include the Big Mountain Bike Fest, July 27–28, part of the WIM (Washington, Idaho, Montana) Point Series, with downhill and cross-country racing, $18/1-day early registration, $22/late registration, $32/2-day early registration, $36/late registration; mountain bike handling and technique workshop, August 10–11; free Adventure Mountain Bike Ride for kids 11–17, Saturdays, noon–2, July–August.

Emergency Facilities: Fire Department with ambulance at resort; hospital is 8 miles from the resort in Whitefish

Accommodations: Economy, single-family homes, condos, and deluxe hotel at resort; call 800/858-5439.

Dining: Restaurants open daily at summit and base area; other options in Whitefish

Off-the-Bike Activities: Hiking, tennis courts with free equipment use, volleyball courts, concerts, plays, microbrew festival, running races, gondola ride to summit, Forest Service Interpretive Center, golf, fishing, boating, horseback rides, 2-week Flathead Music Festival

Other Services and Features: The Big Mountain is located near Glacier National Park. Miles of mountain bike trails are available in the area.

Maverick Mountain

Maverick Mountain Road
P.O. Box 460475
Polaris, MT
(406) 834-3454

Located on the Pioneer Mountain Scenic Byway and hidden away in the mountains of southwest Montana and Beaverhead National Forest, Maverick Mountain is a small, day-use resort with lift-served mountain biking.

Location, Hours, and Prices

General Location: Southwest Montana in Beaverhead National Forest

Getting There: Take Interstate 15 to Dillon and continue 35 miles west on Highway 278, following signs to Maverick near the town of Jackson. By car, it is 2–3 hours from the Butte, Bozeman, or Idaho Falls airports.

Biking Season: July–October

Elevation: Base 6,800′; summit 8,750′

Hours: Open daily during daylight hours

Prices: No charge

The Rides

Known for its tree skiing, Maverick Mountain offers cyclists singletrack and access roads with a combination of technical, rocky, and smooth terrain. Some access roads are open to mountain maintenance traffic, so be alert.

Terrain Description: Combination
Mileage/Number of Trails: 10 miles
Difficulty: 20% easiest, 50% more difficult, 30% most difficult
Trails Under Development: New singletrack trails are added each year.
Recommended Trails: Not indicated
Mountain Bike Lift: 1
Trails Accessible from Lift: All
Biggest Vertical Drop: 1,950′
Longest Trail: 3.5 miles
Other Local Trails: There is more riding in Beaverhead National Forest. Contact the Beaverhead National Forest Supervisor's Office, 610 North Montana, Dillon, MT 59725, 406/683-3900.
Trail Map: No

Local Services

Most services are 38 miles away in the town of Dillon, although you can find natural hot springs nearby.

Mountain Bike Services: Nearby
Special Events: Phun Hog Bike Races in September, co-sponsored with the Patagonia Outlet Store
Emergency Facilities: Nearby
Accommodations: Grasshopper Inn, 406/834-3456; Elkhorn Hot Springs Lodge, 406/834-3434
Dining: Available at the lodges listed above
Off-the-Bike Activities: Natural hot springs pools nearby

WILLIAM SALLAZ PHOTO COURTESY GRAND TARGHEE SKI & SUMMER RESORT

Wyoming

Grand Targhee Ski and Summer Resort

Box SKI
Alta, WY 83422
(800) TARGHEE
(307) 353-2300

Located in the heart of Targhee National Forest next to Grand Teton National Park, Grand Targhee features panoramic views spanning three states. Fields of mountain wildflowers surround the area and their awesome backdrop is Grand Teton Mountain, which soars to almost 14,000'. Resort personnel speak of the special magic that comes from Grand Targhee's combination of inspiring scenery, abundant sun, clear mountain air, and intimate lodges.

Location, Hours, and Prices

General Location: 42 miles north of Jackson Hole, Wyoming, 12 miles east of Driggs, Idaho, and 82 miles east of Idaho Falls, Idaho

Getting There: From Jackson Hole, take Highway 22 across the Teton Pass to Victor, Idaho, then take Highway 33 to Driggs. Follow the signs to Grand Targhee. From Idaho Falls, there are two ways to get to the resort. One is to take Highway 20 to Idaho 33 and follow the signs to Grand Targhee. The second way is to take Highway 26 to Swan Valley, then Highway 32 to Victor, then Highway 33 to Driggs, and follow the signs to Grand Targhee.

Biking Season: Summer bike season opens June 1 (if all snow has melted) and closes mid- to late September.

Elevation: Resort base 8,000'; summit 10,200'

Hours: Daily

Prices: $5/daily adult trail pass, $5/children 6–12, children under 5 are free; $10/chair ride with bike and trail pass

Regulations/Restrictions: Trail pass required; helmets strongly recommended

The Rides

Beginner through advanced riders will want to check out the rolling single- and doubletrack in Rick's Basin, a Nordic ski area during winter, while intermediate and advanced riders can tackle the singletrack and doubletrack on Fred's Mountain and Peaked Mountain.

Terrain Description: Combination

Mileage/Number of Trails: Total not known

Difficulty: 25% easiest, 50% more difficult, 25% most difficult

Trails Under Development: Quakie Ridge Trail beyond Rick's Basin, overlooking South Leigh Canyon

Recommended Trail: Rick's Basin

Mountain Bike Lift: 1

Trails Accessible from Lift: 1

Biggest Vertical Drop: 2,200′

Longest Trail: 2.8 miles (Teton Vista Trail), 3 miles (Teton Overlook Trail on Peaked Mountain)

Other Local Trails: Ski resort trails open onto unmarked and undeveloped trails for advanced riders only. A Forest Service map is recommended.

Trail Map: Contact Targhee's Activity Center

PHOTO COURTESY GRAND TARGHEE SKI & SUMMER RESORT

Local Services

A destination resort, Grand Targhee has on-site lodging, dining, and lots of outdoor activities and events. As for mountain biking services, you can find rentals, tours, and special events. Plus, the resort makes a great jumping-off point for exploring nearby Grand Teton and Yellowstone National Parks.

Mountain Bike Services: Rentals available at base for $22/full day or $15/half-day, reservations suggested; guided tours also available by reservation.

Special Events: Jimmy Huega Mountain Bike Express, August 24, 1996; possible race event in July 1996.

Emergency Facilities: Fully equipped emergency facility in the town of Driggs, 12 miles west of Grand Targhee.

Accommodations: Hotel accommodations on-site. For full lodging information, call 800/TARGHEE.

Dining: On-site dining includes Skadi's Restaurant for fine dining; Snorkel's restaurant for deli-style meals, home-baked pastries, and espressos; Trap Bar for sandwiches, burgers, etc.

Off-the-Bike Activities: Full-service spa facility, pool, hot tub, horseback riding, scenic chairlift rides, climbing wall, soaring, day trips to Yellowstone and Grand Teton National Parks, river rafting, tennis. Two music festivals take place on the mountainside amid wildflowers: the Sixth Annual Rockin' the Tetons Music Festival, a weekend of rock, blues, and reggae; the Ninth Annual Grand Targhee Bluegrass Festival, August 9–11, 1996, featuring Grammy winner Alison Krauss

Other Services and Features: Grand Targhee is a full-service, year-round resort offering the beauty of nature, fun, and excitement for people of all ages.

Colorado

Aspen

P.O. Box 1248
Aspen, CO 81612
(800) 525-6200
(800) 262-7736 (lodging)

Aspen is a historic mining town with approximately 300 retail stores, 30 art galleries, and 100 restaurants and bars. The Aspen Skiing Company runs four resorts in the area, all of which allow mountain biking: Aspen Mountain in the heart of downtown Aspen, Aspen Highlands (2 miles outside of town), Buttermilk Mountain (3 miles outside of town), and Snowmass (see separate listing). At press time, Aspen's plans for mountain biking were not set. Aspen Mountain may offer gondola-served mountain biking in the summer of 1996. Lift or not, Aspen's miles and miles of trails should not be overlooked.

PAUL HILTS PHOTO COURTESY ASPEN SKIING COMPANY

Location, Hours, and Prices

General Location: In the White River National Forest, 220 miles southwest of Denver

Getting There: Denver International Airport offers air and ground service to Aspen. Or you can fly into Aspen's airport, 3 miles from town, or Eagle Airport, 70 miles from Aspen. Driving from Denver, take I-70 west to Glenwood Springs and Highway 82 south to Aspen.

Biking Season: Mid-June to mid-September

Elevation: Base 7,900'; summit 11,212'

Hours: TBD

Prices: \$15/day for gondola if in use

Regulations/Restrictions: Helmets mandatory

The Rides

Aspen's backcountry roads and trails appeal to all levels of cyclists; you can find downhill tours, overnight hut trips, and half- and full-day trips over a variety of terrain. On the mountain, terrain varies from dirt roads to technical singletrack.

Terrain Description: Combination

Mileage/Number of Trails: TBD

Difficulty: TBD

Trails Under Development: TBD

Recommended Trails: Smuggler Mountain Road leads to Hunter Creek Valley and a variety of singletracks for the intermediate to advanced rider; Rio Grande Trail, part paved and part dirt, is suitable for beginner/intermediate riders.

Mountain Bike Lift: Possibly gondola

Trails Acessible from Lift: TBD

Biggest Vertical Drop: TBD

Longest Trail: TBD

Other Local Trails: The Aspen/ Snowmass area is filled with roads and trails suitable for mountain biking. Beginner to advanced riders will find terrain to suit their ability.

Trail Map: Available free from bike shops in Snowmass Village

Local Services

While the resort itself does not offer much in the way of mountain biking services, you can find just about everything you need in the town of Aspen or in nearby Snowmass Village.

Mountain Bike Services: Shops in Aspen and Snowmass Village rent and sell equipment. Several shops also offer clinics. Call for more information: Hub of Aspen, 970/925-7970; Ajax Bike and Sports, 970/925-7662; Aspen Bicycle Rentals, 970/925-1360; Aspen Ski Mart, 970/925-9169; Aspen Sports, 970/925-6331; Aspen Velo, 970/925-1495.

GREGG ADAMS PHOTO COURTESY ASPEN SKIING CO.

Special Events: Town race series on Tuesday nights; Hub of Aspen Mountain Bike Festival, July 6-7, 1996.

Emergency Facilities: Hospital located between Aspen and Snowmass Village, clinic at base of Snowmass, doctors in Aspen and Snowmass Village.

Accommodations: Aspen has a bed base of nearly 9,000 in a variety of hotels, inns, bed and breakfasts, lodges, and condominiums. Call 800/262-7736 for information.

Dining: 100+ restaurants, from casual to fine dining to ethnic food

Off-the-Bike Activities: Aspen features a world famous summer music festival, June-August; International Design Conference, June; Food and Wine Classic, June; Dance Aspen, July-August; Theater in the Park, June-August; FilmFest, September. Other outdoor activities include: hiking, whitewater rafting, kayaking, rock climbing, fly fishing, backcountry jeep tours, golf, hot-air ballooning, biplane rides, hang gliding, paragliding, tennis, arts and crafts fairs, 4th of July celebration and fireworks over Aspen Mountain, Ruggerfest rugby tournament, Mother Lode Volleyball Classic.

Beaver Creek

P.O. Box 7
Vail, CO 81658
(970) 845-5725

Located in the Vail Valley, Beaver Creek Resort is often overlooked due to its high profile neighbor, Vail. But Beaver Creek has plenty to recommend it to mountain bikers, including free lift-served biking—at least for 1996. Warm summer days and cool, crisp nights make Beaver Creek a great summer getaway.

Location, Hours, and Prices

General Location: Vail Valley in the central Rockies of Colorado

Getting There: 110 miles west of Denver on Interstate 70; free parking at base area

Biking Season: Early June to mid-October

Elevation: Base (at village) 8,100′; summit 11,440′

Hours: Centennial Lift will be open daily from July 1–August 31, and weekends through September.

Prices: The Beaver Creek Merchant, Culinary, and Lodging Association has sponsored a program for the summer of 1996 in which chairlift rides are complimentary. Stop by any shop, hotel, lodge, or restaurant within the resort for validation.

Regulations/Restrictions: Bikes with child seats not permitted up lift

JACK AFFLECK PHOTO COURTESY BEAVER CREEK

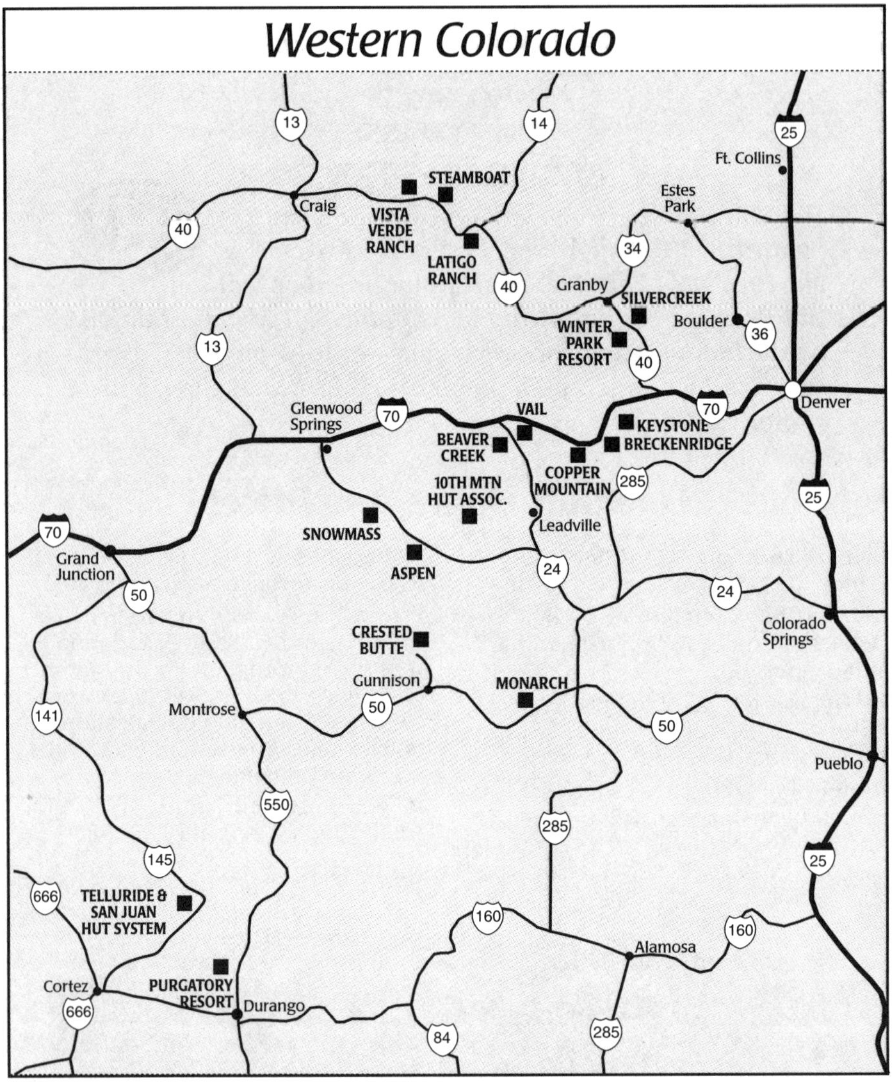

The Rides

Beaver Creek's 20-mile mountain bike trail network consists mostly of singletrack and service roads. Lifts provide access to a variety of terrain for all abilities.

Terrain Description: Combination

Mileage/Number of Trails: 20+ miles

Difficulty: 45% easiest, 20% more difficult, 35% most difficult

Trails Under Development: TBD

Recommended Trails: Village Loop and Oxford (beginner); Bachelor's Trail (intermediate, will be re-opened in 1996); Grouse Mountain Climb (advanced)

Mountain Bike Lift: 1

Trails Accessible from Lift: 8

Biggest Vertical Drop: 3,340′

Longest Trail: 4.5 miles (both Cinch and Dally)

Other Local Trails: Beaver Creek has limited access to other Forest Service trails and lands.

Trail Map: Available at bottom of mountain for no charge

Local Services

Beaver Creek offers mountain bike services as well as dining and lodging options. What you don't find on the actual mountain, you can find in Beaver Creek Village.

Mountain Bike Services: Mountain bike rentals available at the top of Centennial Lift and at the base area, $8/first hour, $5/second and third hour, $25/day.

Special Events: None at this time

Emergency Facilities: Medical services provided by Beaver Creek on-mountain employees

Accommodations: Beaver Creek Resort is in full swing in the summer with a wide range of hotels and lodges open. Call 800/525-3875 or 800/622-3131. Internet address: http//vail.net/summer

Dining: Lunch and refreshments served at Spruce Saddle (top of lift); complete menus are available in Beaver Creek Village.

Off-the-Bike Activities: Separate hiking trails, 4WD tours, horseback riding, whitewater rafting, and hot-air ballooning

Breckenridge Ski Resort

P.O. Box 1058
Breckenridge, CO 80424
(800) 789-7669
(970) 453-5000

During summer months, Breckenridge Ski Resort operates the Peak 8 Fun Park, featuring a super slide, miniature golf, lift rides, horseback riding, a human maze, mountain BBQs, nature walks, and, of course, lift-served mountain biking. Situated in Summit County between Keystone and Copper Mountain (see those two listings for more information), Breckenridge is the oldest continuously occupied town on Colorado's western front. The town's restored Victorian architecture and its Main Street, full of great restaurants and shops, give it a distinctive atmosphere.

Location, Hours, and Prices

General Location: Blue River Valley in the central Rockies

Getting There: From Denver, take Interstate 70 West for 75 miles to the Frisco exit, and then go south on Route 9 for 9 miles.

Biking Season: Mid-June through the end of September

Elevation: Base 9,950'; Vista Haus 11,200'

Hours: Mid-June to early September, 9:30–4:30; September, 10–3:30. Daily schedule is weather dependent.

Prices: Lift and trail pass, 1 ride with own bike, $7/adult, $5.50/child age 10–12; 2 rides with own bike, $11/

adult, $8/child age 10–12; unlimited rides with own bike, $16/adult, $11/child age 10–12; mountain biking season pass (interchangeable with Keystone Resort), $80/adult, $80/child. Rates subject to change without notice.

Regulations/Restrictions: Helmets required. Appropriate shoes, clothes, and gloves recommended.

The Rides

Mountain bikers can choose from four challenging lift-served singletracks at Peak 8. Terrain varies from gnarly switchbacks to wide ski runs. Most of the trails in the surrounding Blue River Valley and at Breckenridge are multi-use trails, so be courteous and yield the right-of-way to horseback riders and hikers.

Terrain Description: Mostly downhill

Mileage/Number of Trails: 4

Difficulty: 25% easiest, 50% more difficult, 25% most difficult

Trails Under Development: None

Recommended Trails: Pioneer Trail (beginner); Klinko Falls (intermediate); Frosty's Challenge (advanced)

Mountain Bike Lifts: 2

Trails Accessible from Lifts: All

Biggest Vertical Drop: 1,250′

Longest Trail: Pioneer Trail

Other Local Trails: For additional information on local trails and bike paths, stop at the Mountain Bike Rental Shop at the base of Peak 8. A paved bike path winds along the Blue River for 40 miles, all the way to Vail.

Trail Map: Available at the resort

Local Services

In addition to lift-served biking and bike rentals, Breckenridge's Peak 8 Fun Park has activities for the whole family. Plentiful lodging and dining choices exist in the Breckenridge/Keystone area.

Mountain Bike Services: Bike rentals include bikes with front suspension, lift and trail pass, and helmet. 1-hour rentals $14/adult, $9/child 10–12; 2-hour rentals $18/adult, $12/child; 3-hour rentals $22/adult, $15/child; day rentals $28/adult, $18/child; $6 additional/overnight bike rental. Rentals not available for children under 10. Helmets can be rented separately.

Special Events: TBD

Emergency Facilities: First aid room located at base; emergency telephones at Vista Haus and other selected spots on the mountain—see trail map for details.

Accommodations: A variety of options in the Breckenridge/Keystone area. See the Keystone listing for more details.

Dining: The Vista Haus and Bergenhof Restaurant are on-site. You can find more options in the Breckenridge/Keystone area. See the Keystone listing for more details.

Off-the-Bike Activities: A Superslide, scenic Superchair lift rides, Superputt miniature golf, horseback riding at Breckenridge Stables, Amaze'n Breckenridge (Colorado's largest human maze), mountain BBQs, Forest Service and self-guided nature walks

Other Services and Features: Variety of activities in the area. Check the Keystone listing for more details.

BOB WINSETT PHOTO COURTESY KEYSTONE RESORT

Copper Mountain Resort

P.O. Box 3001
Copper Mountain, CO 80443
(800) 458-8386

Copper Mountain Resort offers the luxury of a first-class resort located in the heart of the most rugged mountain biking region in the country. Extreme elevation changes (the summit is over 12,000') make for rigorous riding—and spectacular views.

Location, Hours, and Prices

General Location: 75 miles west of Denver and 20 miles east of Vail on Interstate 70

Getting There: From Denver, take I-70 West to exit 195. Parking is free.

Biking Season: June–September

Elevation: Base 9,712'; summit 12,313'

Hours: Daily, 10–3

Prices: Free lift rides for foot traffic; $10/day for bicyclists

Regulations/Restrictions: Helmets required

The Rides

Located along the paved bike path between Frisco and Vail and on the free Summit Stage shuttle route, Copper Mountain is a centrally located jumping-off spot for all levels of mountain biking. A scenic lift ride on the American Eagle high-speed quad chairlift provides access to 17.5 miles of gentle fire roads for the novice. The experienced rider can easily hop onto the 460-mile Colorado Trail, which stretches from Denver to Durango.

Terrain Description: Combination

Mileage/Number of Trails: TBD

Difficulty: TBD

Trails Under Development: Extensive cross-country and downhill trails, trials center, dual slalom course

Recommended Trails: An open-pit BBQ at Solitude Station at the top of the American Eagle chairlift highlights the spectacular views of the Ten Mile and Gore Mountain Ranges. The Ten Mile Canyon ride is great for intermediates and follows the old railroad grade along Ten Mile Creek. Stream crossings and gradual inclines build skills for some of the more challenging routes. Searle Pass begins at Copper, passes through a willow-filled valley, and eventually climbs into high alpine meadows on top of the pass. Steep, rocky sections add a significant level of difficulty to this advanced intermediate ride.

Mountain Bike Lifts: 1 or 2, depending on the snow pack

Trails Accessible from Lifts: TBD

Biggest Vertical Drop: 2,300'

Longest Trail: TBD

Other Local Trails: Lots of riding opportunities in the surrounding Arapaho National Forest; over 50 miles of paved bike paths in the area. Contact the Arapaho National Forest, Dillon Ranger District, P.O. Box 620, Silverthorne, CO 80498, 970/468-5400.

Trail Map: Available during summer months

Local Services

From brandname outlet shopping to rugged 4WD backcountry touring, Copper Mountain has it all. Visitors will find lodging and dining options for a variety of tastes and budgets.

Mountain Bike Services: Rentals available

Special Events: TBD

Emergency Facilities: On-site medical clinic, ambulance, emergency response team

Accommodations: Extensive lodging with free health club access for guests. Call 800/458-8386.

Dining: Plentiful dining options in the village. Call for details. On-mountain open pit BBQ.

Off-the-Bike Activities: Racquet and Athletic Club, golf course, horseback riding, hiking, tennis, chairlift rides, paddleboat rides, fishing, whitewater rafting, 4WD backcountry trips, canoe tours.

Other Services and Features: Restrooms and nature center on the mountain. Excellent shopping with over 25 shops in the village; over 70 brandname outlet stores in the town of Silverthorne, just 10 minutes east of Copper Mountain.

Crested Butte Mountain Resort

12 Snowmass Road
Crested Butte, CO 81225
(800) 544-8448

CRESTED BUTTE

Home to one of the longest running fat tire festivals and the Mountain Bike Hall of Fame, Crested Butte is among the most storied mountain bike destinations. Some of the best mountain biking terrain in the United States is easily accessible from the town center. Brilliant high-alpine scenery and a lack of crowds greet those fit enough to challenge the area's high altitude and rugged terrain.

Location, Hours, and Prices

General Location: About 230 miles southwest of Denver

Getting There: From Highway 50 in Gunnison, drive north 31 miles on Highway 135. There is air service to Gunnison, and the Alpine Express Shuttle (970/641-5074) transports visitors from Gunnison Airport to crested Butte.

Biking Season: Opens as soon as the snow melts, usually sometime from mid-May to mid-June; lift service closes Labor Day; all other trails open until the snow falls

Elevation: Town 8,889′; resort base 9,100′; summit 12,162′

Hours: Daily

Prices: None

Regulations/Restrictions: No bikes on chairlifts

TOM STILLO PHOTO COURTESY CRESTED BUTTE MOUNTAIN RESORT

The Rides

Surrounded by over a million acres of Forest Service land, Crested Butte boasts numerous biking trails, mainly singletrack, for all skill levels. On your rides, expect to find wildflowers, meadows, and stands of aspen. The quality of the riding and the scenery more than make up for the lack of lift service.

Terrain Description: Combination

Mileage/Number of Trails: Numerous

Difficulty: Predominately intermediate

Trails Under Development: None

Recommended Trails: Farris Creek Loop Trail #736/Upper Loop (beginner); Paradise Divide (advanced)

Mountain Bike Lift: None

Biggest Vertical Drop: 2,600′

Longest Trail: Not indicated

Other Local Trails: All surrounding roads lead to Forest Service land and maintained trails.

Trail Map: Available free from local ski shops, Chamber of Commerce. and Crested Butte Mountain Resort

Local Services

Most visitor services can be found in the Victorian town of Crested Butte.

Mountain Bike Services: Available from Butte & Co., Eflin Sports, The Alpineer, Flatiron, and Christy Sports. Flatiron rents bikes for $5/hour or $22/day; overnight and multi-day rates available. Christy Sports also rents bikes for $5/hour, $22/day adult and kids.

Special Events: Fat Tire Bike Week, June 24–30, 1996, $100/all races, $30/kids; Dirt Camp, June 27–30, 1996, call 800/711-DIRT.

TOM STILLO PHOTO/CRESTED BUTTE

TOM STILLO PHOTO COURTESY CRESTED BUTTE MOUNTAIN RESORT

Emergency Facilities: Mt. Crested Butte Clinic, 2 on-site clinics, 2 clinics in town; nearest hospital is Gunnison Hospital, 32 miles away

Accommodations: Varies from condos to hotels to bed and breakfasts; call 800/544-8448

Dining: Mt. Crested Butte and the town of Crested Butte are known for their fine restaurants.

Off-the-Bike Activities: Fishing, hiking, whitewater rafting, camping, hot-air ballooning, golf, wildflower festival, arts fair weekend

Other Services and Features: Mountain Bike Hall of Fame, P.O. Box 845, Crested Butte, CO 81224, 970/349-7382, houses a museum of mountain bike memorabilia.

Keystone Resort

Box 38
Keystone, CO 80435
(800) 222-0188 (reservations)
(800) 354-4386 (dining and activities)
(970) 468-2316

Woven into the Rocky Mountain tapestry, Keystone takes pains to balance wilderness aesthetics with world-class amenities. Here, everything blends seamlessly with the great outdoors. Though distanced from bustling metropolises, the area retains a feeling of sophistication. From fine dining to river rafting, mountain biking, and golfing, Keystone provides mountain adventures for the whole family.

Location, Hours, and Prices

General Location: 90 miles west of Denver International Airport, 70 miles west of Denver

Getting There: From Denver, take Interstate 70 West through the Eisenhower tunnel, to Dillon. Take Exit #205, and then go east for 6 miles on Highway 6 to Keystone.

Biking Season: Bike trails are generally open from mid-May through mid-October. Early/late season: Opening through mid-June and early September through closing. Regular season: mid-June through early September. Gondola operates from late June through early September.

Elevation: Mountain base at Keystone Village 9,200'; Outpost at North Peak 11,244'

Hours: Skyway and Outpost gondolas operate daily 9:30–3:30

Prices: Mountain bike lift ticket for 1 ride is $15/adult, $11/child age 12 and under; full day ticket is $20/adult, $15/child; season pass (interchangeable with Breckenridge) is $80/adult or child.

Regulations/Restrictions: Helmet, appropriate shoes, cycle clothes, and gloves recommended

The Rides

Keystone offers a wide variety of mountain biking terrain, including both downhill challenges and cross-country rides. With over 100 miles of trails, Keystone and the Snake River Valley area have terrain for all levels of cyclists. Challenge yourself on Radical Hill, ride alongside the Snake River, or let the gondolas whisk you and your bicycle up the mountain to experience challenging descents on old mining roads.

BOB WINSETT PHOTO COURTESY KEYSTONE RESORT

Terrain Description: Combination

Mileage/Number of Trails: 31 trails

Difficulty: 37% easiest, 56% more difficult, 7% most difficult

Trails Under Development: TBD

Recommended Trails: Sportshaq Trail (beginner); West Ridge Trail (intermediate); Frey Gulch Trail (intermediate and advanced)

Mountain Bike Lifts: 2 gondolas (Skyway and Outpost)

Trails Accessible from Lifts: All 31

Biggest Vertical Drop: 2,120'

Longest Trail: 14 miles (Peru Creek)

Other Local Trails: Over 100 miles at Keystone and in the surrounding Snake River Valley. More lift-served mountain biking is available at Breckenridge. (See the Breckenridge listing for more details.) Refer to the *Mountain Bike Guide to Summit County, Colorado* by Laura Rossetter, available at the SportShaq and the Activities and Dining Center at Keystone, and at bookstores and bike shops throughout Summit County.

Trail Map: The resort produces a comprehensive trail map with resort trails and other local rides.

Local Services

Very upscale, Keystone offers fine dining, golf, and tennis for adults, but does not neglect families, offering daycare and other programs for children. The SportShaq and River Run SportShaq II provide all kinds of bicycling services, from rentals to tours to sales.

Mountain Bike Services: Keystone's SportShaq provides basic repair services and sells bike parts and accessories. Guided tours on select terrain are also offered through SportShaq. A downhill tour runs $40. Call for more information or reservations, 970/468-4245. The shop rents 18-, 21- and 24-speed mountain bikes. Low season rates (early June and late September) for standard mountain bikes are $5.50/hour child and $7.50/hour adult, $17/half day, $20/full day, $17/day for multi-day rental; low season premium mountain bikes with suspension go for $8/hour adult, $19/half day, $22/full day. High season (midsummer) rates for standard mountain bikes are $6.50/hour child and $9.00/hour adult, $21/half day, $24/full day, $21/day for multi-day rental; high season premium mountain bikes with suspension go for $11.50/hour adult, $24/half day, $28/full day. Children's bikes are available only by the hour and are not available with suspension. The SportShaq is located in Keystone Village on the southeast end of the lake; hours are 9 a.m. - 8 p.m. daily during high season, and 9-6 daily during low season. The River Run SportShaq II at the base of the Skyway Gondola also offers rentals from mid-June to early September, and is open daily from 9:30-4:30.

Special Events: In conjunction with the Arapaho Warriors Cycling Club, Keystone sponsors The Snake River Mountain Bike Challenge in early September. Call 800/354-4386 for times, registration, and information.

Emergency Facilities: Emergency phones are marked on the bike trail map.

Accommodations: Keystone offers a variety of accommodations; among them are the Keystone Lodge, the Inn, condominiums, and private homes. Call 800/222-0188.

Dining: The Outpost atop North Peak features an outdoor summer barbecue from 11:00-2:30 during high season. In Keystone Village, Edgewater Cafe serves breakfast and lunch on a patio overlooking Keystone Lake, Ida Belle's Bar and Grille serves lunch and dinner, Pizza on the Plaza serves lunch and makes box lunches to go, The Keystone Ranch serves lunch, and Razzberry's at the Inn offers a breakfast buffet. More dining options are available nearby. Call 800/354-4FUN or 970/468-4FUN.

Off-the-Bike Activities: Children's programs, breakfast horseback rides, llama lunch rides, dinner hay rides, Thursday night Barn Dances, country dance lessons, fitness center (features exercise/aerobics room, weight room, massage, tanning, sauna, steam room, outdoor heated swimming pool and 2 hot tubs), fly fishing lessons, nature walks, 4WD tours, golf, scenic gondola rides, game room and arcade, stable and horseback riding, petting farm and pony rides, tennis, sailing tours, river rafting, various boating activities on Keystone Lake, Village entertainment, 4th of July concert and activities, Arts and Crafts Celebration, Annual Fiddle Contest, Colorfest '96, Taste of Keystone, and more

Other Services and Features: The Keystone Children's Center provides on-site daycare for children 2 months and older. At Kamp Keystone, kids 3 and up experience the mountains with nature hikes, gold panning, gondola rides, and other fun activities. Call for more information and reservations, 970/468-4181.

Latigo Ranch

P.O. Box 237
Kremmling, CO 80459
(970) 724-9008

Offering cross-country and downhill skiing in winter—and functioning primarily as a horse ranch in summer—Latigo Ranch offers mountain bikers more than 200 miles of old logging roads on the Routt and Arapaho National Forests that adjoin ranch property. The ranch provides clearly marked trail maps. Besides lodging and dining on-site, you can find plenty of horseback riding and other ranching activities, as well as fishing, swimming, rafting, hiking, and special children's programs.

Monarch Ski Resort

#1 Powder Pl.
Monarch, CO 81227
(800) 332-3668
(719) 539-3573

Located in the Upper Arkansas River Valley, Monarch Ski Resort sits atop Monarch Pass (11,386′) on the eastern flank of the Continental Divide. Surrounded by the 14,000′ peaks—15 of them—this area has become known as the 14ers Region. While the ski resort itself offers limited services to mountain bikers, the area is full of fantastic riding, with trailheads for such long-distance routes as the Colorado Trail and the Continental Divide Trail.

Location, Hours, and Prices

General Location: In central Colorado on U.S. Highway 50 at Monarch Pass

Getting There: From Denver, Monarch is 157 miles southwest via Highway 285 South and Highway 50 West. From Colorado Springs, it's 120 miles west via Highway 24 West, 285 South, and 50 West. From Gunnison, it's 43 miles east on U.S. 50.

Biking Season: Late June–August

Elevation: Resort/base 10,790′; summit 11,950′

Hours: Not indicated

Prices: Not indicated

The Rides

Most of the riding in the area is on the San Isabel National Forest. The Upper Arkansas River Valley's mining and railroading past has left a legacy of abandoned railroad beds that now make great biking and hiking trails. The trailhead for the Monarch Crest Trail sits at the base of the Monarch Scenic Tram. Named one of the top 5 downhill trails in the United States by *Bicycling* magazine, this trail is a must ride.

Terrain Description: Cross-country

Mileage/Number of Trails: Various

Difficulty: Varied

Trails Under Development: None

Recommended Trails: Monarch Crest Trail, Rainbow Trail

Mountain Bike Lift: No

Biggest Vertical Drop: Unknown

Longest Trail: Epic loops and one-way routes possible

Other Local Trails: Hundreds of miles of mountain biking on Forest Service land surrounding resort. Terrain varies from beginner to advanced. For more information, contact the local mountain bike group, Banana Belt Fat Tracks Mountain Bike Club, at Otero Cyclery, 719/539-6704.

Trail Map: Forest Service maps available locally. A free *Mountain Bike Guide to the 14ers Region*, outlining 15 rides, is available locally as well.

TOM STILLO PHOTO COURTESY CRESTED BUTTE MOUNTAIN RESORT

Local Services

Lodging and dining are available at the Monarch Mountain Lodge, 3 miles from the resort. More lodging and dining options as well as bike services are available in the nearby towns of Poncha Springs and Salida, 12 miles east, and Buena Vista beyond that.

Mountain Bike Services: For sales, service, parts, accessories, maps, rentals, and tours, try Otero Cyclery in Salida, 719/539-6704.

Special Events: Monarch is the site of the Monarch Mountain Challenge, a NORBA-sanctioned race and traditionally part of the Colorado Off-Road Points Series, which bills itself as the highest race in the United States. In September the local bike club sponsors the Banana Belt Loop fun ride. Call 719/539-6704 or 719/539-3573 for race information.

Emergency Facilities: Call 911. Local Sheriff's number is 719/539-2814. Most medical services are in Salida or Buena Vista.

Accommodations: Monarch Mountain Lodge, 800/332-3668, is 3 miles from the resort and offers 100 rooms, an indoor pool, outdoor hot tub, sauna, tennis and racquetball courts, and an outdoor activities center. Nearby Heart of the Rockies campground has RV sites, tent sites, a heated outdoor pool, horseback riding, whitewater rafting, a playground, miniature golf, and more.

Dining: Syncline Restaurant at Monarch Mountain Lodge

Off-the-Bike Activities: Rafting, fishing, Monarch Scenic Tram, hiking, backpacking, hot springs, golfing, ghost towns, 4WD tours, museums.

Other Services and Features: Contact the Buena Vista Chamber of Commerce at 719/395-6612, and the Salida Chamber of Commerce at 719/539-2068. For more trail information, contact the Salida Ranger District of the San Isabel National Forest at 325 West Rainbow Blvd., Salida, CO 81201, 719/539-3591.

Purgatory Resort

#1 Skier Place
Durango, CO 81301
(800) 525-0892 (central reservations)
(970) 247-9000

Primarily devoted to downhill skiing, Purgatory is a year-round resort with lift-served mountain biking, over 36 miles of trails on-site, and literally hundreds of miles of singletrack and trails in the surrounding National Forest. Condos, restaurants, and shops at the slopeside village and in nearby Durango make Purgatory a great mountain bike vacation destination.

Location, Hours, and Prices

General Location: 25 miles north of Durango in the San Juan Mountains of southwest Colorado

Getting There: The nearest airport is the Durango/La Plata Country Airport, an all-weather, jet-served commercial airport served by United Express from Denver International (7 times daily) and America West Express from Phoenix Sky Harbor International Airport (3 times daily). The nearest town to Purgatory Resort is Durango (pop. 14,000). The closest city is Albuquerque, New Mexico, 212 miles to the south.

Biking Season: Mid-June through Labor Day for lift-served mountain biking; trails are open until the first snow, usually in mid-October

Elevation: Base 8,793'; summit 10,822'

Hours: Chairlift runs daily, 9-4

Prices: $5/single lift ride, $12/all-day lift pass

Regulations/Restrictions: Helmets required with lift use. Helmets are provided with mountain bike rentals.

The Rides

How good is the riding at Purgatory? Well, the Purgatory and Durango area has more world champion mountain bikers per capita than any other place on earth. No less than Ned Overend, John Tomac, Greg Herbold, Juli Furtado, Ruthie Matthes, and Missy Giove train here. Area highlights include the World Championship Course on the ski mountain and the Hermosa Creek Trail just off of the mountain. Beginning riders and those not accustomed to Purgatory's elevation can make use of the chairlift for altitude gain without the pain.

Terrain Description: Combination

Mileage/Number of Trails: 36 miles on the mountain

Difficulty: 9% beginner, 65% intermediate, 26% advanced; trails that are not part of the ski system are not rated.

Trails Under Development: None for 1996

Recommended Trails: Columbine Loop (beginner); Hermosa Cliffs Overlook (intermediate); World Mountain Bike Championships Course (loop) or the Hermosa Creek Trail (point-to-point singletrack, shuttle required)

Mountain Bike Lift: 1

Trails Accessible from Lift: 6 on the mountain and many more outside the ski resort permit area

Biggest Vertical Drop: Depends where you go

Longest Trail: You could ride to Durango on a 45-mile trail if you have the legs and lungs for it, but most people can't do it in a day. Most advanced riders opt for either the 24-mile Hermosa Creek Trail or ride out and back on the Cascade Divide Road.

Other Local Trails: Literally hundreds of miles of jeep trails, Forest Service dirt roads, multiple-use trails, and singletrack. These rides fan out in all directions from Purgatory like spokes from a hub.

Trail Map: Available at the resort, or by calling 970/247-9000. The best resource is the booklet "Bicycle Routes on Public Lands of Southwest Colorado," published by the San Juan National Forest Association. Now in its expanded second edition, the book has information on 37 different road bike and mountain bike rides in the region. It costs $5 and is available at Purgatory Sports, or by calling the association at 970/385-1210.

Local Services

At the resort, you can find lodging and dining, and you can rent bicycles from Purgatory Sports. Purgatory and the western-themed town of Durango offer a full schedule of summer events, from classical music festivals to motorcycle rallies to cowboy poetry readings.

Mountain Bike Services: Available from Purgatory Sports (970/385-2183) at the resort, rental bikes are available in 2 models. The basic (non-suspension) bike costs $18/half day or $28/full day; performance (full suspension) bikes run $25/half day or $40/full day. Bike rentals include a water bottle and helmet; half-day rentals include 1 chairlift ride, and all-day rentals include an all-day chairlift pass.

BYRON HETZLER PHOTO COURTESY WINTER PARK RESORT

Special Events: The Durango Cup is a locals-oriented race series with dates TBD. The Iron Horse Bicycle Classic, a stage race that has riders competing on the road and in the dirt, is held Memorial Day weekend. Among the longest running mountain bike races, the Iron Horse Classic also includes the spectator friendly Budweiser Roostmaster Shootout, a circuit race which combines cross-country, downhill, and dual slalom terrain in a BMX-type track. For information, call 970/259-4621.

Emergency Facilities: Medical clinic staffed by EMTs for basic first aid located at the base of the lift

Accommodations: The slopeside Purgatory Village Hotel is the premier place to stay. For the price of a hotel room in Durango, you can get a mountain condominium. Rates are $70–$130. Numerous condos are available at the resort. Call 800/525-0892. The town of Durango has a bed base of 10,000+.

Dining: At the resort, Purgatory Creek serves lunch and dinner, mid-June to Labor Day; the Rocky Mountain Chocolate Factory has breakfast service; and you can get snacks at a deli/general store. There are a number of evening dinner restaurants at the resort, and Durango has over 40 restaurants, diners, cafes, and delis.

Off-the-Bike Activities: Alpine slide, scenic chairlift rides, horseback riding, wildflower walks, birding, backcountry jeep tours, hiking, fly fishing, and whitewater rafting on the Animas River. Scheduled events include: Songwriters' Rendezvous, Four Corners Backcountry Horseman Poker Run, Southern Ute Indian Tribe Bear Dance, Great Western Air Show, Champion International Whitewater Series, Art on the Animas Arts and Crafts Fair, Animas River Days Whitewater Festival, Fiesta Days/Parade and Rodeo, Annual Trimble Hot Springs Jazz Festival, Music in the Mountains/Classic Musical Festival, La Plata Country Fair, Annual Main Avenue Arts Festival, Four Corners Iron Horse Motorcycle Rally, Southern Ute Tribal Fair and Pow Wow, National Narrow Gauge Convention, Cowboy Poetry Gathering.

Other Services and Features: The Durango and Silverton Narrow Gauge Railroad takes passengers on a scenic ride along the Animas River gorge and on to Silverton, an authentic Old West town. Also nearby is Mesa Verde National Park, where you can explore the cliff dwellings of the ancient Anasazi Indians.

SilverCreek Ski Area

P.O. Box 1110, Granby, CO 80446

(800) 448-9458

(970) 887-3384

Known as a budget friendly destination during the winter months, SilverCreek Resort offers a variety of activities in the summer, including hot-air balloon rides, miles of mountain biking trails, hiking, and much more. Close to Denver, the resort makes a nice weekend getaway, or a convenient stop on the way to Rocky Mountain National Park.

Location, Hours, and Prices

General Location: 78 miles west of Denver

Getting There: From Denver take I-70 West to exit 232. Then take U.S. 40 West to SilverCreek, 15 miles past Winter Park.

Biking Season: Memorial Day weekend to Labor Day

Elevation: Base 8,202'; summit 9,202'

Hours: Daily

Prices: No charge to use trails

Regulations/Restrictions: None

The Rides

SilverCreek's dedicated trail system combines singletrack and doubletrack over terrain that is less demanding than what you'll find at many of the other Colorado resorts. Share trails winding through beautiful mountain pastures with coyote, elk, moose and deer—you might even catch sight of a bald eagle.

Terrain Description: Cross-country

Mileage/Number of Trails: 40 K

Difficulty: Not rated

Trails Under Development: None

Recommended Trails: Loop 13

Mountain Bike Lift: None

Biggest Vertical Drop: 1,000′

Other Local Trails: Trails connect directly to those at neighboring Snow Mountain Ranch/YMCA of the Rockies. In addition, access to the 600-mile Fraser Valley mountain bike trail network is just minutes away. See the Winter Park listing for more information on riding in the Fraser Valley.

Trail Map: Free maps available, call 800/448-9458

Local Services

SilverCreek itself has limited services, but you can find others in the nearby town of Granby. The resort does have rentals, and hosts several biking events.

Mountain Bike Services: Equipment rental available at the Inn at SilverCreek and Grand Cycles

Special Events: SilverCreek Fat Tire Classic, July 13, 1996; Courage Classic, September 7-8, 1996

Emergency Facilities: Timberline Clinic located 2 miles from the resort

Accommodations: At SilverCreek and in the town of Granby, 800/754-7458

Dining: In Granby

Off-the-Bike Activities: Fireworks, BBQ and parade, July 4; rodeo, July 20, 1996; Granby Arts and Crafts Fair, August 10-11, 1996.

Other Services and Features: Known as a family resort, SilverCreek was purchased by a Brazilian family in 1995.

PAUL HILTS PHOTO COURTESY ASPEN SKIING COMPANY

Snowmass

Aspen Skiing Company
P.O. Box 1248
Aspen, CO 81612
(800) 525-6200
(800) 598-2003

Operated by the same people who run Aspen (see the Aspen listing for more details on the area), Snowmass has better-developed lift service for mountain biking than its sister mountain.

Location, Hours, and Prices

JOHN BING PHOTO COURTESY ASPEN SKIING COMPANY

General Location: In the White River National Forest, 220 miles southwest of Denver, Colorado

Getting There: Denver International Airport offers air and ground service to Aspen/Snowmass. You can also fly into Aspen's airport, 3 miles from town, or Eagle Airport, 70 miles from Aspen. By car, take U.S. 70 to Glenwood Springs and drive south on Highway 82.

Biking Season: Mid-June to mid-September

Elevation: Base 8,114′; summit 11,325′

Hours: Daily, 10:30–5

Prices: No charge

Regulations/Restrictions: None indicated

The Rides

At press time, Snowmass had not decided which chairlifts would be open to mountain bikers in 1996. At least two will be open, most likely Funnel and Elk Camp. What's open in 1996 may not be what's open in upcoming years. Check with the resort for updates.

Terrain Description: Combination

Mileage/Number of Trails: TBD

Difficulty: TBD

Trails Under Development: TBD

Recommended Trails: Government Trail from Snowmass to Aspen

Mountain Bike Lifts: 2

Trails Accessible from Lift: TBD

Biggest Vertical Drop: TBD

Longest Trail: TBD

Other Local Trails: The entire Aspen/Snowmass area is filled with roads and trails suitable for mountain biking. See the Aspen listing for more information, or contact the White River National Forest, Aspen Ranger District, 806 West Hallam, Aspen, CO 81611, 970/925-3445.

Trail Map: Free at local bike shops

Local Services

You can find all sorts of lodging, dining, and nightlife in Snowmass Village and Aspen. Both areas also have recreational support services and outdoor gear suppliers.

Mountain Bike Services: Several shops in Aspen and Snowmass Village rent and sell equipment. Prices vary. Some shops also offer clinics; for details call Snowmass Shop at 970/923-6111, Snowmass at 970/923-5507, Gene Taylor Sports at 970/923-4336, or Sidewinder Sports at 970/923-3708.

Special Events: Tuesday night town race series; Hub of Aspen Mountain Bike Festival, July 6–7, 1996.

Emergency Facilities: Hospital located between Aspen and Snowmass Village; clinic at base of Snowmass; medical offices located in Snowmass Village and Aspen

Accommodations: Snowmass has a bed base of 6,000. Call 800/598-2003 for lodging information.

Dining: On-site, Cafe Suzanne is right in the middle of the lift-served terrain; Snowmass Village has more than 20 restaurants.

Off-the-Bike Activities: Snowmass hosts jazz concerts all summer. Other area activities include: hiking, whitewater rafting, kayaking, rock climbing, fly fishing, backcountry jeep tours, golf, hot-air ballooning, bi-plane rides, hang gliding, paragliding, tennis, arts and crafts fairs, 4th of July celebration and fireworks over Aspen Mountain, Ruggerfest rugby tournament, Mother Lode Volleyball Classic.

Other Services and Features: See the Aspen listing for more details on mountain biking in the area.

Steamboat

2305 Mt. Werner Circle
Steamboat Springs, CO 80487
(800) 922-2722 (reservations/lodging)
(970) 879-6111

Steamboat.

Not simply a resort, Steamboat actually encompasses a complete mountain range: Sunshine Peak, Storm Peak, Thunderhead Peak, and Christie Peak. About 2,500 acres of permitted terrain offer a diversity of trails for all ability levels. The trails take you through gentle rolling mountains to the rugged peaks of the Continental Divide, past waterfalls, rivers, streams, and lakes abundant with fish, and across fields, meadows and pastures resplendent with flowers, wheat, or native grasses. But you don't need to be an expert naturalist to appreciate all the land has to offer because there's more to do per square mile in and around Steamboat Springs than just about any other resort community.

Location, Hours, and Prices

LARRY PIERCE PHOTO COURTESY STEAMBOAT SKI CORP.

General Location: In northwest Colorado, 157 miles northwest of Denver

Getting There: Accessible by daily air service into Hayden Regional Airport on United Express with connecting service from over 100 other cities through Denver International Airport. Steamboat is an easy 3-hour drive from Denver. Take I-70 West through the Eisenhower Tunnel to the Silverthorne exit (#205), then go north on Colorado Highway 9 to Kremmling, then west on U.S. 40 to Steamboat Springs.

Biking Season: Weekends in early June; daily from mid-June through early September; weekends through the end of Sept.

Elevation: Downtown Steamboat 6,695′; ski area base 6,900′; mid-mountain 9,080′; summit/Mt. Werner 10,568′

Hours: The Silver Bullet gondola operates from 10–4, with the last down load at 4:30.

Prices: $19/adult gondola ride with own bike; $7/adult with current gondola pass and own bike; $50/passholder mountain bike book of 10 tickets; $75/passholder summer mountain bike season pass (for bike lift). Silver Bullet Gondola Prices are $12/adult day (good for same evening); $6/seniors 65–69 day (good for same evening, ID required); seniors 70 and over ride free day and evening (ID required); $6/evening-only adult or seniors 65–69; $6/kids 6–12 day and evening; kids 6–12 with paying adult (1 child per adult) ride free; kids 5 and under ride free; $75/summer 1996 season pass (for gondola rides); $10/summer 1996 senior season pass, 70 and over (for gondola rides); Steamboat ski season pass holders ride free.

Regulations/Restrictions: Helmets are required on the mountain and are included with all rentals; children under 18 must have parent's signature on liability release form; children 12 and under must be accompanied by an adult. Rental pricing does not include sales tax; all rentals require a credit card deposit. Due to extreme fire dangers, smoking is strictly prohibited in all areas.

The Rides

Steamboat's high-speed Silver Bullet Gondola transports cyclists and bikes to mid-mountain, accessing more than 40 miles of trails. Highlights include the new Pete's Wicked Trail, Duster/Broadway Loop, Zig Zag Trail, Valley View Trail, Storm Peak Challenge, Duster/Sunshine Loop, Creekside Loop, Short Cut Loop, Tenderfoot Loop, and Yoo Hoo Loop.

Terrain Description: Combination

Mileage/Number of Trails: 15 trails, 40+ miles

Difficulty: Not rated

Trails Under Development: Pete's Wicked Trail, a 4-mile mostly single-track adventure with creek crossings, switchbacks, expansive views, and lots of wildflowers

Recommended Trails: Any trails listed in "The Rides" introduction

Mountain Bike Lift: Silver Bullet Gondola

Accessible from Lift: All 15 trails

Biggest Vertical Drop: 2,100′ (Zig Zag Trail)

Longest Trail: 5.5 miles (Valley View Trail)

Other Local Trails: Contact the Routt National Forest, 29587 West US 40, Suite 20, Steamboat Springs, CO 80487, 970/879-1722

Trail Map: Free map available at base area of resort or the Summer Activities Center

Local Services

For on-mountain services, head to one of the Summer Activities Centers, located at the base area (open 8-5) across from the Silver Bullet Gondola exit and at the upper Silver Bullet Gondola terminal (open 10-3:45 p.m.). The Centers provide directions, daily activities, ticket sales, Hazie's brunch/dinner reservations, accessory sales, community happenings, and general Steamboat information.

Mountain Bike Services: Mountain bikes are available for rent at the Summer Activities Center or at the top of the Silver Bullet gondola. The fleet includes front-suspended bikes as well as standard KHS bicycles. Mountain bike packages include bike rental, gondola ride, bike lift, and helmet for $22/1-hour standard package, $25/1-hour suspension package; $31/3-hour standard package, $37/3-hour suspension package; $6/additional hours standard package, $9/additional hours suspension package. Mountain bike rentals include helmet, but no lifts: $6/1-hour standard package, $10/1-hour suspension package; $13/3-hour standard package, $19/3-hour suspension package; $6/additional hours standard package, $9/additional hours suspension package.

Special Events: Steamboat Mountain Bike Challenge, August 3-4, 1996, held on Pete's Wicked Trail

Emergency Facilities: For emergencies only, dial 911 for an emergency operator for fire, police, and ambulance services. Routt Memorial Hospital, located in downtown Steamboat Springs, provides medical care 24 hours a day, including emergency care, radiology, lab, respiratory therapy, family practice, general surgery, sports medicine, and more. If you need medical care during your visit, call 970/879-1322.

Accommodations: For on-site lodging, call 800/922-2722.

Dining: On-site, Thunderhead Sundeck BBQ atop Thunderhead Peak, open daily 10-4, for beverages and snacks, BBQ served daily from 11:30-2:30. Hazie's offers an à la carte menu Friday and Saturday night, with a stunning sunset view of the valley.

LARRY PIERCE PHOTO COURTESY STEAMBOAT SKI CORP.

Dinner includes a complimentary Silver Bullet gondola ride. Reservations available from 6:30 until 8:45. Reservations recommended, call 970/879-6111. In addition, Steamboat has over 60 bars and restaurants to choose from, with a wide variety of menus and pricing.

Off-the-Bike Activities: 1996 events include the 15th Annual Steamboat Marathon/Half-Marathon/10K, 16th Annual Yampa River Festival, Steamboat Carriage Classic, ProRodeo Series, 11th Annual Steamboat Western Weekend, Perry-Mansfield Performing Arts School and Camp, Jubilee Family Festival, Strings in the Mountains Music Festival, 93rd Annual Cowboy Roundup Days and Fourth of July Celebration, Rainbow Weekend/16th Annual Hot Air Balloon Rides, 22nd Annual Art-in-the-Park, Broken Skull Cattle Drive, Steamboat Mountain Youth Soccer Tournament, Perry-Mansfield Evening of Dance, Routt County Fair and Rodeo, Steamboat's PRCA ProRodeo Finals, Steamboat Springs Sidewalk Sale, Mountain Lumberjack Festival, Steamboat Derby Classic Cutting Horse Competition, Steamboat Wine Auction and Festival, 13th Annual Steamboat Vintage Auto Race and Concours d'Elegance, Literary Sojourn: Steamboat Festival of Authors, 16th Annual Steamboat Motorcycle Week, Steamboat's Fall Foliage Festival and BrewFest, 8th Annual Environment 2000 Conference.

Other Services and Features: Steamboat is on the World Wide Web at http://www.steamboat-ski-com. A wide variety of information is available through Steamboat Online, including facts about the mountain, prices, mountain bike rentals, lodging, and dining.

Telluride and the San Juan Hut System

Telluride Visitor Services
666 W. Colorado Ave.
P.O. Box 653 , Telluride, CO 81435
(800) 525-3455

Many journalists have written that Telluride is actually two towns in one—the Historic District, known for its laid-back atmosphere, spontaneity, and unique cultural opportunities, and the Mountain Village, the mid-mountain, European-style luxury resort. Telluride is one of the few places where you can enjoy the solitude of a backcountry camping trip and then go out for a five-star dinner and a night at the ballet. The town of Telluride sits at the base of the Telluride Ski Resort and is surrounded by more than 250 miles of hiking and biking trails. This is mostly public land and is therefore always "open." However, the ski area does not, as of now, provide lift service in the summer for mountain biking. Telluride makes a great base for exploring the area by bike, and can be used as a jumping-off point for the world-famous, multi-day bike trek from Telluride to Moab, Utah.

Location, Hours, and Prices

General Location: In the heart of the Uncompahgre National Forest in the Rocky Mountains of southwest Colorado, Telluride is 330 miles southwest of Denver, and 450 miles northeast of Phoenix.

Getting There: From Durango or Cortes, drive to Dolores and continue northwest on Highway 145 to Telluride. From Grand Junction, drive south on Highway 50 to Highway 550, continue south to Ridgway, drive west on Highway 62 to Highway 145, and then go south to Telluride. Telluride Regional Airport is 5 miles west of Telluride. Montrose County Airport, Telluride's alternate, is a scenic 67 miles northeast of Telluride. Telluride is serviced by United and American West Express.

PAGE TEAHAN PHOTO COURTESY TELLURIDE VISITOR SERVICES

Several ground shuttles operate in the area, as do major rental car agencies.

Biking Season: May to October

Elevation: Telluride 8,750'; Mountain Village 9,450'

Hours/Prices: Not indicated

Regulations/Restrictions: U.S. Forest Service regulations apply

The Rides

More than 250 miles of hiking and biking trails lead from town to pristine forests, alpine lakes, wildflower meadows, and mining ruins. Many of the old mining trails are open for jeep tours. Experienced cyclists can embark on a 70-mile loop around the Sneffels Range from Telluride to Ouray to Ridgway. But the area's crowning jewel is probably the San Juan Hut System. Originally developed for backcountry skiers, this hut-to-hut system has been expanded to a 215-mile trail network that links Telluride with Moab, Utah. Cyclists can travel lightly on this week-long trek, with their gear transported to overnight huts. Contact the San Juan Hut System at P.O. Box 1663, Telluride, CO 81435, 970/728-6935.

Terrain Description: Combination

Mileage/Number of Trails: 250+ miles

Difficulty: Varies

Trails Under Development: None

Recommended Trails: San Miguel River Trail (beginner); Bear Creek (intermediate); Silver Pick Road (advanced)

Mountain Bike Lift: None

Biggest Vertical Drop: Not indicated

Longest Trail: 215 miles (to Moab)

Other Local Trails: See below for information sources

Trail Map: Contact the Uncompahgre National Forest, Ouray Ranger District, 2505 South Townsend, Montrose, CO 81401, 970/249-3711, or the Norwood Ranger District, 1760 East Grand Avenue, P.O. Box 388, Norwood, CO 81423, 970/327-4261. You can also obtain the Telluride Mountain Biking and Hiking Trail Map from the Visitor Center.

Local Services

You can find bike rentals, tours, and hut-to-hut support in Telluride. The Victorian town boasts plenty of lodging and dining options.

Mountain Bike Services: Painted bright pink and yellow, town bikes are available free for tooling around town—just return them when you're done. San Juan Hut System for Telluride to Moab trek runs from June to October, $425/person, includes use of hut facilities, 3 meals a day, sleeping bag at each hut, trail descriptions, and maps. Guide service and vehicle shuttle available for additional fee. Rental bikes and panniers also available. Call 970/728-6935 for more information. Telluride Outside (800/831-6230 or 970/728-3895) offers downhill mountain bike tours for $55, including rental bike, shuttle, and refreshments. The tours run from Lizard Head Pass, 10,222', down 17 miles of the Galloping Goose Railroad grade for a 2,000' descent. Bike rentals available at local sport shops: Freewheelin' Bike Shop, 970/728-4734; Paragon Ski & Sport, 970/728-4525; Telluride Sports, 970/728-4477.

Special Events: Annual Melee in the Mines Mountain Bike Race, a NORBA-sanctioned event that is one of the most grueling legs of the 10-part Colorado Off-Road Point Series. The circuit race speeds through the streets and alleyways of Telluride's historic district and into Bear Creek Basin, while the cross-country race climbs nearly 3,000' through the Telluride ski area to Prospect Basin. Contact event organizer E. Dan Smith at Freewheelin' Bike and Board Shop, P.O. Box 3089, Telluride, CO 81435, 970/728-4734. Dates for the 1996 race are July 27-28. Telluride is also a stop on the Jimmie Heuga Mountain Bike Express, September 8, 1996.

Emergency Facilities: Call 911 for emergencies, or contact Telluride Medical Center, 970/728-3848.

Accommodations: Telluride Central Reservations offers several lodging specials with as much as a 15% discount on 3-night stays. Call 800/525-3455 or 800/525-2717. You can find standard to luxury accommodations in town and in the Mountain Village, including inns, hotels, lodges, homes, condominiums, a guest ranch, full-service luxury spa, and campsites in 6 areas.

Dining: Specializing in everything from pizza to gourmet wild game, Telluride has more than 40 cafes and restaurants, including delis, bakeries, vegetarian-only restaurants, coffee houses, street vendors, and catering.

Off-the-Bike Activities: Recreation opportunities include ballooning, four-wheeling, golf, horseback riding, river rafting, swimming, summer camps, glider rides, health clubs, rock climbing, tennis, camping, gold panning, hiking, mountain climbing, scenic drives, wagon dinner rides, fishing, geology tours, hut-to-hut tours, nature walks, spa services.

Other Services and Features: Numerous cultural events. A free gondola connecting the National Historic District of Telluride with the Mountain Village will open sometime in 1996.

PAGE TEAHAN PHOTO COURTESY TELLURIDE VISITOR SERVICES

10th Mountain Hut Association

1280 Ute Avenue, Suite 21
Aspen, CO 81611
(970) 925-5775

Formed for cross-country ski touring, the 10th Mountain Hut Association is open to mountain bikers in the summer months. The series of huts, spread over 300 miles of singletrack, allows for rugged backcountry mountain bike treks. The system is easily accessed from Vail, Leadville, or Aspen. Huts are open for summer use from early July through September. Current rates are $22 per person per night. The Association can help book privately owned lodging, too. Call for information and reservations. Guide service is also available for additional charge.

Please note that the Association is non-profit and relies heavily on memberships ($25) and donations to help construct, maintain, and operate the system. Consider joining or contributing if you use the system. For more details on planning a trip, consult *Colorado Hut to Hut: A Guide to Skiing and Biking Colorado's Backcountry* by Brian Litz, available from the Association or Westcliffe Publishers, Inc., 2650 South Zuni, Englewood, CO 80110. Maps and other publications are also available from the Association.

Vail

P.O. Box 7, Vail, CO 81658
(970) 476-5601

In the summer, Vail Mountain changes from a world-class ski resort to a mecca for mountain bikers and hikers. Instead of being knee deep in powder, outdoor enthusiasts find themselves knee deep in wildflowers on over 60 miles of hiking and biking trails. The only things that don't change are the scenery, terrain, and amenities—which definitely remain world-class.

JACK AFFLECK PHOTO COURTESY VAIL

Location, Hours, and Prices

General Location: Central Rocky Mountains of Colorado

Getting There: Vail is 100 miles west of Denver on Interstate 70. Parking is free at the town of Vail parking structures during the summer months.

Biking Season: Early June to mid-October

Elevation: Base 8,120'; summit 11,450'

Hours: Vista Bahn and Chair 3 run daily from early July to early September; the gondola runs Saturday, Sunday, and Monday from Memorial Day to mid-June, daily mid-June to mid-September, and weekends through mid-October.

JACK AFFLECK PHOTO COURTESY VAIL

Prices: $12/adults, $8/children, $7/bike, subject to weather and on-mountain construction

Regulations/Restrictions: Bicycles with child carriers are not allowed on the lifts and not recommended on the trails.

The Rides

Vail's trails are well known to racers, the resort having hosted several national and international competitions, including the 1994 World Championships. Advanced riders will want to try their luck on the championship courses. Others need not be intimidated—Vail offers easy bike paths for the beginner and plenty of intermediate terrain. Most of the mountain biking trails are singletrack and range from smooth to rocky and technical.

Terrain Description: Combination

Mileage/Number of Trails: 55 miles

Difficulty: 25% easiest, 30% more difficult, 45% most difficult

Trails Under Development: TBD

Recommended Trails: Village Trail and Gitalong Road (beginner); Grand Traverse, Kloser's Klimb, and Lion Down (intermediate); World Championship cross-country and downhill courses (advanced)

Mountain Bike Lifts: 3

Trails Accessible from Lifts: 18

Biggest Vertical Drop: 3,330'

Longest Trail: 11 miles (Grand Traverse)

Other Local Trails: Access to Forest Service trails; contact the White River National Forest, Holy Cross Ranger District, P.O. Box 190, 24747 US 24, Minturn, CO 81645, 970/827-5715. You can ride a paved bike path to Copper Mountain, Frisco, and Breckenridge, with side trips to Dillon and Keystone possible. See these resort listings for more information on biking in the area.

Trail Map: Free maps available at the bottom of the mountain at ticket offices

Local Services

Vail is top-notch all the way. You'll find mountain bike services on the mountain and in town. The Bavarian Vail Village hosts numerous restaurants, accommodations, and shops.

Mountain Bike Services: Mountain bikes available for rent at the base and top of the mountain for $8/first hour, $5/second and third hours, $25/day. Bike terrain park at the top of the gondola.

Special Events: Jimmie Heuga Mountain Bike Express mountain bike marathon to fight against Multiple Sclerosis, tentative dates for regionals, June 29, 1996, and for national finals, September 26–29, 1996.

Emergency Facilities: Vail Valley Medical Center at bottom of mountain; medical service is provided during the summer months by employees of Vail Associates.

Accommodations: Lodging is available in Vail, 800/525-3875 or 800/622-3131, or on the Internet at http://vail.net/summer.

Dining: Lunch and refreshments are served at the top of the gondola and at Mid-Vail. More options are available in the town of Vail at the base of the mountain.

Off-the-Bike Activities: In the Vail Valley you'll find hiking trails, 4WD tours, horseback riding, whitewater rafting, and hot-air balloon rides.

Vista Verde Ranch

P.O. Box 465
Steamboat Springs, CO 80477
(970) 879-3858
(800) 526-7433

A destination guest and ski ranch, Vista Verde provides casual rides and backcountry tours for their guests only. Mountain biking guests will find 50 miles of cross-country ski trails in addition to the hundreds of miles of roads and trails available in the nearby Routt National Forest. Lodging and dining is on-site, while nearby you'll find fishing, hiking, horseback riding, hot air ballooning, river rafting, rock climbing, and swimming. Biking season runs from late May to mid-September.

BYRON HETZLER PHOTO COURTESY WINTER PARK RESORT

Winter Park Resort

P.O. Box 36
Winter Park, CO 80482
(970) 726-5514

Winter Park Resort is a major year-round resort adjacent to a small mountain town along Colorado's Continental Divide. In addition to the many recreational activities here such as mountain biking and miniature golf, there is a full schedule of special events from June to September. Music festivals highlight the summer events, while the Winter Park Resort Mountain Bike Series and Chili Cookoff round out the summer competitions. Aside from the myriad activities, the views are spectacular and the people friendly and down-to-earth.

Location, Hours, and Prices

General Location: Only $1\frac{1}{2}$ hours from Denver and 40 miles from the west entrance of Rocky Mountain National Park, Winter Park Resort is located in the Arapaho National Forest.

Getting There: 67 miles northwest of Denver via Interstate 70 and Highway 40; 85 miles from Denver International Airport

Biking Season: June through September

Elevation: Base 9,000′; summit 10,700′

Hours: Daily, 10–5, mid-June to early September; weekends only through the end of September

Prices: One time up Zephyr Express Chairlift with bike is $11, $16/all day

Regulations/Restrictions: You must wear a helmet and sign a liability form. If you are 18 or under, your parent or guardian must sign liability form.

BYRON HETZLER PHOTO COURTESY WINTER PARK RESORT

The Rides

The towns of Winter Park and Fraser have worked with the resort, local Forest Service personnel, and the area mountain bike club to create a 600-mile trail network that rivals the finest trail systems in the country. At the resort, most of the trails are intermediate singletrack. In the surrounding Fraser Valley, there are paved bike paths and dirt trails for every ability level. Free maps and trail descriptions are available in boxes along many of the routes.

Terrain Description: Combination

Mileage/Number of Trails: 45 miles at the resort; hundreds of miles in surrounding areas

Difficulty: Resort trails are rated 10% easiest, 70% more difficult, and 20% most difficult.

Trails Under Development: March Hare

Recommended Trails: Sorenson Park/ Bike Path/Long Trail (beginner); Upper and Lower Roof of the Rockies (intermediate); Mountain Goat (advanced)

Mountain Bike Lift: 1—Zephyr Express

Trails Accessible from Lift: 9

Biggest Vertical Drop: 2,000′ (Upper Roof of the Rockies to base)

Longest Trail: 9.3 miles (Upper Roof, Lower Roof, Long Trail, Arapaho)

Other Local Trails: Over 600 miles of interconnected trails. For the inside scoop on trails and other mountain bike events, contact the Winter Park Fat Tire Society (FATS) at P.O. Box 1337, Winter Park, CO 80482, 970/726-8044, or 800/521-BIKE.

Trail Map: Summer trail maps are available free of charge at the base of Winter Park Resort.

Local Services

Winter Park has all sorts of bicycle services, from rentals to lessons to races, including the famous King of the Rockies Festival in August. The area boasts a full roster of special events slated for the summer months.

Mountain Bike Services: Bike rental rates are $5.50/1 hour standard bike, $9/1 hour front-suspension model, $12/1 hour full-suspension bike; $13/ half day standard bike, $22/half day front-suspension model, $30/half day full-suspension bike; $20/all day standard model, $32/all day front-suspension model, $44/all day full-suspension bike. Bike lessons run $14/ 2 hours, $25/4 hours. Bike patrol on duty during operating hours.

Special Events: Winter Park Race Series, $18 in advance, $20 on race day, $80 for series. 1996 dates are Sunday, June 23, circuit race; Sunday, July 7, cross-country race; Sunday, July 21, circuit race; Sunday, August 4, finals. Other events include Family Hike and Bike Festival, Saturday, June 22, free; Sixth Annual American Red Cross Fat Tire Classic, June 29-30, $45/person plus $150 in pledges; Women's Mountain Biking Weekend, July, TBA; King of the Rockies Mountain Bike Festival, Friday-Sunday, August 9-11, $40/person.

Emergency Facilities: 7 Mile Medical Clinic at the base of the resort

Accommodations: Winter Park Central Reservations handles more than 100 condos, family-style mountain inns, hotels, bed and breakfasts, European-style lodges, and motels. For information/reservations, call 800/729-5813.

Dining: More than 30 restaurants and bars within 4 miles of Winter Park

Off-the-Bike Activities: Alpine slide, human maze, chairlift rides, miniature golf, horseback riding, rodeo, golf, hiking, backpacking, camping, fishing, tennis, whitewater rafting, rock climbing, kayaking, boating, windsurfing, and in-line skating. Special events for 1996 include: Sixth Annual Great Western Shootout (archery competition), June 28-30; Run for Independence (5 mile and 10K run), July 6; Winter Park American Music Festival (with Big Head Todd and the Monsters), July 13-14; Priscilla Welch Running Camp, July 14-20 and September 15-21; Winter Park Jazz Festival, July 20; 23rd Annual Alpine ArtAffair (outdoor art festival), July 27-28; 11th Annual Rocky Mountain Wine, Beer and Food Festival, August 2-4; Fourth Annual Fraser Valley Railroad Days Festival, August 30-September 1; 18th Annual Winter Park Famous Flamethrower High Altitude Chili Cookoff, September 1; Fall Fest, September 14-15.

Other Services and Features: Summer camps for skiers and snowboarder.

CHAPTER 4

THE SOUTHWEST

Utah

Brian Head Resort

223 Hunter Ridge Rd.
Brian Head, UT 84719
(800) 272-7426 (24 hours for lodging)
(801) 677-2035

Brian Head RESORT

Located in spectacular southern Utah, Brian Head Resort is fast becoming one of the United States' premier mountain biking destinations. In the winter, the resort offers some of the best Utah powder skiing available. In the summer, Brian Head shifts gears into a mountain bike program, offering chairlift and shuttle access to the area's trails, bike rentals, major mountain bike festivals, competitions, and over 100 miles of world class mountain bike trails.

PHOTO COURTESY BRIAN HEAD RESORT

Location, Hours, and Prices

General Location: Southern Utah by Bryce and Zion National Parks

Getting There: From Las Vegas, less than a 3-hour drive up Interstate 15 North. From Salt Lake City, less than a 4-hour drive down I-15 South. Take I-15 to Parowan and exit on Highway 143. Continue 12 miles up to the resort.

Biking Season: June to early October, depending on weather conditions

Elevation: Some of the highest elevation riding available in the country, rides can begin above 11,000′ and drop over 5,000′.

Hours: Chairlift, bike shop, and shuttle operations offered during the day; regular mountain bike services are usually open from 9- 5. Trails are always open.

Prices: Estimated prices for 1996 are $10-$12/all-day lift pass, $5/single lift ride, $3/child sightseeing lift, $60/ summer season pass; shuttles available for $8/all-day-lifts per person for groups of 20 or more all day, $9-$12/ shuttle round-trip for Bunker Trail or Dark Hollow (group rate is $8/each), Sightseeing group rates: $4/each for adults, $2/each for children

Regulations/Restrictions: Helmets required

The Rides

Thanks to the lift and shuttle services, Brian Head is a downhiller's dream. The majority of trails are downhill routes, dropping 3,000′ to 5,000′ over distances of 15 to 20 miles, mostly on singletrack. Routes at the resort range from easy, beginner trails to advanced, rocky challenges, while the surrounding Dixie National Forest offers miles of roads and trails. Landscape varies from aspen groves to red rock formations. Who needs Moab when you can have all this—and no crowds?

Terrain Description: Cross-country and downhill

Mileage/Number of Trails: 20+ trails

Difficulty: 20% easiest, 60% more difficult, 20% most difficult

Trails Under Development: Dixie National Forest is expanding the trail systems in the southern Utah area.

PHOTO COURTESY BRIAN HEAD RESORT

Recommended Trails: Left Fork of Bunker Creek (beginner/intermediate, 12 miles, 2.5 hours, singletrack, shuttle required) is an absolute must for everyone. Beautiful overlooks and a thrilling variety of riding terrain make this route especially enjoyable. Elk frequent the area when the aspens turn gold. *Snow Country* magazine called it one of the top 5 mountain bike trails in the country. Dark Hollow/Second Left Hand Canyon (intermediate/advanced, 13 miles, 2.5 hours, shuttle required) features two outstanding attractions: more than a mile of vertical descent and colorful rock formations similar to those found in Bryce National Park. Abrupt descents, rocky stretches, and a stream crossing offer opportunities to sharpen your technical skills. Scout Camp Loop (intermediate, 9 miles, 1½ to 3 hours, loop) offers numerous delights: historical sites, a steam engine used in the 1879s, and incredible singletrack. One unforgettable section takes you on a zig-zagging plunge through an eye-boggling maze of aspen on a singletrack downhill.

Mountain Bike Lift: 1 (Giant Steps Chairlift)

Trails Accessible from Lift: 6 singletrack trails; top of the lift is also the trailhead for the majority of all the destination singletrack trails available, such as Bunker Creek and Dark Hollow.

Biggest Vertical Drop: Top of Giant Steps Chairlift at almost 11,000′ down to Dark Hollow at 6,000′

Longest Trail: Singletrack resort trails average 4 miles; 16 miles from Brian Head to Panguitch

Other Local Trails: Resort trails access other trails in Dixie National Forest

Trail Map: Free trail map available through the resort, Brian Head town, and Chamber of Commerce

Local Services

Brian Head, both the resort and the town, caters to mountain bikers in a big way. Despite a population of just 100, the area has all the bike services you could want. The area is particularly famous for its festivals and races. Lodging and dining options are more limited, but still surprisingly good for such a sparsely populated area. Be sure to ask about the resort's budget-minded lodging/biking packages.

Mountain Bike Services: 60 miles of singletrack, round-trip mountain bike shuttles, mountain bike clinics, guided bike tours, bike patrol/medical, free trail maps, 2 bike wash stations, Cannondale bike rentals, lodging and bike packages available. The small, bike-friendly town of Brian Head has 3 bike shops that offer rentals, sales, repairs, and riding tips.

Special Events: 1996 mountain bike events include the Utah Summer Games, June 18–19, downhill, uphill, and cross-country racing; Brian Head/ Bud Light Cannondale Cup, July 20–21, cross-country and downhill racing; Brian Head Bash (fat tire festival) August 2-4—southwestern Utah's biggest recreational mountain bike festival with guided tours, games, clinics, shuttles, BBQ, live entertainment; Brian Header (mountain bike race), August 31, cross-country racing; Fall Colors Fat Tire Festival, September 20–22—guided rides, shuttles, chairlift rides, picnics, clinics, live entertainment, prizes, all against the colors of autumn and in conjunction with Octoberfest. A summer mountain bike camp is also being scheduled for July.

Emergency Facilities: Giant Steps Mountain Bike Park medical EMT staff is available when lifts are open. Other medical support is available 24 hours a day from the town of Brian Head.

Accommodations: Brian Head Resort has many different accommodations available, including lodging with shuttle/lift service starting at $39.95 per person. Lodging is located right at the base of the ski/bike area. Call 800/ 272-7426 for lodging information, and 801/677-2035 for activity information.

Dining: 5 restaurants in town during prime summer season; grill and snack area at the resort

Off-the-Bike Activities: Fly-fishing lessons, guided horseback rides, hiking trails, babysitters available, Giant Steps BBQ, rock climbing, hot tubs, sight seeing, and shopping. The Utah Shakespeare Festival (rated one of the top 3 Shakespeare festivals in the United States) is a short 35-minute drive from Brian Head in the town of Cedar City. Cedar Breaks National Monument is 4 miles up the road from Brian Head, while Bryce and Zion National Parks are a short drive away.

Other Services and Features: Brian Head is located within The Grand Circle of the Four Corner states. Within the circle are 7 National Parks, 7 National Monuments, 5 National Forests, 5 American Indian reservations, and numerous State Parks and historical sites dotted with ancient petroglyphs.

Deer Valley Resort

P.O. Box 1525
Park City, UT 84060
(800) 424-DEER
(801) 649-1000

Upscale Deer Valley Resort hardly seems the place for panting, dirt-stained mountain bikers. But with 25 miles of lift-served terrain and high profile events like Downhill Mania, it draws more and more fat tire vacationers each year.

Location, Hours, and Prices

General Location: Park City, Utah

Getting There: 45 minutes from Salt Lake International Airport. Take Interstate 80 East to Kimball Junction exit, Highway 224. Take Highway 224 to Deer Valley Drive, and turn right, continuing to the resort. No charge for parking during summer months.

PHOTO COURTESY DEER VALLEY RESORT

Biking Season: Mid-June through Labor Day

Elevation: Base 7,200′; mid-mountain at Silver Lake 8,400′; summit 9,400′

Hours: Wednesday-Sunday and holidays, 10-5:30

Prices: $14/all day, $7/single ride; kids 4 and under ride free; $6 for foot passengers or scenic ride

Regulations/Restrictions: Children must be accompanied by a paid adult. Signed liability releases (by parent or guardian if under 18) required. Helmets mandatory.

The Rides

The Sterling Lift provides access to the top of Bald Mountain, where most of Deer Valley's trails begin. Most trails are custom-made singletrack, some linked by roads or ski runs. Much of the singletrack winds through aspen groves, twisting and turning on the way down the mountain. But there are also doubletracks and dirt roads for the less skilled. All the trails are well marked and well maintained.

Terrain Description: Downhill

Mileage/Number of Trails: 25 miles

Difficulty: 5% easiest, 45% more difficult, 50% most difficult

Trails Under Development: Constantly building new trails, usually 1-2 per season

Recommended Trails: McHenry's (beginner); Naildriver (intermediate);

Twist and Shout (advanced)

Mountain Bike Lift: 1

Trails Accessible from Lift: 17

Biggest Vertical Drop: 1,189' from Sterling chairlift

Longest Trail: 6 miles

Other Local Trails: Trails connect to Great Western Trail, Rails to Trails, Telemark Park, Wasatch Mountain State Park, and many other local trails

Trail Map: Call 800/424-DEER to request a free summer brochure and trail map.

Local Services

After a 5-year absence from the National Championship Series, Deer Valley will host a series event in 1996. The resort is also a stop on the Downhill Mania race circuit. Non-racers will find rentals and lessons on-site at Silver Lake Village, and plenty of lodging and dining choices when the riding is done.

Mountain Bike Services: Equipment rental available on the mountain through Cole Sports, prices TBD. Lessons are also available, prices TBD. Full-time bike patrol in place.

Special Events: 1996 events include the Pedalfest, June 22–23; Downhill Mania, August 17–18; and the NORBA National Championship Series, August 24–25.

Emergency Facilities: EMTs on staff, ambulance service to Park City Clinic

Accommodations: Lodging at the resort—call 800/424-DEER. Lodging and lift packages are available.

Dining: McHenry's Restaurant, located mid-mountain adjacent to the Sterling chairlift, is open for lunch. Lots of dining options in nearby Park City.

Off-the-Bike Activities: Scenic chairlift rides, hiking, outdoor concerts and events, horseback riding, golf, tennis, swimming, fishing, rodeo, shopping

Other Services and Features: The resort just completed a $10 million expansion to the Snow Park Lodge base facility. Deer Valley is the site of the 2002 Winter Olympics slalom, combined slalom, and freestyle aerial and mogul events.

Elk Meadows Ski and Summer Resort

P.O. Box 511
Beaver, UT 84713

(800) 248-7669

(801) 438-5433

On the Fishlake National Forest in the Tushar Mountains, Elk Meadows offers shuttle services to mountain bikers, seven designated mountain biking trails, rentals, guided tours, and access to miles of riding in the surrounding forest. Lodging, camping, and limited dining is available on-site, with more options in the town of Beaver.

The Homestead

P.O. Box 99, 700 North Homestead Drive
Midway, UT 84019

(801) 654-1102
(800) 327-7220

Less than an hour's drive from Salt Lake City, this resort offers bike rentals and over 20 miles of trails, but its primary concern is its 18-hole golf course. Other activities include hay rides, horseback riding, hot-air balloon rides, swimming, tennis, cross-country skiing, and snowmobiling. The Homestead also provides lodging and dining.

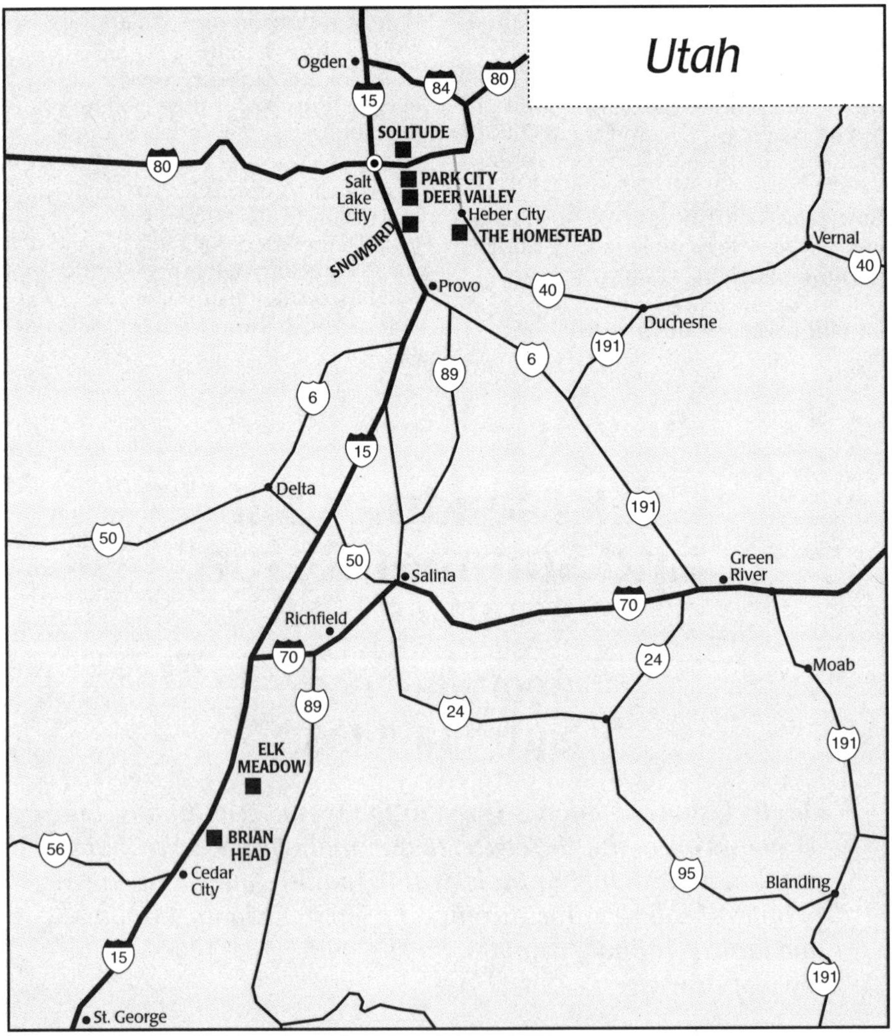

Park City Ski Area

P.O. Box 39
Park City, UT 84060
(801) 649-8111

Utah's largest ski resort, Park City Ski Area boasts 2,200 acres of terrain. The resort is currently expanding its mountain biking program. That can only mean even more riding opportunities in an area that already offers the mountain biker great terrain and scenery.

Location, Hours, and Prices

General Location: Northeast of Salt Lake City in the beautiful Wasatch Mountains.

Getting There: A 40-minute drive east from Salt Lake City International Airport via Interstate 80

Biking Season: Late May through late September

Elevation: Base 6,900'; summit 10,000'

Hours: All day, everyday

Prices: No charge to use trails

PHOTO COURTESY DEER VALLEY RESORT

The Rides

Park City Ski Area has both doubletrack and singletrack trails, and bikers will be on and off access roads and ski runs with the terrain varying between grassy slopes and rocky steeps. Trails are dedicated hiking/biking trails and are not open to vehicle traffic. Along these trails, you pass weathered mining buildings and historic relics from the area's silver mining past.

Terrain Description: Combination

Mileage/Number of Trails: 2 trails

Difficulty: Both trails rated difficult

Trails Under Development: Mountain biking program is currently being expanded, details TBD.

Recommended Trails: Sweeney Switchbacks and Shadow Lake Loop (both difficult)

Mountain Bike Lift: No

Biggest Vertical Drop: Not indicated

Longest Trail: 10.5 miles (Sweeney Switchbacks)

Other Local Trails: Numerous trails branch off from the two dedicated trails. All are rated difficult. Since Park City Ski Area is privately owned, any other terrain accessed off the designated trails is owned by the same mining company that owns the resort. However, there is a Ridge Ride along Jupiter Bowl, on the uppermost part of the mountain, that allows access to neighboring resorts of Deer Valley and Wolf Mountain.

Trail Map: "Park City Hiking and Biking Guide" provided by the Park City Chamber/Bureau and the Mountain Trails Foundation: 801/649-6100.

Local Services

Currently, there's not much in the way of bike services on-site, but you can certainly find what you need in the town of Park City. Both the town and the resort center have a variety of lodging and dining choices.

Mountain Bike Services: Several outfitters in the town of Park City rent mountain bikes/equipment and host workshops.

Special Events: Pedalfest and Tour d'Suds; for dates and prices contact the Mountain Trails Foundation at 801/649-6100.

Emergency Facilities: Medical clinic on-site; University of Utah Family Health Center in the town of Park City

Accommodations: There's plenty of lodging at the resort and in town; call 800/222-PARK

Dining: There are several restaurants at the resort center, and Main Street, which is a short ride away, is home to numerous other eateries.

Off-the-Bike Activities: Little Miners' Park offers amusement rides for youngsters. Other activities include an alpine slide, miniature golf, horseback riding, hiking, shopping, summer concert series, Music in the Mountains, and arts festivals.

Other Services and Features: Park City's colorful mining past is present today in the area's historic architecture on and off the slopes.

Snowbird Ski and Summer Resort

Snowbird, UT 84092

(801) 742-2222 • (801) 742-3344

Surrounded by rugged mountains in lovely Little Cottonwood Canyon, Snowbird is an alpine-style resort with condominiums, full service hotel, conference center, and 12 restaurants. In the summer, you can enjoy tram-served mountain biking on advanced-level trails.

Location, Hours, and Prices

General Location: 25 miles from Salt Lake International Airport in the Wasatch Cache National Forest

Getting There: Take Exit 6 off of Interstate 215 and then go south on State Road 210. Plenty of free parking available.

Biking Season: Mid-June to mid-October

Elevation: Salt Lake Valley 4,500'; resort base 8,100'; summit at Hidden Peak 11,000'

Hours: Daily, 11-7

Prices: $9/single lift ride, $12/all-day lift ticket

Regulations/Restrictions: Advanced riders only; helmets required; waiver signed by adult required

The Rides

Snowbird's Aerial Tram whisks riders to the top of 11,000' Hidden Peak for a challenging descent. Trails are old mining service roads of mixed dirt and gravel. Traffic is restricted to hikers, cyclists, and official resort vehicles only.

Terrain Description: Downhill
Mileage/Number of Trails: 4 miles
Difficulty: All trails rated difficult
Trails Under Development: As of spring 1996, one low elevation intermediate trail was almost complete, and construction on a second top-to-bottom advanced trail had just started.
Mountain Bike Lift: 1
Trails Accessible from Lift: 1
Biggest Vertical Drop: 2,900′
Longest Trail: 3 miles
Other Local Trails: Contact the Wasatch-Cache National Forest
Trail Map: Available throughout the resort

PHOTO COURTESY SNOWBIRD SKI & SUMMER RESORT

Local Services

A full-service destination resort, Snowbird provides plenty of lodging and dining choices, and on-site mountain bike services at the Snowbird Activity Center.

Mountain Bike Services: Rental bikes with front suspension available for $35/day; instruction is $35/4 hours. Bike patrol on mountain.
Special Events: Outdoor Sports Festival, July 4th weekend, includes a bike race that is part of the Fat Tire Series.
Emergency Facilities: Bike patrol and ambulance service available. Nearest hospital is 8 miles away.

Accommodations: Approximately 2,000 beds, condos, and hotels on property. Call 800/453-3000.
Dining: 12 restaurants
Off-the-Bike Activities: Assorted weekend festivals, aerial tram to 11,000′ peak, spa in Cliff Lodge, hiking, rock climbing, tennis ($4 for lodge guests)
Other Services and Features: Day care available. Largest private collection of Persian rugs on open display under one roof.

Solitude Ski Resort

12000 Big Cottonwood Canyon
Solitude, UT 84121
(801) 534-1400
(801) 536-5707

In the past, Solitude has offered lift-served access to a 25-mile trail network. However, Solitude is suspending mountain biking operations for 1996 because of construction, but should resume them in 1997. The improvements should increase both skiing and mountain biking opportunities.

Location, Hours, and Prices

General Location: 28 miles southeast of downtown Salt Lake City

Getting There: From Salt Lake City, take I-80 East to I-215 South. Take Exit 6 and follow the signs to Solitude.

Biking Season: June to October

Elevation: 7,988′

Hours: Not indicated

Prices: Not indicated

Regulations/Restrictions: Helmets mandatory

The Rides

Solitude currently has 6 miles of signed, marked, and patrolled singletrack and service road for biking. The dedicated biking and hiking trails are very technical, and you may encounter service vehicle traffic on some routes. An extensive cross-country ski network is also available.

Terrain Description: Combination

Mileage/Number of Trails: 3 trails

Difficulty: 80% more difficult, 20% most difficult

Trails Under Development: An additional 2 miles of trail will be in place for summer 1997.

Recommended Trails: Silver Fork Trail (beginner); Solitude Canyon (intermediate); Wasatch Crest (advanced)

Mountain Bike Lift: 1

Trails Accessible from Lift: 3

Biggest Vertical Drop: 900′

Longest Trail: 6 miles

Other Local Trails: Approximately 25 miles of trails in and around Solitude

Trail Map: Free at base area

Local Services

Because of Solitude's expansion, mountain bike services are very limited at this time. Expect that to change in the near future. Meanwhile, you can find accommodations and dining on-site and nearby.

Mountain Bike Services: Should be available in 1997

Special Events: Solitude Sizzler, July 14, 1996

Emergency Facilities: On-site

Accommodations: Creekside and Solitude offer 1-, 2-, and 3-bedroom condo rentals, call 801/536-5787.

Dining: Creekside at Solitude restaurant; Silver Fork Lodge, 1 mile down canyon

Off-the-Bike Activities: Hiking and fishing

Other Services and Features: The epic Great Western Trail runs through the area.

PAUL PETERSEN PHOTO COURTESY BEAR VALLEY X-C SKI & ADVENTURE CO.

Arizona

Flagstaff Nordic Center

P.O. Box 40
Flagstaff, AZ 86002
(520) 779-1951

When summer comes to northern Arizona, the Flagstaff Nordic Center (FNC) puts away the cross-country skis and brings out a new fleet of mountain bikes. Enjoy cool summer temperatures on FNC's marked trail system, and experience scenic views from the western slope of Arizona's highest point, Humphreys Peak (12,633').

Location, Hours, and Prices

General Location: 16 miles northwest of Flagstaff

Getting There: Take Highway 180 northwest of Flagstaff for 16 miles to mile 232. Parking is free.

Biking Season: June through October

Elevation: Base/resort 8,000'; summit 8,600'

Hours: Friday–Sunday, 9–5

Prices: Hourly $8/adult, $5/junior; daily $23/adult, $19/junior

Regulations/Restrictions: Helmets mandatory

The Rides

FNC's doubletrack trails are smooth, "family friendly," and well marked. Some 25 miles of trails wind through pine-clad forest and open up to scenic views.

Terrain Description: Cross-country

Mileage/Number of Trails: 25 miles

Difficulty: 50% easiest, 50% more difficult

Trails Under Development: Numerous unmarked doubletrack trails are located in the area

Mountain Bike Lift: No

Biggest Vertical Drop: Not indicated

Longest Trail: Not indicated

Other Local Trails: Miles of doubletrack in the area

Trail Map: Free at the center with bike rental

Local Services

FNC rents bikes for adults and children, and provides instruction and tours for all age groups. The area's lodge has day-use facilities; lodging and other dining options are found in Flagstaff.

Mountain Bike Services: Bike tours, bike and helmet rentals, kids camp

Special Events: Kids Mountain Bike Camp on Fridays; Eat, Drink and Bike Merry in the fall; mountain bike races, run/bike races

Emergency Facilities: First aid at lodge

Accommodations: In Flagstaff, call 800/828-7285

Dining: Food and beverages available at lodge; restaurants in Flagstaff

Off-the-Bike Activities: Hiking, scenic chairlift ride to 11,000' at nearby Arizona Snowbowl

Other Services and Features: 60 miles from the Grand Canyon; fall colors (aspens) are particularly nice

Sunrise Park Resort

P.O. Box 217
McNary, AZ 85930
(800) 554-6845
(520) 735-7669

Spread across three mountains, Sunrise Park Resort is Arizona's largest ski resort. A full-service area, Sunrise has approximately 65 trails for biking—a combination of logging roads, marked trails, and service roads. The resort is unique in that it sits on the White Mountain Apache Reservation and is run by the White Mountain Apache Tribe.

Northern and Central Arizona

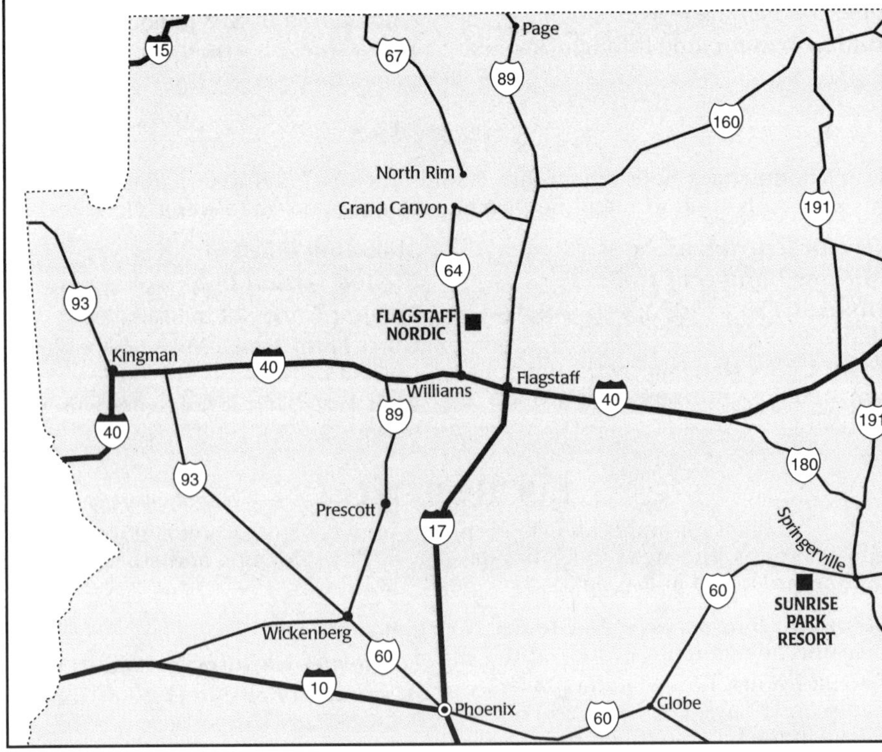

Location, Hours, and Prices

General Location: White Mountain area, central eastern part of the state; 200 miles northeast of Phoenix, 200 miles north/northeast of Tucson, 225 miles west of Albuquerque, New Mexico.

Getting There: Located off Highway 260 between the communities of Pinetop and Springerville (near the New Mexico border). Map and detailed driving instructions are included with reservations.

Biking Season: June through September

Elevation: Resort 9,100′; base 9,200; summit 11,000′

Hours: Trails open daily, 9–4; lifts operate on select weekends only

Prices: Land use permit $6

Regulations/Restrictions: Stay in approved areas, certain areas restricted

The Rides

The resort is in the early stages of developing more of the area for summer biking and hiking uses. Currently trails consist of doubletrack or singletrack and some access or service roads (service roads are not open to public vehicle traffic). Trail surfaces vary from gravel to loose rock to dirt. The trails are rated the same as the ski terrain—beginner, intermediate, advanced. Note: In 1996, lifts will be running on set weekends only—June 7–9, July 4–6, and August 31–Sept. 2.

Terrain Description: Combination

Mileage/Number of Trails: 65 trails

Difficulty: 40% easiest, 40% more difficult, 20% most difficult

Trails Under Development: Approximately 15 additional miles of trails in development

Recommended Trails: Poleknoll, Paradise Creek, Green's Peak

Mountain Bike Lifts: 2 (open on select weekends only; see above)

Trails Accessible from Lifts: About 40

Biggest Vertical Drop: 1,800′

Longest Trail: 5 miles

Other Local Trails: Adjacent to National Forest land with access to 26 miles of semi-developed multi-use trails

Trail Map: Included with purchase of land use permit

Local Services

Sunrise Park is a self-contained resort with lodging, dining, and bike rentals on-site. For those who want to rough it, camping and RV facilities are available.

Mountain Bike Services: Bike and safety equipment rental through Sunrise Sports Center

Special Events: NORBA downhill championship races, June 7–9, 1996.

Emergency Facilities: Licensed EMT on-site; nearest hospital 25 miles away

Accommodations: Call 800/554-6835 or 520/735-7669

Dining: Dining facilities available on mountain on the weekends lifts are operating. Full food service available at hotel 7 days a week.

Off-the-Bike Activities: Camping, RV hook-ups, hiking, fishing (boat rental and equipment available), horseback riding, Indian Casino 17 miles away. Scheduled 1996 events include archery tournament, June 21–22; Marathon/50 mile race, July 6; indoor dart tournament, August 2–3; Indian Pow Wow, July 29–30.

Other Services and Features: Located on the White Mountain Apache Reservation

New Mexico

Angel Fire Resort

P.O. Drawer B
Angel Fire, NM 87710
(505) 377-6401
(800) 633-7463

ANGEL FIRE
NEW MEXICO'S PREMIER FAMILY RESORT

Perched in the Sangre de Cristo Mountains, Angel Fire is a four-season resort offering golf, skiing, horseback riding, fishing, rafting, snowmobiling, mountain biking, and other fun activities. If the stunning backdrop of the Sangre de Cristos isn't enough to entice you, maybe the picture-perfect summer weather will—the average summer high is 72 degrees. Angel Fire has the added benefit of being close to Taos and its famous galleries.

Location, Hours, and Prices

MICHAEL MANTHEI/LEGENDARY PHOTO COURTESY ANGEL FIRE

General Location: 150 miles north of Albuquerque and 22 miles east of Taos

Getting There: Head north out of Albuquerque on I-25, through Santa Fe and up to Taos. Go east on Highway 64 and follow signs to the resort.

Biking Season: April to November

Elevation: Resort 8,500'; base 8,700'; summit 10,680'

Hours: Daily, 10 hours a day; chairlift service weekends, 10–3

Prices: $7/unlimited lift rides

Regulations/Restrictions: Tread lightly, stay out of restricted areas, and wear a helmet.

The Rides

All trails are closed to motor vehicle traffic. Trails are predominately singletrack with technical sections, but are joined with access roads. All ski run are considered smooth, dedicated trails. Keep your eye on Angel Fire in the coming years, as an expansion plan calls for a 20% increase in skiing and biking terrain.

Terrain Description: Combination

Mileage/Number of Trails: 60 miles

Difficulty: 25% easiest, 35% more difficult, 40% most difficult

Trails Under Development: The area is currently expanding the ski/bike terrain with the addition of a high-speed detachable quad chairlift, which should add approximately 20% more terrain.

Recommended Trails: Angel Fire Green Belts (beginner); Chili Challenge Race Course (intermediate); South Boundary Trail or The Three Passes (advanced)

Mountain Bike Lift: 1 (more will be open after construction)

Trails Accessible from Lift: 51

Biggest Vertical Drop: 2,180′

Longest Trail: 3.7-mile downhill, 8.6-mile cross-country

Other Local Trails: Angel Fire is a gateway to incredible mountain biking in the Carson National Forest. With expansive terrain and a variety of difficulty levels, this is the premier mountain biking area in northern New Mexico. There are about 80 miles of trails within 1 mile of the ski area boundaries, including the awesome South Boundary singletrack. For more information, contact the Carson National Forest, Camino Real Ranger District at P.O. Box 68, Penasco, NM 87553, 505/587-2255.

Trail Map: Contact the resort at 800/633-7463 or 505/377-6401, or call Mountain Sport at 505/377-3450.

Local Services

Angel Fire is a completely appointed resort with expanding bicycle services and a variety of accommodations and restaurants. If nothing right here grabs you, you can find fabulous Southwestern cuisine and an array of activities in Taos.

Mountain Bike Services: Rental equipment is available within the resort area. The resort is getting serious about mountain biking and, as of spring, 1996, plans to develop a full array of classes, tours, and services in the base area. Check with the resort for the latest information.

Special Events: The Chili Challenge VIII, September 21–22, 1996, is the final stop of the New Mexico State Off-Road Championship Series. Call 505/377-4237 for more information.

Emergency Facilities: Ambulance and EMTs on hand at all times

Accommodations: The resort hotel, The Legends, is located at the bottom of the ski mountain. Call 800/633-7463 for information on The Legends or the numerous resort-managed condominiums.

Dining: The Legends has 2 dining facilities and a lounge; several other facilities are located at Angel Fire, many within walking distance.

Off-the-Bike Activities: Golf, tennis, fishing, river rafting, horseback riding, gold panning, Taos Pueblo and gallery tours, balloon rides, wine tasting events, concerts, art festivals, and more. The Legends has a spa with indoor swimming pool, hot tub, and exercise equipment.

Other Services and Features: Angel Fire offers supervised child care for children 6 weeks to 6 years. For children 7-12, they offer the Summer Mountain Adventure, a day full of activities for active youngsters, Monday–Friday, 8–5.

MICHAEL MANTHEI/LEGENDARY PHOTO COURTESY ANGEL FIRE

Sandia Peak Ski Company

#10 Tramway Loop NE, Albuquerque, NM 87112

(505) 242-9133 (ski area)
(505) 856-6419 (business office)

Conveniently located just outside of Albuquerque and easily accessible, Sandia Peak is a family area offering scenic summer chairlift rides to the top of the mountain. From the summit, visitors can enjoy an unparalleled view of the 11,000-square-mile Land of Enchantment. Guests may take advantage of the mountain biking trail system, hiking, sand pit volleyball, or horseshoes. A full-service base facility, including the Double Eagle II Outdoor Grill, makes Sandia Peak a perfect place for family reunions, company picnics, club gatherings, or just getting together with friends.

Location, Hours, and Prices

General Location: Located in the Cibola National Forest, approximately 30 minutes from Albuquerque. The Ski Area is also accessible by the Sandia Peak Aerial Tramway from far north-east Albuquerque. Note that bikes are not allowed on the Tramway, but rental bikes are available at the top of the chairlift where the Tramway and ski lift meet.

Getting There: From Albuquerque, take I-40 East into the east mountain area and exit Cedar Crest, Highway 14 North to Highway 536. Proceed up Highway 536 to the Sandia Peak Ski Area base lodge. Parking is available in the Ski Area lot free of charge.

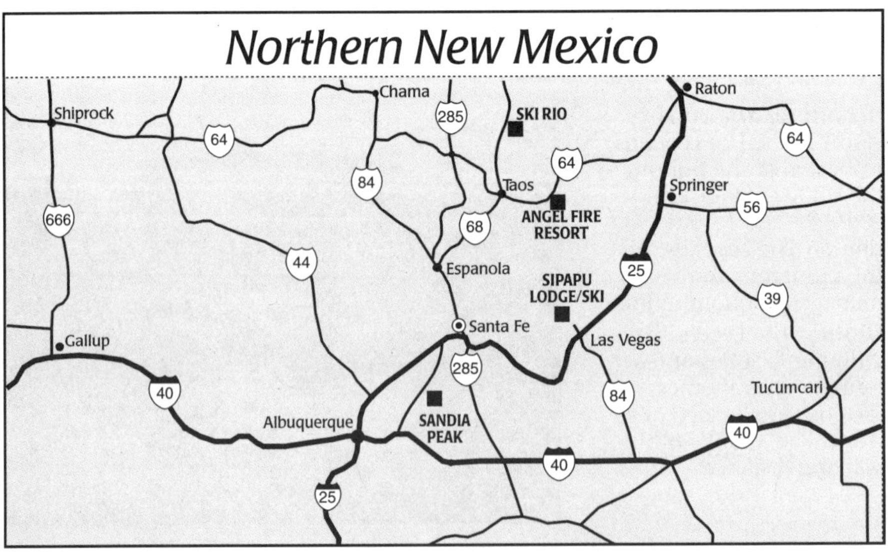

Biking Season: Sandia Peak's traditional mountain biking season begins Memorial Day weekend and ends with the final weekend of the Kodak International Balloon Fiesta in mid-October.

Elevation: Base 8,600'; summit (Sandia Peak) 10,378'

Hours: Thurs.-Sun. and holidays, 10–4. Trails open at 12:30 on race days; reduced rates available on those days.

Prices: \$6/round-trip chairlift; \$4/one-way lift; \$4/with tram ticket; \$6/one way with bike, \$10/all day with bike.

Regulations/Restrictions: Helmets mandatory. Children must be accompanied by an adult. No bikes allowed on tram.

The Rides

Sandia Peak offers nine bike routes for various skill levels, including Kids Circuit. Lift service eases the pain for those not accustomed to the altitude (the summit is over 10,000'), but those with the legs and lungs are welcome to tackle the King of the Mountain uphill, which includes over 5 miles of climbing over 9,000'.

Terrain Description: Combination

Mileage/Number of Trails: 9 trails, ranging from 0.8 mile to 8.3 miles

Difficulty: 45% easiest, 33% more difficult, 22% most difficult

Trails Under Development: None at this time

Recommended Trails: Golden Eagle Downhill, Service Road, Capulin Spring Road, The Kids Circuit (beginner); King of the Mountain Downhill, Falcon Ridge Uphill Climb, Mule Deer Uphill Climb (intermediate); King of the Mountain Uphill Climb, Competition Loop (advanced)

Mountain Bike Lift: 1

Trails Accessible from Lift: All

Biggest Vertical Drop: 1,500'

Longest Trail: 8.3 miles (King of the Mountain)

Other Local Trails: Contact the Cibola National Forest at 505/243-8443

Trail Map: Sandia Peak Trail Maps are available free of charge by writing or calling the Sandia Peak Ski Company. Forest Service Trail Maps are available from the Forest Service office for a minimal fee.

Local Services

Sandia Peak attracts racers with its full schedule of competitive events. Recreational riders will find rentals and bike services at both the top and bottom of the mountain. While the resort offers all the necessary day facilities, Albuquerque is the place for overnight lodging and dining.

Mountain Bike Services: Full-service bike rental shop, including front-suspension rental bikes for adults, children's bike rentals, safety equipment rentals, parts, supplies, repair, and maintenance. Rentals available at the top and bottom of chair #1. Professional bike patrol on mountain.

Special Events: Sandia hosts a 6-race Mountain Bike Challenge Series; 1996 dates are May 27, July 7, July 27–28, August 18, September 8, October 6. Other events include the Watermelon Mountain Classic, part of the New Mexico Off-Road Series in June.

Emergency Facilities: Professional and volunteer staff on duty to offer first aid or medical service. The Ski Patrol building is located at the base area.

Accommodations: Some in nearby Cedar Crest and the east mountain area; most hotels and activities are in Albuquerque, about 30 miles away.

Dining: Full-service outdoor grill (open 11–3), picnic facilities, group rates, and group food service for 75 or more on-site. Other restaurants in Albuquerque.

Off-the-Bike Activities: In early October, Albuquerque hosts the renowned Kodak Albuquerque International Balloon Fiesta.

Sipapu Lodge and Ski Area

Route Box 29
Vadito, NM 87579
(505) 587-2240

Nestled in the mountains on the banks of the Rio Pueblo, Sipapu provides a comfortable, affordable haven for a relaxing vacation. The mountain location brings cool breezes during the summer, clear, crisp air for fall hiking and backpacking, and skiing in the winter.

Location, Hours, and Prices

General Location: On Highway 518 between Las Vegas (New Mexico) and Taos

Getting There: Albuquerque is the nearest airport. Go north on I-25 to Santa Fe, then north on Highway 285/84 towards Espanola. From there, take Highway 68 towards Dixon, then Highway 75 towards Penasco, and then Highway 518 toward Las Vegas. Sipapu is about 15 miles from that point on Highway 518.

Biking Season: April–November

Elevation: Base/resort 8,200′; summit 9,065′

Hours: 8–4

Prices: No charge to use trails

The Rides

New Mexico's oldest ski area, Sipapu offers a trail network of 19 cross-country runs of varied difficulty. In general, the terrain is steep and the elevation can be a bit daunting.

Terrain Description: Cross-country

Mileage/Number of Trails: 19 trails

Difficulty: 20% easiest, 50% more difficult, 30% most difficult

Trails Under Development: None

Mountain Bike Lift: No

Biggest Vertical Drop: 865′

Longest Trail: 1.3 miles

Other Local Trails: 150 miles of forest trails in and near the resort, including trails in the Pecos Wilderness and the Carson National Forest

Trail Map: Free

Local Services

Although the lodge offers accommodations and food, you will otherwise be on your own. No bicycling facilities exist at this time, nor are there many other local services.

Mountain Bike Services: None

Special Events: None

Emergency Facilities: Ambulance available

Accommodations: At the lodge—call 505/587-2240

Dining: Food service and groceries available at the lodge

Off-the-Bike Activities: Motorcycle trails, hiking, backpacking, fishing, picnic areas, camping, skiing, cross-country skiing

Other Services and Features: Excellent family resort

Ski Rio

P.O. Box 159
Costilla, NM 87524
(505) 758-7707

Boasting 810 skiable acres with 83 trails on 8,300 acres, Ski Rio offers a total winter experience without any crowds. In summer, this northern New Mexico resort opens its trail system for lift-served mountain biking. From the top of the chairlift, you can see north into Colorado.

Location, Hours, and Prices

General Location: 48 miles north of Taos

Getting There: From Albuquerque take I-25 North to Santa Fe, and continue on State Route 68 to Taos. From Taos go 40 miles north on Highway 522 and then 8 miles east on State Road 196.

Biking Season: June through August

Elevation: Base 9,500'; summit 11,650'

Hours: Weekends and holidays, 10–3

Prices: \$5/Bravo chairlift ride, 50¢ for kids 6 and under

Regulations/Restrictions: Helmets required. Stay on marked trails.

The Rides

Biking the backcountry at Ski Rio is an exciting adventure for both novice and expert riders. The Bravo chairlift provides access to over 13 miles of designated trails in both the ski basin and the cross-country touring area. In the Nordic area, you ride through groves of fir, pine, and aspen, where you might catch sight of deer, elk, rabbit, squirrels, and woodpeckers.

Terrain Description: Combination

Mileage/Number of Trails: 13 miles

Difficulty: 60% easiest, 20% more difficult, 20% most difficult

Trails Under Development: None

Recommended Trails: Night Wind (beginner); Over Easy (intermediate); Winter Hawk (advanced)

Mountain Bike Lift: 1

Trails Accessible from Lift: All

Biggest Vertical Drop: 900'

Longest Trail: Racer's Edge

Other Local Trails: No access

Trail Map: Available from resort

Local Services

From suites with private hot tubs to kitchen units, Ski Rio provides a variety of accommodation choices. You will find dining on-site, too. Basic bike repair and bike rentals are also available.

Mountain Bike Services: Bike rental, including helmet, is \$15/half day and \$20/full day. Bike repair also available.

Special Events: No

Emergency Facilities: Yes

Accommodations: At Ski Rio, the Silver Tree condos, Paradise Hotel, Stone Bridge Inn; call 800/2 ASK RIO (227-5746)

Dining: Silver Tree Restaurant, Day Lodge Cafeteria; picnic areas at

Evergreen Lake, Westlake, and Aspen Lake

Off-the-Bike Activities: Hiking, camping, fishing, sightseeing in nearby Taos. Lodging guests have access to hut tubs and saunas.

Other Services and Features: During the winter, the resort offers 5 on-snow sports as well as snowmobiling, dogsled tours, and sleigh rides.

PHOTO COURTESY NORTHSTAR-AT-TAHOE

CHAPTER 5

THE SOUTH

North Carolina

Sugar Mountain Resort

P.O. Box 369
Banner Elk, NC 28604
(704) 898-4521
(800) SUGAR MT (during ski season)

Beginning in the late summer of 1993, Sugar Mountain started allowing mountain bike enthusiasts access to its slopes. Since that time the system has grown to over 10 miles of trails. All the trails are intermediate to advanced with a vertical rise of 1,200'. Most trails are open year-round, but some are closed during the ski season. North Carolina's largest ski area, Sugar Mountain does not charge a trail fee.

Location, Hours, and Prices

General Location: Near the Kentucky border in the northeasten part of the state

Getting There: From Charlotte, take U.S. 77 north and U.S. 40/Highway 70 west to Morgantown. Head north on Highway 181 to Highway 105, then Highway 184 for 1 mile to the resort.

Biking Season: Mid-April through mid-October; some trails open year round

Elevation: Base 4,100'; summit 5,300'

Hours: Mountain biking allowed during daylight hours, Monday–Sunday

Prices: No charge

Regulations/Restrictions: Helmets mandatory; ride at your own risk.

The Rides

Sugar Mountain has over 10 miles of doubletrack and numerous singletracks for intermediate and advanced riders. You can ride to the top for a nice view. For trail access, go to the bottom of Easy Street or the brown lift at the base of Sugar Mountain Resort, locate the green trail marker, and begin riding. There are a series of green, yellow, and orange trails. Organized group rides are welcome.

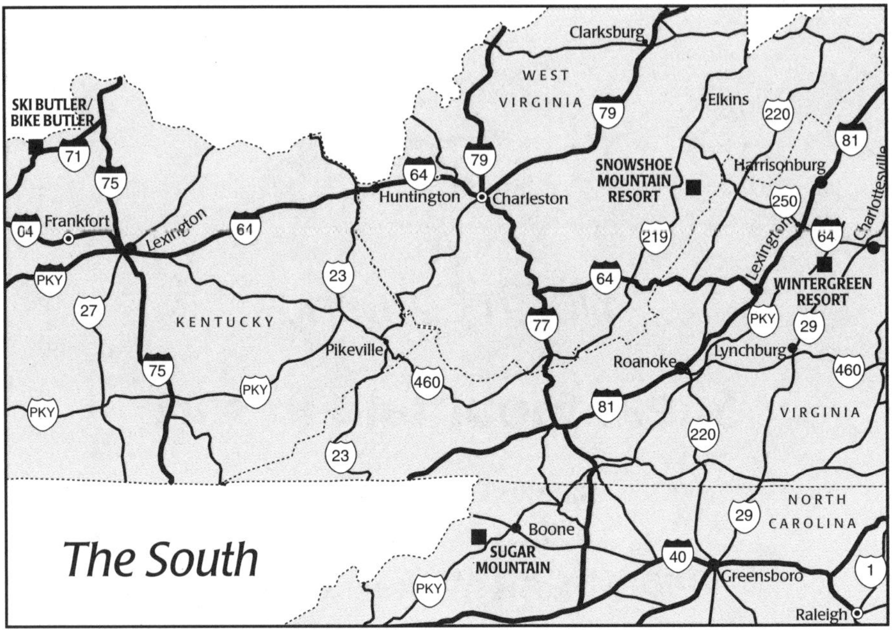

Terrain Description: Combination
Mileage/Number of Trails: 10+ miles
Difficulty: Intermediate and advanced
Trails Under Development: None
Recommended Trails: Not indicated
Mountain Bike Lift: No

Biggest Vertical Drop: 1,200′
Longest Trail: Not indicated
Other Local Trails: No
Trail Map: Available for free from the Administration Office in the Base Lodge, Monday–Friday, 8–4.

Local Services

Although there are no bicycle services at the resort, you can find lodging, and golf and tennis facilities at Sugar Mountain. Dining and other services are available nearby.

Mountain Bike Services: None on-site

Special Events: Annual Showdown At Sugar Mountain Bike Race in August, for all abilities and ages, merchandise and cash prizes. Call 704/898-4521 for more details.

Emergency Facilities: Hospital 3 miles away

Accommodations: Call 800/438-4555

Dining: Everything from fast food to fine dining within 3 miles of resort

Off-the-Bike Activities: Golf and tennis at the resort; whitewater rafting, tourist attractions, movies, and shopping nearby

Other Services and Features: North Carolina's largest ski area

PETE WINKEL PHOTO COURTESY WINTERGREEN RESORT

Virginia

Wintergreen Resort

P.O. Box 706
Wintergreen, VA 22958
(800) 325-2200
(804) 325-2200

A four-season resort and conference center in Virginia's Blue Ridge Mountains, Wintergreen offers luxurious accommodations, 36 holes of championship golf, and distinctive dining. Nightly, weekend, and weekly rates and packages are available.

Location, Hours, and Prices

General Location: 43 miles southwest of Charlottesville in the Blue Ridge Mountains

Getting There: USAir Express, United Express, American Eagle, and Com Air (Delta Connection) serve the Charlottesville Airport. Transportation to Wintergreen from the Charlottesville and Lynchburg airports is available through Wintergreen Transportation Services, 804/325-2200, ext. 850. By car from areas east and northeast, including Charlottesville/ Albemarle Airport, follow Route 29 South to I-64 West to Exit 107 (Crozet, Route 250). Take Route 250 West to Route 151 South, and turn left. Follow Route 151 South to Route 664, 14.2 miles. Turn right, and Wintergreen is 4.5 miles ahead on Route 664. From areas west, northwest and southwest, take I-81 to I-64 East to Exit 99 (Route 250). Take Route 250 East to Route 151 South, and turn right. Continue by following the previous directions. From areas south, including Lynchburg airport, take Route 29 North to Route 151 North, and turn left. Follow Route 151 for 21 miles to Route 664. Turn left and Wintergreen is 4.5 miles ahead on Route 664. From the Blue Ridge Parkway, take Reeds Gap exit (between mileposts 13 and 14) on Route 664 and go east 1 mile to the Wintergreen entrance.

Biking Season: Memorial Day to Labor Day

Elevation: Base 600′; resort 3,600′; summit 3,800′

Hours: Daily, 10–8

Prices: No charge for guests to use trails; visitors must pay $3 trail fee.

Regulations/Restrictions: Helmets required; riders must register at the Mountain Bike Center at Lake Monocan.

The Rides

Wintergreen's valley foothills offer singletracks through a rich variety of terrain, from very beautiful wooded glens and meadows, to peaceful stream banks. These dedicated mountain biking trails are not part of the ski trails.

PETE WINKEL PHOTO COURTESY WINTERGREEN RESORT

Terrain Description: Cross-country
Mileage/Number of Trails: 8.5 miles
Difficulty: 33% easiest, 33% intermediate, 33% advanced
Trails Under Development: None
Recommended Trails: None indicated
Mountain Bike Lift: No
Biggest Vertical Drop: Not indicated
Longest Trail: Not indicated
Other Local Trails: No
Trail Map: Available free to resort guests; included in $3 trail fee for visitors

Local Services

Guided rides and mountain bike rentals are available weekends in May, September, and October, weather permitting, and daily Memorial Day through Labor Day. Guided rides must be arranged in advance.

Mountain Bike Services: Bicycle rental available $9/hour, $21/half day, $30/full day for resort guests; $30/half-day guided ride for resort guests; rentals for non-guests $12/hour, $25/half day, $36/full day, $36/half-day guided ride.

Special Events: None

Emergency Facilities: Rescue squad on property

Accommodations: Wintergreen offers 340 rental homes and condominiums ranging in size from studios to 6 bedrooms. More than 1,000 guests can be accommodated in overnight lodgings. Most accommodations have fireplaces and fully-equipped kitchens, and many have spectacular views. Call the resort at 800/325-2200.

Dining: Coppermine, Cooper's Vantage, Garden Terrace, Verandah, and Rodes Farm Inn on-site

Off-the-Bike Activities: Golf, tennis, swimming, hiking, canoeing and fishing on Lake Monocan, equestrian center and stables, spa with indoor/outdoor sports facilities, sports and therapeutic massage, nature program, children's programs, fly fishing stream, wine festival, micro brewery festival, special holiday weekends, shopping.

Other Services and Features: Wintergreen is considered one of the

PETE WINKEL PHOTO COURTESY WINTERGREEN RESORT

country's most environmentally sensitive resorts and is a former winner of the National Environmental Quality Achievement Award from the American Hotel and Motel Association. The Wintergreen Nature Center offers a year-round outdoor program and teaches conservation education to both children and adults.

West Virginia

Snowshoe Mountain Resort

P.O. Box 10
Snowshoe, WV 26209
(304) 572-1000 (information)
(304) 572-5252 (reservations)
Internet: http://wvweb.com/www/snowshoe.html

Tucked away in the Allegheny Mountains, Snowshoe Mountain Resort harbors over 100 miles of maintained mountain biking trails and two full-service mountain bike centers. In fact, Snowshoe's Mountain Bike Centers are one reason that Pocahontas County, West Virginia, has been hailed as the East's answer to Moab, Utah. The mountain biking here has rightly been heralded in a number of bicycling publications, and the area is quickly becoming one of the premier mountain bike vacation destinations in the United States.

Location, Hours, and Prices

General Location: Central West Virginia, 45 miles south of Elkins and 26 miles north of Marlinton

Getting There: From Lewisburg, drive north on Highway 219 past Marinton and on to the resort. Closest airports are Lewisburg (USAir), 1½-hour drive, and Clarksburg (USAir), a 2-hour drive. Plenty of free parking at both of the resort mountain biking centers.

Biking Season: Mid-April to late October

Elevation: Base 3,250′; summit/resort 4,848′

Hours: Daily, 8–sunset

Prices: $8/all-day trail pass; $12/two-day pass; $15/3-day pass; $75/season pass; fees include trail map

Regulations/Restrictions: Trail pass required. Helmets always mandatory.

The Rides

All types of rides are available, from meandering along easier country backroads and trails to barreling down 1,500 vertical feet, dodging rocks and trees along the way. Plenty of wide-open riding as well as expert and beginner singletrack make Snowshoe a good choice for any level or rider.

Terrain Description: Combination

Mileage/Number of Trails: 125 miles of maintained trails

Difficulty: 30% easiest, 45% more difficult, 25% most difficult

Trails Under Development: None at this time

Recommended Trails: Greenbrier River Trail (beginner); Bald Knob Road (intermediate); The Plunge (advanced)

Mountain Bike Lift: Only for special events

Biggest Vertical Drop: 1,500′

Longest Trail: Bald Knob, 25 miles round trip

Other Local Trails: There is mountain biking access from Snowshoe Mountain Resort to 309,000 acres of the Monongahela National Forest in Pocahontas County, West Virginia.

Trail Map: Available at the Snowshoe and Silver Creek Mountain Biking Centers for $2

Local Services

Snowshoe has two top-notch Mountain Biking Centers, one located at the base of the mountain and one at the Silver Creek Lodge. Staffed with trained professionals, the centers offer guided tours, trail advice, bicycle rentals and sales, as well as service. The centers carry top-of-the-line mountain bikes, including rigid, front suspension and full-suspension models, and tandems.

Mountain Bike Services: Rigid bike rentals cost $30/all day, $50/2 days, $70/3 days, $20/additional day, $10/hour, $15/2 hours, $20/3 hours; front-suspension models cost $36/all day, $60/2 days, $85/3 days, $25/additional day, $15/hour, $20/2 hours, $25/3 hours; full-suspension models cost $42/all day, $70/2 days, $100/3 days, $30/additional day, $20/hour, $25/2 hours, $30/3 hours; tandems run $50/all day, $80/2-days, $115/3-days, $35/additional day, $25/hour, $30/2 hours, $35/3 hours. Reservations recommended, call Snowshoe at 304/572-1000, ext. 165, or call Silver Creek at 304/572-6766. Weekend expeditions ($20, trail pass must be purchased separately) leave the Silver Creek shop at 10 a.m. on Saturday and Sunday. These 3-hour tours require advance reservations. Call the above number for information. Private tours are also available (trail pass must be purchased separately): 2-hour tours run $30/person, $45/2 people, $60/3 or more; 3-hour tours cost $40/person, $60/2 people, $80/3 or more; 4-hour tours cost $50/person, $75/2 people, $100/3 or more; all-day tours (6 hours) run $60/person, $90/2 people, $120/3 or more. Shuttle service for you and your bike leaves the Mountain Bike Center at The Inn at Snowshoe on the hour, stops at Silver Creek and the Timberline parking lot, and then returns to the bottom; operates daily from Memorial weekend to early October, 9-5:30, and on weekends from late April to late May, and early October to early November; costs $5/ride or $20/all day.

PETE WINKEL PHOTO COURTESY WINTERGREEN RESORT

Special Events: 1996 events include the Get It In Gear Weekend, June 22-23 (singletrack skills instruction, mechanical and nutritional clinics, $75, event and lodging package $125); Wild Hare Mountain Bike Festival, July 26-28 (3-day festival with guided rides and fun events $115, event and lodging package $165); NORBA American Mountain Bike Challenge, August 10-11 (cross-country, downhill, dual slalom, and trials competitions, prices TBD); Master the Mountain Weekend, September 14-15 (lift-serviced riding, guided rides, and fun events $95, event and lodging package $145).

Emergency Facilities: Daily bike patrol, 3 medics, 3 EMTs, and fully staffed clinic on the mountain

Accommodations: Snowshoe Lodging Reservations can be reached at 304/ 572-5252. Super Saver Mountain Bike Packages are available and include meals, trail pass, trail map, lodging, bike rental, and a souvenir water bottle. One-night packages run from $52–$87, depending on type of bike rented; 2-night packages run from $95–$155, depending on type of bike rented.

Dining: Skidder Restaurant at Timberline Lodge, Brandi's Restaurant at The Inn at Snowshoe, Terrace Restaurant at Silver Creek Lodge

Off-the-Bike Activities: 4 pools, 3 workout facilities, 2 Jacuzzis, horseback riding, golf, tennis, hot tubs, shopping, hay rides, nature programs, canoeing, fishing, hiking, whitewater rafting, chili cook-off, Snowshoe Symphony Festival, Cass Scenic Railroad, National Radio Astronomy Observatory, Cranberry Glades Botanical Center, the Falls of Hills Creek (one of the highest waterfalls in West Virginia), Beartown State Park, Watoga State Park, Droop Mountain Civil War battle site, Highland Scenic Highway, Pearl S. Buck birthplace, 75-mile Greenbrier River Trail

Other Services and Features: It's tough to break a sweat at Snowshoe since summer temperatures rarely reach or exceed 80 degrees.

Kentucky

Ski Butler/Bike Butler

General Butler State Resort Park
4770 Squiresville Road
Owenton, KY 40359-8516
(502) 484-2998

The General Butler State Resort Park houses a ski lodge at the summit of the resort. Adjacent is a first-class lodge and restaurant, golf course, tennis courts, and swimming pool. Also on-site are luxurious lakeside cottages, full-service campgrounds, and other recreational facilities. Mountain biking, however, is limited to organized events.

Location, Hours, and Prices

General Location: On Interstate 71, 1 hour south of Cincinnati, Ohio, 1 hour north of Louisville, and 2 hours from Indianapolis, Indiana

Getting There: From Cincinnati or Louisville, take I-71 to Exit 44. From Indianapolis, take Highway 7 to Madison, Indiana, and turn left.

Biking Season: April–October

Elevation: Base 450′; summit/resort 800′

Hours: 8-5 during scheduled festivals

Prices: $25/1 day, $35/2 days if preregistered; $5/recreational riders and kids

Regulations/Restrictions: Riding allowed only during festivals. You must preregister before riding and wear a helmet at all times while riding.

The Rides

All trails are off-road singletrack and doubletrack except where trails cross ski slopes. Trail surface is generally hard pack, and most routes have technical challenges.

Terrain Description: Combination

Mileage/Number of Trails: 5 miles

Difficulty: 40% easiest, 60% more difficult and most difficult

Trails Under Development: None

Recommended Trails: Trail map indicates suitable trails for beginner, intermediate, advanced riders.

Mountain Bike Lift: No

Longest Trail: 5 miles

Other Local Trails: No

Trail Map: Free at events; everyone who registers receives one.

Local Services

Bike Butler's organized mountain bike events cater strongly to racers, but also include fun rides and events for new riders and racers.

Mountain Bike Services: Local MTB units (patrol)

Special Events: Bike Butler hosts 5 events a year. The 1996 schedule includes: MudFest IV, April 13-14, with cross-country, hill climb, slalom racing, and fun events; Fat Tire Boogie, June 8-9—cross-country and 8-hour team relay races; Mud, Sweat and Gears, July 13-14—slalom and cross-country racing; The Kentucky Open, August 31-September 2, includes the General Butler Off-Road Triathlon and the Nine to Five Off-Road Relay; 1996 National Collegiate Mountain Bike Championship, October 19-20, collegiate and open cross-country racing. Events include a free women's clinic, free first-timers guided tour, special race categories for Clydesdales (200 pounds and over), police, juniors, and first-timers.

Emergency Facilities: Hospital 2 miles from site; ambulance on call; first aid on-site by EMTs on duty

Accommodations: For the resort, call 800/325-0078; nearby lodging, 800/325-4290; primitive cabins, 502/732-5333

Dining: Food vendor on-site, restaurant adjacent, fast food facilities within a mile

Off-the-Bike Activities: Golf, tennis, basketball, miniature golf, recreational lake (swimming, fishing, canoe and paddle boat rentals), playgrounds, swimming pool, museum

PETE WINKEL PHOTO COURTESY WINTERGREEN RESORT

Florida

Hardrock Mountain Bike Park/ Gone Riding!

10915 SW 58th Ave. Rd.
Ocala, FL 34476
(904) 873-9279

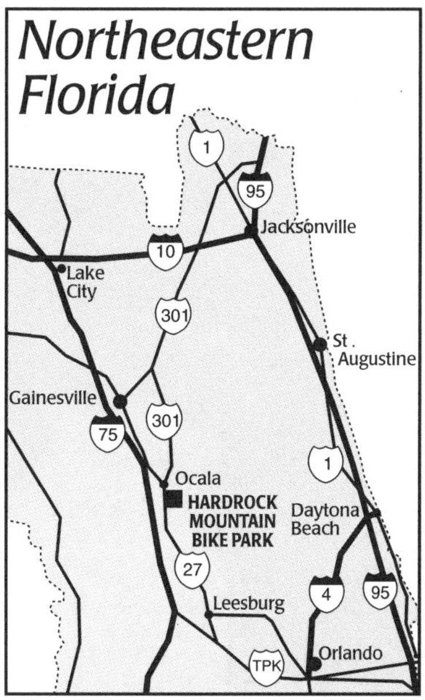

OK, OK, there's probably no skiing here at all, but why leave out Florida's hot mountain bike park? Primarily a motocross track since it closed as a quarry, this park now caters to mountain bikers with its 150 acres of mostly singletrack riding ($5/day to use trails, open weekends). Gone Riding! manages the park and organizes races and other events. In 1996 Hardrock played host to the opening round of the AMBC eastern circuit of races. The best time to ride is in winter. You must wear a helmet and sign a waiver. Facilities on-site include parking area, restrooms, and hoses. Camping permitted during race events only. Other services are available in Ocala; call the Ocala Chamber of Commerce at 904/629-8051.

MIKE TROY PHOTO

CHAPTER 6

THE MIDWEST

Minnesota

Buck Hill Ski Area

15400 Buck Hill Road
Burnsville, MN 55306
(612) 435-7174
(612) 435-7511 (fax)

Conveniently located near the Twin Cities, Buck Hill boasts the highest point in five counties. The rolling terrain includes cross-country routes across from Crystal Lake.

Location, Hours, and Prices

General Location: South central Minnesota, just outside the metropolitan Twin Cities area at the southern junction of Interstate 35 West and I-35 East

Getting There: 21 miles south of downtown Minneapolis on I-35 West, 23 miles south of downtown Saint Paul on I-35 East. Take the County Road 42 exit and follow the west frontage road (Buck Hill Road) of I-35 West approximately 1 mile south to Buck Hill.

Biking Season: Early May to end of September

Elevation: Base 930'; summit 1,235'

Hours: Wednesday-Sunday, 9-sunset; closed during race events

Prices: $5/day trail pass, $75/season pass

Regulations/Restrictions: Trails are one way, bicycles only. Helmets required.

The Rides

Buck Hill's dedicated trails are both double- and singletrack, with some technical routes. About half the area is smooth, open terrain, and about half is wooded and more technical.

Terrain Description: Cross-country

Mileage/Number of Trails: 14 named trails with several different loops from 1 mile up to 4 miles

Difficulty: 20% easiest, 50% more difficult, 30% most difficult

Trails Under Development: New climb up the south ski runs, 4 new singletracks or extensions being planned

Recommended Trails: Saidor, Myitkyina, and Wizards Way (adv.)

Mountain Bike Lift: None
Biggest Vertical Drop: 200′
Longest Trail: 4-mile loop
Other Local Trails: No access
Trail Map: Brochure with map available from ski area or local bike shop

Local Services

Primarily a day-use area, Buck Hill provides bike rentals, hosts special events, and sells snack food. You can find lodging and dining nearby in Burnsville.

Mountain Bike Services: Bike rental for $6/hour for front-suspension model, $10/hour for high-performance dual-suspension model; helmet rental $3/day
Special Events: Thursday evening race series throughout the summer, cyclocross events in October; Twin Cities Cycling Expo in May, Jimmy Heuga Mountain Bike Express in July, Bennett's Mountain Bike Race in August, Habaneros/Hoigaards 24 Hours of Buck in August. (In 1995, this endurance event raised funds for troubled and disadvantaged youth.)
Emergency Facilities: Fairview Hospital, 201 E. Nicolet Blvd., Burnsville, 612/892-2000, 2 miles away
Accommodations: No lodging at the resort, but many hotels nearby

PHOTO COURTESY LUTSEN MOUNTAIN BIKE PARK

Dining: Sandwiches, drinks, energy bars at the area. Nearby restaurants offer fare from fast food to fine dining.
Off-the-Bike Activities: None
Other Services and Features: None

Giants Ridge Resort

County Road 138
P.O. Box 190, Biwabik, MN 55708
(800) 688-7669
(218) 865-4143

Located north of Duluth in the Iron Range, Giants Ridge has over 60 miles of trails, including a cross-country course that the U.S. Ski Team trains and races on. While there is no lift service, there's also no charge to use the trail system.

Location, Hours, and Prices

General Location: On the Superior National Forest in northeastern Minnesota; 3½ hours north of Minneapolis/St. Paul, 1 hour north of Duluth. Both have major airports.
Getting There: From Duluth, take

Highway 53 north and follow signs east onto Highway 37 and Gilbert. Continue past Gilbert to Highway 135, which continues north to Biwabik and the resort. From Minneapolis/St. Paul, take U.S. 35 north to Cloquet and cut north to Highway 53. Continue north following instructions from Duluth.

Biking Season: Beginning of May through October

Elevation: Base 950′; summit 1,450′

Hours: Daily, daylight hours

Prices: No charge to use trails

Regulations/Restrictions: Helmet required

The Rides

With over 60 miles of its own trails and access to another 40 miles of Forest Service roads and trails, Giants Ridge lives up to its name. Trails are primarily smooth cross-country ski trails with long hills and lots of trees.

Terrain Description: Combination

Mileage/Number of Trails: About 65 miles

Difficulty: 40 miles (beginner/intermediate); 15–20 miles (advanced); 6 miles of singletrack

Trails Under Development: 5 miles of alpine singletrack and cat track trails

Recommended Trails: Laurentian and Bronze Trails (beginner); Silver and Lake Trails (intermediate); Gold and Cedar Trails (advanced)

Mountain Bike Lift: No

Biggest Vertical Drop: 500′ (downhill run on Placid Alpine Trail)

Longest Trail: 15-mile loop

Other Local Trails: Over 20 miles of Forest Service logging and forest roads, and 15–20 miles of abandoned mine roads

Trail Map: Purchase on site for $5

Local Services

Giants Ridge is one-stop shopping, with lodging and dining, bike rentals, bicycle sales and service, and special events all on-site.

Mountain Bike Services: Trek bike rentals available; sales and service

Special Events: Giants Ridge Mountain Bike Festival, Labor Day weekend, cross-country racing, downhill racing, hill climb, fun events

Emergency Facilities: Giants Ridge ski patrol

Accommodations: On-site, Giants Ridge Sports Dorm, Laurentian Resort (condos); hotels within 4 miles; camping 3 miles from resort on trails

Dining: On-site food service

Off-the-Bike Activities: In-line skating with rentals, canoeing with rentals, fishing, swimming, tennis, hiking, berry picking, golf

Other Services and Features: Timber wolf pack, whitetail deer, moose; site of cross-country skiing World Cups and National Championships

Golden Eagle Lodge, Inc.

325 Gunflint Trail
Grand Marais, MN 55604
(800) 346-2203 (reservations)
(218) 388-2203
(218) 388-9417 (fax)

The only resident on Flour Lake, Golden Eagle Lodge has lakefront cabins with fireplaces. It offers 28 miles of trails to mountain bikers, and another 300 miles of roads and trails await exploration in the surrounding forest.

Location, Hours, and Prices

General Location: Central Gunflint area on the north shore of Flour Lake

Getting There: Drive up the Gunflint Trail out of Grand Marais at Lake Superior 27 miles to Clearwater Road/ Cook County #66. After 3 miles follow signs to the lodge. Parking fee of $5/ day; parking free to lodge or campground guests.

Biking Season: April to October

Elevation: Resort 1,680′; highest elevation on trails 1,940′

Hours: Daily, 7:30 a.m. to 8:30 p.m.

Prices: No charge to use trails

Regulations/Restrictions: None

The Rides

The lodge's ski trails are for foot and bike traffic only. These doubletracks range from easy and smooth to difficult and rocky. The routes are primarily old logging roads; new roads are open to vehicle traffic but are seldom used.

Terrain Description: Cross-country

Mileage/Number of Trails: 28 miles

Difficulty: 10% easiest, 30% more difficult, 60% most difficult

Trails Under Development: None

Recommended Trails: Logging Camp, Wolf Point, Poplar Creek (beginner); Beaver Dam, Flour Vista, Red Pines (intermediate); Red Pines, Cross Fox, Moose Ridge, Bear Cub (advanced)

Mountain Bike Lift: No

Biggest Vertical Drop: Not indicated

Longest Trail: 9-mile loop

Other Local Trails: Over 200 miles of trails on the Superior National Forest are open to bikes. Check with the lodge the for most suitable areas.

Trail Map: Available at Lodge for $3, or $4.95 for larger maps of the area

PHOTO COURTESY LUTSEN MOUNTAIN BIKE PARK

Local Services

Visitors have a choice of on-site accommodations, from deluxe cabins to camping, but will have to ride or drive at least 4 miles to find dining. Some bike services are available on-site.

Mountain Bike Services: Bike rentals for adults and children, helmets included, $5/hour or $25/day

Special Events: None at this time

Emergency Facilities: Lodge has 1 EMT and 2 First Responders. Report any accidents to the Lodge.

Accommodations: Campsites and cabin rentals, including deluxe cabins with fireplaces, whirlpool tubs. Call 800/346-2203. Campground open May to September.

Dining: Located within 4 to 20 miles of the lodge

Off-the-Bike Activities: Fully staffed nature center with naturalist program, Indian Teepee, campfires, fishing, canoeing, hiking, berry picking, vista points, wildlife, lake tours on pontoon boats, free fishing seminar, variety of boat rentals available, fishing guides, winter activities

Other Services and Features: This is the only facility on Flour Lake. Two cabins are handicapped accessible.

Lutsen Mountain Bike Park

Box 129
Lutsen, MN 55612
(218) 663-7281

THE STAR OF THE NORTH
LUTSEN
MOUNTAINS

Located 90 miles northeast of Duluth on Lake Superior's north shore, Lutsen is mid-America's largest ski area—and now its largest mountain bike park, with over 30 miles of trail and a gondola and chair to the upper trailheads.

Location, Hours, and Prices

General Location: Lake Superior's north shore

Getting There: 90 miles northeast of Duluth on Highway 61

Biking Season: Mid-May through October

Elevation: Base 600'; resort 1,200'; summit 1,688'

Hours: Daily, 10–5

Prices: $10/all-day trail pass with 1 gondola ride; $20/all-day trail pass with unlimited gondola and chairlift rides

Regulations/Restrictions: Helmets required

The Rides

The Lutsen Mountain Bike Park extends over 4 mountains and includes over 28 miles of marked trails with gondola and lift service. Terrain varies from casual riding to advanced, technical descents with a combination of forest roads, singletrack, and open ledge rock. In 1995, Lutsen added a 6-mile loop at the top of Moose Mountain, offering less experienced riders easier access to the spectacular mountaintop vistas.

PHOTO COURTESY LUTSEN MOUNTAIN BIKE PARK

Terrain Description: Combination
Mileage/Number of Trails: 30 miles
Difficulty: 20% easiest, 40% more difficult, 40% most difficult
Trails Under Development: None
Recommended Trails: White Trail (beginner); Red Trail (intermediate); Yellow Trail (advanced)
Mountain Bike Lifts: 3
Trails Accessible from Lift: 5 marked trails
Biggest Vertical Drop: 800′
Longest Trail: 14 miles
Other Local Trails: None
Trail Map: Free from the park

Local Services

Lutsen offers trailside dining and lodging. By all reports, it's worth the view to stop for lunch at the Mountain Top Deli—the name says it all. Bike services include rentals and special events.

Mountain Bike Services: Rental bikes available for $8/hour, $24/day
Special Events: Lutsen Mountain Bike Festival in June; Moose Mountain MTB Classic in September
Emergency Facilities: Lutsen First Responder; Cook County North Shore Hospital in Grand Marais
Accommodations: Trailside lodging at Eagle Ridge, 800/360-7666
Dining: Mountain Top Deli and Restaurant has deli sandwiches, soups, salads, ice cream, coffee, pop, beer, wine, and 100-mile views.
Off-the-Bike Activities: Alpine slide, hiking, and picnic area
Other Services and Features: *Ski* magazine ranked Lutsen's mountain scenery, including Poplar River Gorge and the Sawtooth Mountains, as the most spectacular east of the Rockies.

PHOTO COURTESY LUTSEN MOUNTAIN BIKE PARK

Wisconsin

Chequamegon Area Mountain Bike Association (CAMBA) Trail System

P.O. Box 141
Cable, WI 54821
(800) 533-7454

While many of the CAMBA trails are used by skiers and snowmobilers in winter months, the trail system was primarily built by and for mountain bikers. The town of Cable bills itself as the mountain bike capital of the Midwest, while CAMBA considers its trail system the Midwest's premier trail network. It's hard to argue with them. They could probably call themselves the best in the United States and still not get much of an argument. Why all the superlatives? Imagine six communities working together with U.S. Forest Service personnel and local mountain bikers to build, map, mark, and promote mountain biking trails and tourism.

Location, Hours, and Prices

General Location: Northwest area of Wisconsin

Getting There: Trailheads are in the communities of Cable, Delta, Drummond, Hayward, Namakagon, and Seeley. The main thoroughfare is U.S. Highway 63.

Biking Season: Mid-April through November

Elevation: Not indicated

Hours: 24 hours a day

Prices: No charge to use trails, but donations are appreciated.

Regulations/Restrictions: Forest Service regulations apply; please follow IMBA's Rules of the Trail.

The Rides

The CAMBA Off-Road Trail System consists of over 200 miles of marked and mapped routes. The system is divided into six clusters, each with one or more trailheads. The routes follow a variety of paths, including logging roads, fire lanes, snowmobile trails, ski trails, and singletrack. The terrain lends itself to riders of all abilities, from beginners to experts. One thing you won't find—paved bike paths.

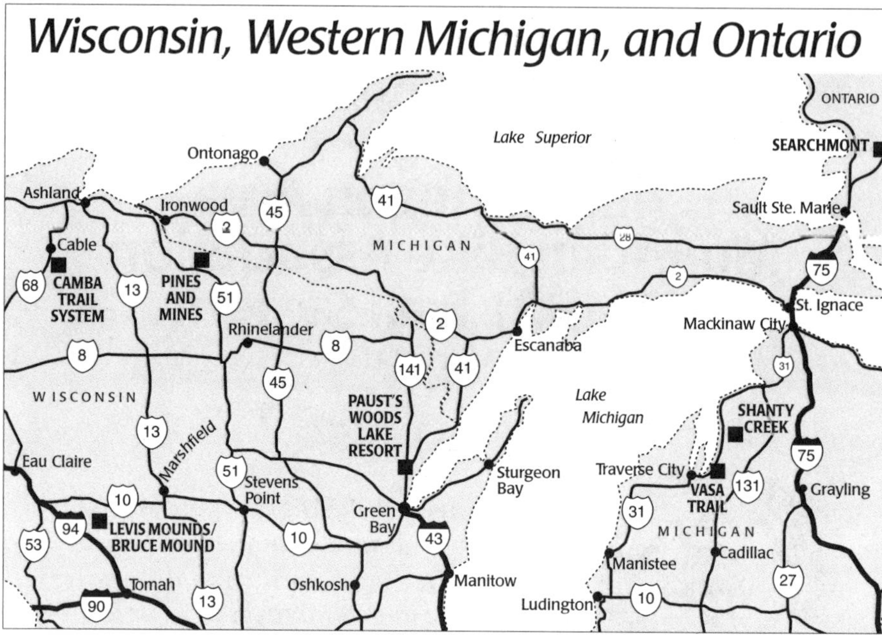

Terrain Description: Cross-country
Mileage/Number of Trails: 200+ miles
Difficulty: Trails range from beginner to advanced
Recommended Trails: Chequamegon 40 route from Hayward to Cable
Mountain Bike Lift: No
Biggest Vertical Drop: Not indicated
Longest Trail: Lots of options possible
Other Local Trails: Contact Chequamegon National Forest, 715/762-2461.
Trail Map: Overview map, more detailed maps and ride narratives, and a trail guide are available from CAMBA or the Cable Area Visitor Center. Contact the Cable Area Chamber of Commerce at P.O. Box 217, Cable, WI 54821, 800/533-7454, 715/798-3833. For a complete set of maps, send $5 plus $1.50 shipping and handling to CAMBA.

Local Services

The six communities around the CAMBA system all promote and support mountain biking. You can find lodging, dining, and bike services throughout the area. Perhaps the best-known resort here is Telemark Resort (800/472-3001 or 715/798-3811), host of the famed Birkebeiner cross-country ski race and the terminus of the Chequamegon 40 mountain bike race.

PHOTO COURTESY LUTSEN MOUNTAIN BIKE PARK

Mountain Bike Services: Lots of bike shops in the area. Contact the Cable Area Chamber of Commerce, 800/533-7454 or 715/798-3833.

Special Events: The area hosts one of the country's largest and most popular festivals, the Chequamegon Fat Tire Festival each September. The event includes the epic Chequamegon 40 cross-country race, a shorter Short and Fat cross-country race, a Rough Stuff Rendezvous bicycle orienteering competition, the Cable Criterium, non-competitive trail rides, and other fun events. Contact the Chequamegon Fat Tire Festival, Inc. at P.O. Box 267, Cable, WI 54821, 715/798-3811. Other events include a mountain bike camp, Poker Ride, and the Cable Area Off-Road Classic. Call the Chamber for a complete calendar of events.

Emergency Facilities: In the local communities

Accommodations: Refer to Chamber of Commerce guides

Dining: Refer to Chamber of Commerce guides

Off-the-Bike Activities: Skiing, hiking, backpacking, camping, golf, fishing, hunting, tennis, canoeing, horseback riding, ice skating, snowmobiling, fine arts festival, Native American Pow-wows

Other Services and Features: Established in 1933, the Chequamegon National Forest covers almost 80% of the Cable area.

Levis Mounds/Bruce Mound

Clark County Forestry and Parks Department
517 Court St.
Neillsville, WI 54456
(715) 743-5140

Run by the County Forestry and Parks Department, the Levis Mounds/Bruce Mound cross-country ski network offers mountain bikers over 20 miles of affordable and enjoyable riding.

Location, Hours, and Prices

General Location: Clark County in central Wisconsin

Getting There: 12 miles southwest of Neillsville on State Highway 95

Biking Season: April 1–November 15

Elevation: Not indicated

Hours: 24 hours a day

Prices: Day use $3/adults, $1/children; season pass $15/adults, $10/children

Regulations/Restrictions: IMBA standards

The Rides

This cross-country ski area contains 21 miles of smooth biking trails with scenic overlooks, sandstone bluffs, some doubletrack, and some singletrack.

Terrain Description: Cross-country

Mileage/Number of Trails: About 21 miles

Difficulty: 20% easiest, 40% more difficult, 40% most difficult

Trails Under Development: None

Recommended Trails: Citizen Loop (beginner); Silver Medal Loop (intermediate); World Cup Loop (all singletrack, advanced)

Mountain Bike Lift: No

Longest Trail: Not indicated

Other Local Trails: Good road cycling in Clark County

Trail Map: Free by contacting the Forestry and Parks Department

Local Services

Levis Mounds/Bruce Mound is strictly a day-use park, although trails are open all the time. Other than occasional special events, the area does not offer any services. You'll have to try Neillsville for lodging and dining.

Mountain Bike Services: No

Special Events: Annual Buzzard Buster Bike Race in September, call 715/743-4134 or 715/743-4937

Emergency Facilities: In Neillsville

Accommodations: Contact the Neillsville Chamber of Commerce, 715/743-6444

Dining: Same as above

Off-the-Bike Activities: Ask the Forestry and Parks Department for the brochure "Clark County, Where Memories Are Made" for information on other recreational and sightseeing opportunities in the area.

Other Services and Features: None indicated

Paust's Woods Lake Resort, Inc.

Route 3, Box 375, Crivitz, WI 54114

(800) 468-8025 (reservations only)

(715) 757-3722

In business since 1900, Paust's Woods Lake Resort sits on 3,000 acres of private land in the heart of Wisconsin's cool, beautiful Northwoods. The four-season resort has both cottages and motel rooms, and offers a variety of lodging and dining plans.

Location, Hours, and Prices

General Location: 70 miles northwest of Green Bay, 16 miles northwest of Crivitz

Getting There: From Green Bay, take Highway 43 to Highway 141 to City Highway A to City Highway X to Parkway Road to Ranch Road.

Biking Season: June through August

Elevation: 940′

Hours: Daily, 8–4

Prices: $4/trail fee

Regulations/Restrictions: None

The Rides

Paust's appeals to beginning and intermediate riders with its 30 miles of cross-country ski trails and dirt roads. More roads and snowmobile trails beckon from the adjoining Nicolet National Forest.

Terrain Description: Cross-country

Mileage/Number of Trails: 30 miles

Difficulty: Beginner and intermediate terrain

Trails Under Development: None

Recommended Trails: Flowage Road, Rock Road, Deer Lake (beginner); Thunder Mountain Pass (intermediate)

Mountain Bike Lift: No

Longest Trail: 8 miles

Other Local Trails: Adjoining the resort's 3,000 acres to the north and west are the Caldron Flowage and Nicolet National Forest, with miles of snowmobile trails.

Trail Map: Available with $4 trail fee

Local Services

As a self-contained resort, Paust's provides lodging and dining on-site. While its trails are open to mountain bikers, it does not cater to the fat-tire set with any other bicycle services.

Mountain Bike Services: None at the resort

Special Events: None

Emergency Facilities: None on-site

Accommodations: Motel rooms and cottages with modified American or housekeeping plans. Call 715/757-3722 for information, 800/468-8025 for reservations.

Dining: Breakfast and dinner available at the resort. Convenience store on-site.

Off-the-Bike Activities: Boating, swimming, playground, games, archery course, rifle ranges and trap range, nature trails, hiking, golf, riding stable, whitewater rafting, fishing, fish cleaning facility, hunting, picnic area with charcoal grills. Lots of water sports available on Woods Lake, Deer Lake, and Caldron Falls Flowage.

Other Services and Features: Within 50 miles you can visit scenic stops such as Thunder Mountain, Goodman Park, McClintock Park, fish hatcheries, Mystery Ship, Camp 5 Farm, Crivitz Area Museum, Stephenson Island Museum, Peshtigo Fire Museum, the Lumberjack Special in Laona, Wisconsin, and the cities of Marinette and Peshtigo, Wisconsin, and Menominee and Iron Mountain, Michigan.

Pines and Mines Mountain Bike Trail System

P.O. Box 97
Hurley, WI 54534
(715) 561-2922

The Pines and Mines Mountain Bike Trail System offers over 200 miles of marked and mapped mountain biking routes in the public lands of northern Wisconsin and on the nearby Ottawa National Forest in upper Michigan. Trails incorporate many of the area's historic transportation, mining, and lumbering sites as they wind through forests and around lakes. Write or call for a free trail map.

PHOTO COURTESY LUTSEN MOUNTAIN BIKE PARK

Michigan

Shanty Creek

One Shanty Creek Road
Bellaire, MI 49615
(800) 678-4111

Perhaps the best known Michigan resort for mountain biking, Shanty Creek's facilities include nearly 20 miles of marked trails for biking, lift service, rentals, races, and tours. The resort further caters to cyclists with lodging packages for special events. Bike industry personnel praise the resort for its excellent race organization and its ability to make the most out of its terrain.

Location, Hours, and Prices

General Location: Shanty Creek is located in the northwest quadrant of lower Michigan, 35 miles northeast of Traverse City.

Getting There: Closest major airport is in Traverse City, 35 miles away. Smaller planes and jets may land at Antrim County Airport, 2 miles away. Airport transportation to Traverse City is available for $25 per person. No charge for on-site parking. By car, Shanty Creek is 4½ hours from Detroit. Take I-75 North to Grayling, M-72 West to C-571 to Mancelona. West on M-88 to Shanty Creek.

Biking Season: April–October

Elevation: Base/Schuss Village 675′; Summit Village at summit of Summit Slopes 850′; summit 1,125′

Hours: Daily, 9–9

Prices: $5/trail fee, $45/season pass

Regulations/Restrictions: Helmets strongly recommended

PHOTO COURTESY SHANTY CREEK

The Rides

Over 19 miles of marked interconnecting trails wind between Schuss Village and the Summit Village, featuring expert, sport, and beginner trails. Schuss Mountain trails may be accessed by chairlift. A highlight is the 5.2-mile championship course with 783′ of climbing per lap. The course consists of 35% singletrack and 65% Michigan doubletrack through hardwood forest and open meadow.

Terrain Description: Combination

Mileage/Number of Trails: 19 miles of trails plus 12 miles of alternate paved roads

Difficulty: Alternate paved roads are all suitable for beginners. Of the mountain bike trails: 5% easiest, 75% more difficult, 20% most difficult

Trails Under Development: Ongoing

Recommended Trails: Portions of Michigan Loop, all paved alternate roads (beginner); portions of Michigan Loop, Huron Loop, Erie Loop, and Ontario Loop (intermediate); Superior Loop (advanced)

Mountain Bike Lift: 1

Trails Accessible from Lift: All

Biggest Vertical Drop: 450′

Longest Trail: 7 miles (Michigan Loop)

Other Trails: Jordan Valley State Park is approximately 6 miles from Shanty-Schuss and features a 20-mile state-maintained trail system. The Vasa Trail (see following listing) is a half hour away.

Trail Map: Available from the Summit Fitness Center and Schuss Village Ski, Bike and General Store

Local Services

Well known nationally as a top race site, Shanty Creek has rentals and tours for mountain bikers. The 3,400-acre full-service, year-round resort has all bases covered with over 600 rooms, suites, and condominiums, 54 holes of championship golf, indoor and outdoor swimming pools, 7 tennis courts, children's programs, and meeting space to accommodate groups of up to 1,000 people.

Mountain Bike Services: The Summit Fitness Center (open daily until 9 p.m.) and Schuss Village Ski, Bike and General Store (open daily from 9-5) offer on-site rentals (including helmets). The Summit Fitness Center rents bikes for $6/hour or $22/day; tandems, 12-speed and 5-speed bikes rent for $10/hour or $26 day. Schuss Village Ski, Bike and General Store rents Trek 220 Junior bikes for $12/hour, $20/half day, $28/day; Trek 800 mountain bikes for $14/hour, $25/half day, $35/day; Trek 830 front-suspension bikes for $17/hour, $30/half day, $45/day. Overnight rental $15 additional charge. Private guided tours available locally.

Special Events: Since 1993, Shanty Creek has become a regular stop on the NORBA National Championship Series circuit (the 1995 event was an Olympic qualifier). In 1996, it hosts a national event, June 27-30, during which the Olympic Mountain Bike Team will be announced.

Emergency Facilities: On-site emergency facilities available at mountain bike events. Local clinics available in Bellaire and Mancelona. Closest hospital is in Kalkaska, 25 miles away.

Accommodations: Over 600 rooms, suites, condominiums, and private homes; call 800/678-4111.

Dining: On-site you can find 2 full-service dining rooms, 2 grills at golf shops, and a deli. Within 10 miles are over 20 places to dine, including elegant, casual, family, fast food, and tavern options.

Off-the-Bike Activities: 54-hole championship golf; 7 tennis courts; fitness center/racquetball court, wellness spa, and weight room; jogging/walking trails; swimming pools; children's programs, day care. The resort is minutes from Lake Bellaire, which offers water sports, fishing, and swimming. In winter, Shanty Creek has 29 downhill ski runs and 35 kilometers of cross-country trails.

Other Services and Features: The Main Lodge is located at the top of the Summit Slopes and has breathtaking views overlooking Lake Bellaire and the Chain-of-Lakes. Designed in the theme of a Bavarian village, Schuss Village is located 3 miles from Summit Village with a continuous free shuttle available. The Main Lodge there is located at the base of Schuss Mountain. The chairlift for mountain bikers is located at Schuss Village.

Vasa Trail

P.O. Box 500
Acme, MI 49610
(616) 938-4400
(616) 938-4443 (fax)
E-mail: xcski@vasa.org

V A S A

The Vasa Trail is a dedicated non-motorized trail winding through the Pere Marquette Forest. Primarily a cross-country ski trail and site of the second largest cross-country ski race in the United States, it is maintained by a volunteer group, North America Vasa, Inc.

Location, Hours, and Prices

General Location: Located outside of Traverse City, near Grand Traverse Bay. About 5 hours northwest of Detroit and 6 hours northeast of Chicago.

Getting There: North from Detroit on I-75 to Grayling (M-72), west on M-72 to US-31, south on US-31 to Bunker Hill Road, Bunker Hill Road south onto Bartlett Road to trailhead. Or from the south, take US-31 North from Traverse City, east on Bunker Hill Road, Bunker Hill Road south onto Bartlett Road to trailhead. Follow the signs from either M-72 or US-31.

Biking Season: From when the snow melts to when the snow flies (April through November). North America Vasa, Inc. tries to make sure that the frost is completely out of the ground before opening the trail to bikes.

Elevation: Traverse City 600′; the Vasa Trail has about 200 feet of vertical on the larger hills.

Hours: The Vasa Trail is always open, but it is not lit for night riding.

Prices: No fee, but users are encouraged to "Feed the Fee Pipe" at the trailhead with a donation.

Regulations/Restrictions: Acme Township park rules are posted at the Vasa trailhead.

The Rides

The Pere Marquette State Forest stretches from Traverse City to Kalkaska and contains approximately 400 square miles of forest. Most trails in the forest are "ski trail width" trails (two tracks). The Vasa Trail is marked all year with "You Are Here" maps, directional arrows, and confidence markers on trees. There are numerous two tracks, snowmobile trails, and power lines that criss-cross the Vasa Trail. Singletracks emanate from the main trail; these are unmarked and wind in and out of the Vasa Trail. It is best to ride the singletracks with a local rider who knows the area. The soil is fairly sandy and soft with very few rocks (the sandiest month is July).

Terrain Description: Cross-country

Mileage/Number of Trails: There are 3 dedicated loops of the trail—3K, 10K, 25K. All are open to riders, hikers, joggers, and skiers.

Difficulty: The Vasa Trail is easy to moderate in technical difficulty. Singletracks are moderate to extremely difficult.

Trails Under Development: A marked and signed singletrack has been proposed to the Michigan Department of Natural Resources.

Recommended Trails: All, but North American Vasa, Inc. is partial, of course, to the actual Vasa Trail.

Mountain Bike Lift: No

Biggest Vertical Drop: "The Wall"

Longest Trail: 25K

Other Local Trails: Traverse Area Recreation Trail (TART) is accessible at the foot of Bunker Hill Road, 1 mile from the Vasa trailhead. The TART connects to Traverse City and soon will hook up with the Grand Traverse Resort and Leelanau County.

Trail Map: Available free from the box on the trailhead sign, by writing to North American Vasa, Inc., or at most local motels and bike shops

Local Services

For bike services, you will have to head to nearby Traverse City. Lodging and dining establishments are within riding distance of the trailhead. The Vasa Trail is most famous to mountain bikers as part of the notorious Iceman Cometh mountain bike race, a competitive event infamous for its wicked weather conditions. Some 1,500 hardy competitors brave wind, rain, sleet, and snow to finish the 27-mile race, which concludes with a climb of Mt. Holiday.

Mountain Bike Services: Heated bathroom at Acme Township Park. Four local bike shops in Traverse City offer sales, service, and complete rentals.

Special Events: The Iceman Cometh Challenge (a mountain bike race which attracts over 1,300 riders) is held annually on the first Saturday in November and uses part of the Vasa Trail. The Cherry Festival Mountain Bike Race is held in July on the 25K trail.

Emergency Facilities: Call 911

Accommodations: Grand Traverse Resort (616/938-2100) is 2 miles from the Vasa trailhead. Jellystone Campground has access to the Vasa Trail,, a half-mile away. There is a wide variety of nationwide hotel chains within 5 miles, and Traverse City State Park is only 3 miles away. The Traverse City Visitors and Convention Bureau may be reached at 800/872-8377.

Dining: Approximately 25 restaurants nearby

Off-the-Bike Activities: Vasa Cross-Country Ski Race, held each February, attracts more than 800 skiers. The NORBA National Championship Series stops at Shanty Creek, only half an hour from the Vasa Trail. Watersports, golf, and all kinds of other family activities abound in the area.

Other Services and Features: Near a bustling tourist area, but very peaceful and quiet

CAROL BONSER PHOTO

CHAPTER 7

MID-ATLANTIC STATES

Pennsylvania

Hidden Valley

1 Craighead Drive
Hidden Valley, PA 15502
(814) 443-8000

Nestled in the scenic Laurel Highlands of western Pennsylvania, Hidden Valley is a true four-season resort with fine dining, accommodations from efficiency rooms through luxury townhomes, and activities to suit any taste. In the summer, mountain bikers can explore on their own thanks to well-marked trails and detailed trail maps.

Location, Hours, and Prices

General Location: Laurel Highlands of western Pennsylvania, 1 hour from Pittsburgh and 3 hours from Washington, D.C., Cleveland, and Baltimore

PHOTO COURTESY HIDDEN VALLEY

Getting There: From the west, take 376 East to the Pennsylvania Turnpike East to Exit 9 (Donegal). Follow Route 31 East 8 miles. Hidden Valley Resort is on the right. From the east, take the Pennsylvania Turnpike to Exit 10 (Somerset), then Route 31 West for 10 miles straight to Hidden Valley on the left.

Biking Season: May–October

Elevation: Base 2,380′; summit 3,000′

Hours: Weekends only in spring (prior to Memorial Day), 10–5; daily in summer, 9–6

Prices: No charge

Regulations/Restrictions: Helmets mandatory for rental customers. Yield trails to hikers and bikers.

The Rides

Dedicated trails range from beginner to expert. Among the trails is a 5-mile race course loop, featuring 2 miles of singletrack. But don't stop there—Hidden Valley has over 30 miles of trails to explore, as well as access to state park lands.

Terrain Description: Combination

Mileage/Number of Trails: 30 miles

Difficulty: 30% easiest, 40% more difficult, 30% most difficult

Trails Under Development: Greenbriar Trail expanson in the North Woods, summer of 1996.

Recommended Trails: Kooser Trail (beginner); Jones Mill Run or Cherry Trail (intermediate); Greenbriar (adv.)

Mountain Bike Lift: No

Biggest Vertical Drop: 610′

Longest Trail: Most trails are interconnected.

Other Local Trails: Hidden Valley lies between Kooser State Park and Forbes State Forest, with 30+ miles of riding

Trail Map: Free from the Mountain Bike Center

Local Services

Besides the usual bike rentals, Hidden Valley offers children's bike rentals and camps. For the competitive rider, the resort hosts several races each year. You will find on-site lodging and dining at Hidden Valley.

Mountain Bike Services: 40 GT mountain bikes and 10 suspension bikes available for rent, price varies for type of bike; child's mountain bikes also available; child day camps available throughout the summer—call 814/443-8252 for details.

Special Events: 1996 events include the Fat Tire Stampede, June 15–16, with downhill, dual slalom, observed trials, cross-country racing, $15/preregistration, $20/race day; Fat Tire Fallout, October 15–16, events and prices same as above.

Emergency Facilities: Somerset Hospital, 12 miles east on Route 31

Accommodations: Call Hidden Valley Four Seasons Resort at 800/458-0175.

Dining: On site, Hearthside Restaurant, The Lost Pelican, Mt. Deli

Off-the-Bike Activities: Summer Splash Party, July 4 Celebration, Classic Car Cruise, and skiing all happen at the resort; nearby you'll find whitewater rafting, historical sites, and antiques.

Other Services and Features: The Fat Tire Stampede and The Fat Tire Fallout are celebrating their 10th annual races in 1996.

The Inn at Starlight Lake

P.O. Box 27
Starlight, PA 18461
(800) 248-2519
(717) 798-2519

Established in 1909, the Inn at Starlight Lake originally served as a summer retreat for wealthy patrons from Philadelphia, New York, and New Jersey. Now best-known as a winter retreat, it still offers summer visitors recreation and relaxation in the upper Delaware River Valley.

Location, Hours, and Prices

General Location: Northeast corner of Pennsylvania, northern Wayne County, foothills of Moosic Range of Appalachians; 50 miles southeast of Binghamtom, New York; 50 miles northeast of Scranton, Pennsylvania; 5 miles south of New York Quickway Route 17; 38 miles northeast of I-81 in Pennsylvania

Getting There: From Scranton, take Highway 171 north to Highway 370 and Highway 370 northeast to the Inn, just a few miles from the Delaware River.

Biking Season: Opens April 15

Elevation: Possible elevation change of 1,000′

Hours: Daily

Prices: No charge

Regulations/Restrictions: None

The Rides

The Inn opens its cross-country ski trails and miles of unpaved dirt roads to mountain bikers. The conversion of old railroad beds into trails adds to the generally easy riding opportunities in the area.

Terrain Description: Cross-country

Mileage/Number of Trails: Loops range from 5–30 miles

Difficulty: Easy to moderate

Trails Under Development: The local chapter of Rails to Trails is working to buy and develop existing abandoned railroad beds.

Recommended Trails: Not indicated

Mountain Bike Lift: No

Biggest Vertical Drop: Not indicated

Longest Trail: Not indicated

Other Local Trails: State game lands

Trail Map: Free at Inn

Local Services

Upholding a long New England tradition of inn touring, the Inn at Starlight Lake offers mountain bikers guided tours and inn-to-inn tours. On-site lakeside dining can be enjoyed by inn guests or day visitors.

Mountain Bike Services: Guided tours, inn-to-inn bike tour

Special Events: No

Emergency Facilities: No

Accommodations: Call 800/248-2519 or 717/798-2519

Dining: The inn has a full-service restaurant, open daily for breakfast, lunch, and dinner.

Off-the-Bike Activities: Swimming, boating, fishing, and tennis. Nearby are golf, fly-fishing, and canoeing on the Delaware River. Cross-country ski center in winter, near downhill skiing at Elk Mountain.

Other Services and Features: In operation since 1909, this country inn is listed in many guidebooks. Member, Independent Innkeepers Association.

Whitetail Ski Resort and Mountain Bike Center

13805 Blairs Valley Road
Mercersburg, PA 17236
(717) 328-9400

One of the newest ski resorts in the country, Whitetail opened its Mountain Bike Center in the summer of 1994 and has quickly developed a full mountain biking program. Here you will find lift service, numerous trails on the mountain and through surrounding farmland, and a full schedule of special events.

BOB WILLIAMSON PHOTO

Location, Hours, and Prices

General Location: 1½ hours northwest of Washington, D.C., and Baltimore

Getting There: From Washington, go north on I-270 to I-70 West, and take Exit 18 (Route 68). Go through the traffic light in Clear Spring, Maryland. Follow the snowflake and Whitetail signs 7 miles to the slopes. From Baltimore, take I-70 West, Exit 18 (Route 68), and follow the directions above. From Harrisburg, go south on I-81 and take Exit 3 (Route 16) in Greencastle, Pennsylvania. Take Route 16 West towards Mercersburg and follow the signs 11 miles to the slopes. From points west, take I-76 East to Breezewood, Pennsylvania, then I-70 East into Maryland. Take Exit 18 (Route 68). Go through the traffic light in Clear Spring, Maryland, and follow the snowflake and Whitetail signs 7 miles to the slopes.

Biking Season: Memorial Day–end of October

Elevation: Base 865′; summit 1,800′

Hours: Daily, 9–6; closed Tuesdays for trail maintenance

Prices: \$6/trail pass, \$23/trail and lift pass, \$6/trail and hike pass

Regulations/Restrictions: Helmets mandatory

The Rides

Whitetail's trail network consists of almost 70% singletrack, 20% doubletrack, and 10% dirt roads. All singletrack and doubletrack are dedicated to mountain biking, but the dirt roads are used occasionally by maintenance vehicles.

Terrain Description: Combination

Mileage/Number of Trails: 16 trails make up 26 miles of dedicated mountain biking routes

Difficulty: 10% easiest, 40% more difficult, 50% most difficult

Trails Under Development: New trails are developed as maintenance schedule allows, 1–2 per season

Recommended Trails: All

Mountain Bike Lift: 1

Trails Accessible from Lift: All

Biggest Vertical Drop: 935′

Longest Trail: 9.2 miles

Other Local Trails: All trails are on Whitetail property.

Trail Map: Available free from rental building

BOB WILLIAMSON PHOTO

Local Services

In addition to rentals and several races, Whitetail offers a day camp for kids. Other unique services include complimentary hot showers and a bike wash. On-site accommodations are limited to camping, and on-site dining consists of snack foods and a BBQ.

Mountain Bike Services: Bike rentals \$50/weekends and holidays, \$40/weekdays; helmet rentals \$3. Mountain Bike Day Camp, ages 12–16, \$185, July 24–26 and August 7–9, 1996. Whitetail has a full-service bicycle repair facility, and the retail shop has the latest in mountain bike fashions and gear. Complimentary hot showers and bike wash (bring a towel).

Special Events: 1996 events include Jimmie Heuga's Toyota Mountain Bike Express, June 9; Mountain Laurel Cross-Country Race, June 23; Dog Days at Whitetail Race Series, July 21, August 4, and August 25; NORBA Pennsylvania State Championships, September 28–29; Whitetail Downhill and Cross-Country Race, October 19–20; Leaf Peeper Weekends, October 12–13, 19–20, 26–27.

Emergency Facilities: First aid

Accommodations: On premises, camping at a wooded site with fixed tent platforms and fire rings; toilets, showers, and running water nearby; sites available for couples, families, and small groups for $15. Hotels and bed and breakfast lodging nearby.

Dining: On-deck BBQ each weekend, and sandwiches, fruits, beverages, and breakfast foods each day.

Off-the-Bike Activities: Hiking, camping, and chairlift rides.

Maryland

Wisp Four Seasons Resort

P.O. Box 629
McHenry, MD 21541
(301) 387-4640

Wisp Four Seasons Resort is a complete recreational facility with golf, skiing, mountain biking, in-line skating, tennis, and a fitness center. The resort overlooks Deep Creek Lake, where you can find other recreational opportunities as well.

Location, Hours, and Prices

General Location: 3 hours west of Baltimore, Maryland and Washington D.C.; 2 hours south of Pittsburgh

Getting There: From Pittsburgh, take I-79 South to I-68 East to 219 South Deep Creek Lake. From Baltimore and Washington, take I-70 West to I-68 West to 219 South Deep Creek Lake.

Biking Season: May 1 to October 15

Elevation: Base/resort 2,500′; summit 3,100′

Hours: Daily

Prices: $2.50/trail access fee per day, $25/season; $3.95/per chairlift ride (weekends only)

Regulations/Restrictions: Helmets required. No pets please. No smoking.

The Rides

In addition to its 30 trails, Wisp offers weekend lift service to the top of Marsh Mountain. The terrain includes forest singletrack and meadow trails. The resort's close proximity to five state parks means even more riding opportunities.

Terrain Description: Combination

Mileage/Number of Trails: Over 30 trails

Difficulty: 50% easiest, 40% more difficult, 10% most difficult

Trails Under Development: New trails added each year

Recommended Trails: 1–10, 12, 13, 16, 30–31 (beginner); 2, 4, 10–11, 14–15, 19–21, 23–24, 27 (intermediate); 3,15, 22, 25–26 (advanced)

Mountain Bike Lift: Weekends only

Trails Accessible from Lift: All

Biggest Vertical Drop: 610′

Longest Trail: 15 miles

Other Local Trails: Swallow Falls and Herrington Manor State Parks are accessible from Wisp's trails.

Trail Map: Included with trail pass, or call 301/387-4640

Local Services

Wisp has everything you need in the way of lodging, dining, and bicycling services and events.

Mountain Bike Services: Rudy's Outdoor Adventures at Wisp rents bikes for $13.50/2 hours, $19/half day, $24/all day, $24 for first day and $19 for each additional day for multi-day rentals. Rudy's also leads guided expeditions through Marsh Mountain Wilderness Trails: 2-hour tours run $15/person with bike rental, $10/person without bike rental, $5/person hiking; 4-hour expeditions cost $25/person with bike rental, $15/person without bike rental, $10/person hiking. Guided tours require a minimum of 4 people; private and group rates available upon request and with advance notice. Bicycle sales and service are also available.

Special Events: Mother's Day Marsh Mountain Classic with downhill, dual slalom, and cross-country racing; weekly summer criterium.

Accommodations: Call Wisp Resort Hotel at 800/426-9477.

Dining: Wisp Resort Hotel has restaurants and lounge.

Off-the-Bike Activities: In-line skate rentals and instruction, championship golf, indoor pool and Jacuzzi, tennis, hiking, scenic chairlift rides, whitewater rafting. Nearby Deep Creek Lake offers boating, water skiing, fishing, and other water sports. Lots of antique stores in the area.

Other Services and Features: Close to several state parks

DAVID LAMONDE PHOTO COURTESY HIDDEN VALLEY

New York

The Bark Eater Inn

P.O. Box 139
Alstead Hill Road
Keene, NY 12942
(518) 576-2221
(518) 576-2071 (fax)

Right out the door? You bet! For fun, distance, a challenge, or a workout, you'll find miles of back roads and logging trails at the Bark Eater Inn. Train with the Olympians—or just watch them! Originally a stagecoach stopover, the inn is minutes from the Olympic Village of Lake Placid. Situated on an old farm with rolling meadows and spectacular views of the surrounding mountains, it offers gracious accommodations and memorable dining. It also has a large, year-round riding stable and an extensive cross- country ski program in winter.

Garnet Hill Lodge and Cross-Country Ski Center

13th Lake Road
North River, NY 12856
(518) 251-2444

Built in 1936 overlooking Thirteenth Lake, Garnet Hill is a rustic Adirondack lodge offering warm hospitality and comfortable accommodations. In summer, guests can enjoy water sports on the lake, or take to the area's hiking and biking trails through woodlands to some of the nicest vistas in the East.

Location, Hours, and Prices

BOB WILLIAMSON PHOTO

General Location: Central Adirondacks, west of Lake George, about a 1½-hour drive north of Albany

Getting There: Closest airport is Albany. Take Road I-87 (Adirondack Northway) to Exit 23 (Warrensburg, New York), Route 9 to Route 28, and go left on Thirteenth Lake Road.

Biking Season: May to November

Elevation: Lodge 2,000'; ski shop 1,900'

Hours: Daily, 8–dark

Prices: $5/trail fee

Regulations/Restrictions: Helmets required

The Rides

The cross-country ski trails and the local dirt roads in the area combine to make great bicycling adventures. Generally the novice ski trails are novice bicycles trails, and the expert ski trails become expert-only mountain biking trails. While there is no lift service, the lodge does offer a shuttle bus service that allows you to ride 10 miles downhill and catch a ride back up to the lodge.

Terrain Description: Cross-country

Mileage/Number of Trails: 20 miles, with additional 10 miles on roads in the area

Difficulty: 10% easiest, 60% more difficult, 30% most difficult

Trails Under Development: Some new singletrack in 1996

Recommended Trails: Old Faithful (beginner); Trapper/Cougar (intermediate); Bobcat, Solitaire, Duffany's (advanced)

Mountain Bike Lift: No, but uphill shuttle bus service is available.

Trails Accessible from Shuttle: All

Biggest Vertical Drop: 700'

Longest Trail: 4–5 miles

Other Local Trails: Trails connect to neighborhood dirt roads; Santanoni Preserve is nearby as are state wild forest areas.

Trail Map: Free with trail fee

Local Services

Bike rentals, shuttles, and even racing are available at the lodge. A self-contained destination lodge, Garnet Hill serves scrumptious meals that include fresh baked bread, low-fat and low-cholesterol options, and vegetarian dishes.

Mountain Bike Services: Bike rental $15/4 hours, $25/day; 10-mile downhill ride and bus shuttle back available twice weekly, free to lodge guests

Special Events: Race pending for 1996 season

Emergency Facilities: Nearby

Accommodations: Lodge is a complete resort with 27 guest rooms plus vacation home rentals.

Dining: Complete restaurant on premises; menu includes low-fat and heart-healthy entrees

Off-the-Bike Activities: Hiking, lake activities, canoe and boat rental, nearby Garnet Mine tours, boat tours, Adirondack Museum

Other Services and Features: Lodge is located at the edge of the 50,000-acre Siamese Ponds Wilderness.

Holiday Valley Resort

Route 219
P.O. Box 370
Ellicottville, NY 14731
(716) 699-2345
(716) 699-5204 (fax)

Nestled in the rolling hills and farmland of the Allegheny foothills, Holiday Valley is a year-round resort offering skiing, golf, mountain biking, and hiking. Resort accommodations are convenient for all activities.

Location, Hours, and Prices

General Location: In the Allegheny foothills of western New York directly south of Buffalo

Getting There: From Buffalo International Airport, take 33 West to 90 West. Take Exit 55 to Route 219 South, and follow 219 for 45 miles to Ellicottville. Holiday Valley is 1 mile farther south. Total distance is 50 miles.

Biking Season: May to October

Elevation: Base 1,500′; summit 2,250

Hours: Daily, sunrise to sunset

Prices: No charge to use trails for hiking or mountain biking

Regulations/Restrictions: Helmets required; mountain bikes not allowed on golf course

PHOTO COURTESY HOLIDAY VALLEY RESORT

The Rides

Holiday Valley's 25-mile trail network offers a combination of singletrack, access roads, and open slopes. Some of the paths wind through pine forests where exposed roots offer technical challenges. The property borders the state forest with many more miles of logging roads and paths.

Terrain Description: Combination

Mileage/Number of Trails: Approximately 25 miles of trails are open to cyclists, although about 15 miles are mostly used.

Difficulty: Beginner to intermediate going uphill; intermediate to advanced going downhill

Trails Under Development: None

Recommended Trails: For intermediate and better riders, the Loop is a 4-mile circuit starting at the Training Center, climbing to Cochran Pond (approximately 600'), traversing along the ridgeline to Tannenbaum Downhill and then back to the Training Center.

Mountain Bike Lift: No

Biggest Vertical Drop: 750'

Longest Trail: 4-mile loop

Other Local Trails: Resort trails connect to state forest logging roads. Trails also connect to Holimont Ski Area (private) and the White Trail (hiking).

Trail Map: No charge for map; call Holiday Valley to get one by mail.

Local Services

While Holiday Valley does not see mountain biking as a huge draw right now, the resort does have plans for a mountain bike school. Currently, it offers rentals and races, with lodging and dining on-site.

Mountain Bike Services: Bike rental (helmet included) for $10/hour, $20/day.

Special Events: 1996 events include a 6-week Wednesday evening race series, June 12–July 17, $35/series or $8/race; Roots, Rocks and Ridges Race, July 28, $20/race and BBQ after in Village Park; Fall Festival Race, October 13.

Emergency Facilities: EMTs on staff during races. Nearest hospital is 20 miles away in Olean or Springville.

Accommodations: The Inn at Holiday Valley offers free continental breakfast, indoor/outdoor pool, hot tub, sauna, and weight room. Holiday Valley Rental Management has 170 condominiums with full kitchens; call 800/323-0020. Other accommodations are available in the Village of Ellicottville; call the Chamber of Commerce at 716/699-5046.

Dining: At Holiday Valley, the Hearth Restaurant (lunch/dinner), Cabana Bar (lunch, snacks and refreshments); nearby, the Ellicottville Brew Pub Microbrewery, Gin Mill, Tips Up, The Barn, SilverFox, Dina's, and Burger King.

Off-the-Bike Activities: The resort's primary summer activity is golf. They have an 18-hole, par-72 course, plus a large 3-pool complex, meeting facilities, and day care on weekends. Other 1996 activities include a Summer Festival of the Arts, June 29–30, with art show, theater, Buffalo Philharmonic on the slopes, fireworks; Taste of Ellicottville, August 10–11; Fall Festival, October 12–13.

Other Services and Features: Ellicottville is a great town with excellent restaurants, and nightlife, yet retains a wholesome small town feeling and relaxed pace of life. Just 15 miles to the south is Allegheny State Park, the largest in New York.

Ski Plattekill Mountain Biking Center

Plattekill Mountain Road
P.O. Box 187
Roxbury, NY 12474
(800) GOTTA-BIKE
(607) 326-3500
(607) 326-3034 (fax)
E-mail: Skiplattkl@aol.com

Since its grand opening in May 1995, Plattekill has quickly added services to become what might be New York's finest mountain bike park. Besides offering the state's only lift-served biking, the area caters to the mountain biking crowd with nice Gary Fisher rental bikes, awesome singletrack, on-site camping, and a full roster of special events. A recent story in BIKE *magazine said Plattekill "shouldn't be missed" and described it as "an unexpected gift" for serious riders.*

Location, Hours, and Prices

General Location: Outside of Roxbury, New York, in the Catskills

Getting There: Take the New York State Thruway to Kingston Exit 19. Take Route 28 West approximately 35 minutes to the town of Arkville. Turn right at Crosby's Farm Equipment just before the railroad crossing. Go 1 mile to the end and turn right onto Route 30 North. After driving about 5 more minutes, look for Ski Plattekill signs and turn left onto Cold Springs Road. Follow signs to Ski Plattekill, 4 miles off Route 30.

Biking Season: April to November

Elevation: 1,000′ of vertical

Hours: Weekends and holidays, 10–5

Prices: $18/all-day lift ticket; $10/trail access only; $250/season pass

Regulations/Restrictions: Helmets required. Stay off closed trails.

The Rides

The terrain selection will satisfy every rider's ability. Many of the trails utilize Plattekill's cross-country ski trail, encompassing the entire ridge surrounding the natural bowl where the resort sits. Many of the trails are downhill, but there are miles of cross-country routes as well. The easy novice trails are wide and gently sloping, while the intermediate trails are steeper and narrower and include some singletrack. With vigorous downhills and miles of singletrack, the advanced trails are for the aggressive rider seeking technical, extreme, race-quality riding. All-day, long-distance rides are also available.

Terrain Description: Combination
Mileage/Number of Trails: 40+ miles
Difficulty: Refer to trail map
Trails Under Development: 10 miles of new trail in 1996 with more to come
Recommended Trails: Any singletrack
Mountain Bike Lift: 1 (Sunshine)
Trails Accessible from Lift: It's possible to connect with all trails, although some climbing may be required.
Biggest Vertical Drop: 1,000′
Longest Trail: All-day loops possible
Other Local Trails: None indicated
Trail Map: Free in brochure

TOM STILLO PHOTO COURTESY CRESTED BUTTE MTN RESORT

Local Services

Plattekill has all the services you could want for a day. You can camp here, or Plattekill will help you find local lodging. What Plattekill lacks in frills it makes up for with a full range of bicycle services and special events.

Mountain Bike Services: Bike sales, rentals, and repairs. Rentals run $20/all day, $30/all day front-suspension bike, $40/all day full-suspension bike; $5/helmet rental; beginner rental package ($45) includes all-day lift ticket, bike, and helmet rental, 1-hour lesson, and guide. Lessons and guided tours cost $10/hour. "Mini Bikers" nursery day care runs $5/hour. Locker rental available as well.

BOB WILLIAMSON PHOTO

Special Events: Special night rides (approved lights required) take place the second Saturday of every month at 8:30 and include the use of the chairlift. Four NORBA-sanctioned races are planned for 1996, exact dates TBD. Each event will have downhill, cross-country, dual slalom, and hill climb events; in addition, Plattekill is set to host New York's first ever 24-hour race. Plattekill also has bike swap sales. Call for special group events and prices.

Emergency Facilities: A volunteer bike patrol administers first aid.

Accommodations: Lots of bed and breakfasts, motels, and hotels in the area. Call or fax Plattekill for a list. Plattekill also lets mountain bikers camp in its parking lot. Campsites with showers are scheduled to be built in the summer of 1996.

Dining: On-site picnic facilities. Base lodge facilities include full-service cafeteria, bar, espresso bar, and pizza parlor. Fine dining in the vicinity.

Off-the-Bike Activities: Golf, hiking

Other Services and Features: Good family area. Gift shop, catering and banquet facilities, group functions, live entertainment. Wild raspberries provide trailside food!

Connecticut

Woodbury Ski and Racquet

Route 47, 785 Washington Road
Woodbury, CT 06798
(203) 263-2203

Open for riding year round, Woodbury Ski and Racquet offers a 20-mile trail network to mountain bikers and is in close proximity to the East Coast's major urban centers.

Location, Hours, and Prices

General Location: Central Connecticut

Getting There: From Waterbury, take I-84 West to Exit 17 to Route 64 West to Route 6 North to Route 47 in Woodbury. From Danbury, take I-84 East to Exit 15 Southbury to Route 6 North to Route 47 in Woodbury.

Biking Season: Year round

Elevation: 850′

Hours: Monday–Friday, 10:30–6; Saturday and Sunday, 9–6

Prices: $10/trail fee

Regulations/Restrictions: None

The Rides

Some 36 trails criss-cross Woodbury's mostly intermediate terrain, giving the mountain biker 20 miles of routes to explore. Nearby Steep Rock Park offers additional riding opportunities.

Terrain Description: Combination

Mileage/Number of Trails: 36 trails, 20 miles

Difficulty: 30% beginner, 50% intermediate, 20% advanced

Trails Under Development: None

Recommended Trails: Mystery Trail

Mountain Bike Lift: No

Biggest Vertical Drop: 300′

Longest Trail: 1 mile

Other Local Trails: Steep Rock Park

Trail Map: Yes

Local Services

Woodbury Ski and Racquet offers little in the way of services itself, but you can find lodging and dining nearby. The resort will help you make arrangements.

Mountain Bike Services: No

Special Events: No

Emergency Facilities: None

Accommodations: Try Heritage Inn, Southbury, 203/264-8255; Curtis House, Woodbury, 203/263-2101; Radisson, Southbury, 800/333-3333 or 203/598-7600. Contact the ski area for special package rates.

Dining: Lodge snack bar or local restaurants

Off-the-Bike Activities: Concerts, swimming, tennis, camping, skateboarding, in-line skating, fishing

Other Services and Features: Home of the Rod Taylor Ski School

CHAPTER 8

THE NORTHEAST

Vermont

Bolton Valley Resort/Mountain Bike and Adventure Center

Bolton Valley, VT 05477

(800) 451-3220

(802) 434-4303

Primarily a winter resort but steadily building its summer business, Bolton Valley Resort is a quick 25 minutes from Burlington Airport. The area offers 100 kilometers of cross-country trails, and may soon be adding lift service for cyclists. Meanwhile, you can catch a complimentary shuttle to the top of the mountain.

Location, Hours, and Prices

General Location: 20 miles from Burlington, just off Interstate 89

Getting There: South on I-89 from Burlington to Exit 11, then east on Route 2 for 8 miles. Follow signs for Bolton Valley Ski Resort.

Biking Season: June 1–late September

Elevation: Base 2,000′; summit 3,200′

Hours: Daily, 7–dusk; Mountain Bike Center, 10–8

Prices: $5/adult trail fee, $3/junior; season pass $50/individual, $75/couple, $100/family.

Regulations/Restrictions: Helmets required

The Rides

Bolton Valley's multi-use trails consist mostly of technical wooded singletrack with occasional logging roads. Alpine slopes are also open for biking.

Terrain Description: Combination

Mileage/Number of Trails: 100 kilometers of cross-country trails and work roads

Difficulty: 20% easiest, 30% more difficult, 50% most difficult

Trails Under Development: Constantly expanding maintained trails through mowing, cutting, and building bridges

Recommended Trails: Broadway on resort work road loop and Pond Loop (beginner); Telemark and Bobcat (intermediate); Maple Loop, Beaver Pond, and Spruce Run (advanced).

Mountain Bike Lift: Shuttle available to the top; lift coming soon

Biggest Vertical Drop: 1,200′

Longest Trail: Broadway

Other Local Trails: Trails link up with the Long Trail and Trapp Trail with access to Stowe and Camels Hump.

Trail Map: Free with trail fee; free to hikers. Pick up at Mountain Bike Center in Bumpo Deli and Country Store in base lodge.

Local Services

The Adventure Center at Bolton rents bikes and provides a free shuttle to the top of the mountain. Downhill fans take note of one of the area's special events—a 12-mile, 2,000′ descent billed as the longest downhill in the East. Lodging, dining, and other outdoor activities are plentiful at Bolton.

Mountain Bike Services: Top-of-the-line rentals $24/day, $19/junior 12 and under; $20/4 hours, $15/junior 4 hours; $15/2 hours, $10/junior 2 hours. Helmets included. Complimentary shuttle to top of mountain.

Special Events: Two events scheduled for 1996—Wimps/Weenies/Wackos in July (cross-country); Longest Downhill in the East in August (12 miles with 2,000′ vertical drop). Weekly evening races.

Emergency Facilities: ATV evacuation sled; ambulance 5 miles away

Accommodations: 1,200 beds at resort; call 800/451-3220 or 802/434-2131

Dining: 7 restaurants/dining facilities on-site

Off-the-Bike Activities: Full resort facilities on-site. Trail fee includes use of outdoor swimming pool (after shower), tennis courts, conference facilities, restaurants, cafe, and deli. Hiking, canoeing, picnics, nature walks, and a ropes course are also available.

Other Services and Features: Nearby Burlington, Stowe, and Sugarbush are very active outdoor communities. Camping and child care are available. Don't miss the great swimming holes on cascading mountain brooks.

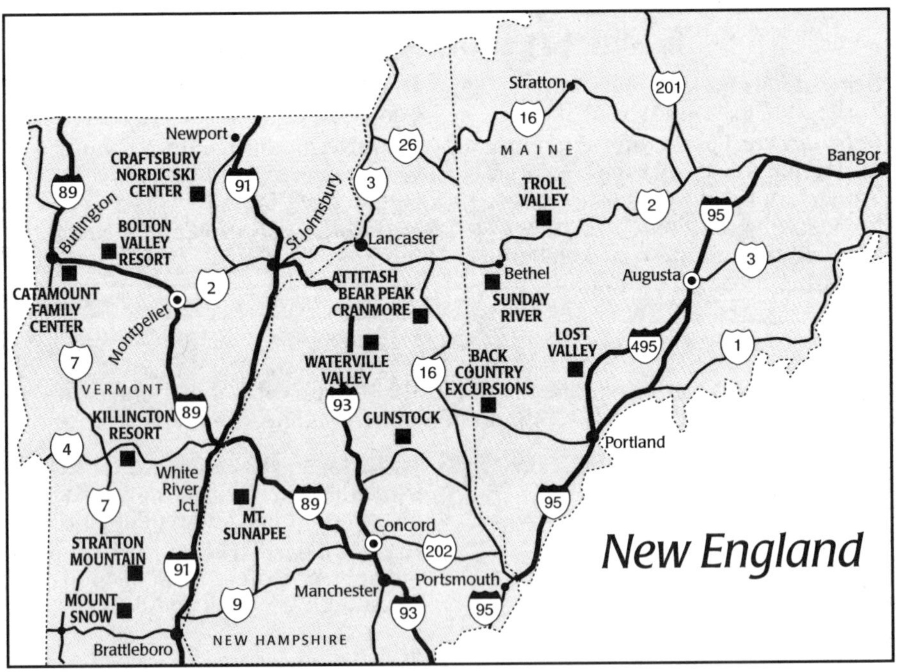

The Outdoor Experience at Catamount Family Center

494 Governor Chittenden Road
Williston, VT 05495
(802) 879-4960
(802) 879-6001

A 450-acre outdoor recreation facility, the Outdoor Experience, operating at Catamount Family Center, has 50 kilometers of groomed and maintained trails for mountain biking, orienteering, running, and walking.

Location, Hours, and Prices

General Location: Northern Vermont, just 20 minutes from Burlington

Getting There: From Burlington Airport, take Route 2 East to North Williston Road (north) to Governor Chittenden Road (east) approximately 10 miles.

Biking Season: May 1–November 1

Elevation: Low, Nordic ski area in winter

Hours: No set hours

Prices: $6/area use fee

Regulations/Restrictions: Helmets mandatory. Follow IMBA Rules of the Trail.

The Rides

If pleasant meadow or wooded trails are your thing, Catamount is the place for you, with mostly gentle terrain for both singletrack and doubletrack.

Terrain Description: Cross-country

Mileage/Number of Trails: 50 kilometers—about 25% singletrack, 75% doubletrack

Difficulty: 10% meadow riding, 60% easy wooded riding, 20% technical, 10% other

Trails Under Development: 30% more singletrack

Recommended Trails: Center marks trails via colored arrows based on ability level. All trails are loops that begin and end at the center.

Mountain Bike Lift: No

Biggest Vertical Drop: 200′

Longest Trail: All interconnected.

Other Local Trails: None indicated

Trail Map: Yes

Local Services

Catamount rents bikes, teaches clinics, and organizes races. The center has developed a number of camps for kids, from half-day to week-long ventures. You can find all the lodging and dining you need in nearby Burlington.

Mountain Bike Services: Rents Gary Fisher bikes for $15. Group lessons, including Learn To Mountain Bike and Women Only groups, $10. Camps include the Catamount Kids Day Camp and Residential Camp for

MICHAEL CLARK PHOTO COURTESY CRAFTSBURY SPORTS CENTER

children 11–15, Girls Only Half-Day Camp for girls 11–15, Tikes Half-Day Camp for kids 8–10. Prices range from $70/half day to $300/week. Call for brochure and details.

Special Events: Weekly cross-country and dual slalom training series; Specialized Eastern Cup American Mountain Bike Challenge, June 1–2, 1996.

Emergency Facilities: Hospital 20 minutes away

Accommodations: 3,500 beds in nearby Burlington area

Dining: Burlington

Off-the-Bike Activities: In Burlington you can find performing arts, waterfront area, tourist train, museums, and movie theaters.

Other Services and Features: Burlington was voted the number one city to live in by *Outside* magazine.

Craftsbury Nordic Ski Center

P.O. Box 31, Craftsbury Common, VT 05827

(800) 729-7751

(802) 586-7767

The Craftsbury Sports Center is a year-round destination resort on Lake Hosmer in the Northeast Kingdom of Vermont, with 60 miles of trails and accommodations for 90 guests.

Location, Hours, and Prices

General Location: Northeast uplands of Vermont

Getting There: From Montreal, take 10 West to 55 South to I-91 South, 58 East, and 14 South. From Burlington Airport, take I-89 South, 100 North, 15 East, 14 North. From New York and Boston, take 91 North to 2 West to 15 West to 14 North.

Biking Season: June to October

Elevation: 800'–2,000'

Hours: Daily, 9–5

Prices: $3/trail use fee

Regulations/Restrictions: Helmets mandatory

The Rides

With nearly 200 miles of mapped roads and trails, Craftsbury has something for all levels of riders. While the terrain can be hilly here in the Green Mountains, there's still plenty of options for the beginning mountain biker.

Terrain Description: Cross-country

Mileage/Number of Trails: 10 kilometers of dedicated singletrack and ski trail (a little wider); 300 kilometers of smooth, public gravel roads within 20 kilometer radius

Difficulty: Singletrack (advanced), ski trails (intermediate/advanced), and public roads (beginner/intermediate)

Trails Under Development: None

Recommended Trails: Lake Loop (beginner/intermediate); Caspian Lake Loop (intermediate); Singletrack Loop, Mud and Sweat Loop (advanced)

Mountain Bike Lift: No

Biggest Vertical Drop: 1,000'

Longest Trail: Mud and Sweat Loop at 40 kilometers

Other Local Trails: Trails on private land open onto lightly traveled gravel town roads.

Trail Map: Purchase at main office

Local Services

Craftsbury makes a great base for guided or self-guided tours. The center will even help you put together an inn-to-inn trip. Craftsbury has everything you need for an extended trek. With lodging and dining on-site, the center is also a good choice for groups.

Mountain Bike Services: 20 Gary Fisher mountain bikes for rent; free weekly beginner clinics for guests; private lessons for beginner to expert riders; guide services for groups. Several 3- and 6-day tours scheduled. The Center can also help you design an inn-to-inn trip on foot, skis, road bike, or mountain bike; book a night at the Center, and they will provide maps and recommend other inns; they also offer shuttle service of your luggage for a fee.

Special Events: 1996 events include the Craftsbury Mountain Bike Race, October 13, and the Craftsbury Triathlon, July 13 (swim ½K, mountain bike 6K, run 6K).

Emergency Facilities: Nearby ambulance rescue service

Accommodations: Lodging available at the center for up to 90 guests; call 800/729-7751

Dining: On-site restaurant serves 3 meals a day buffet style. Meals are hearty and all you can eat, with vegetarian options; all breads and desserts homemade.

Off-the-Bike Activities: Running, rowing/sculling, cross-country ski camps, walking tours, permanent orienteering course, waterfront canoeing, swimming, tennis courts, basketball, volleyball, weight room, sauna, llama walks

Other Services and Features: The Center is used by a combination of adult sports camps, individuals, and groups.

Killington Resort

Killington Road
Killington, VT 05751
(802) 422-3333
(802) 422-4391 (fax)

At Killington, you and your bike can ride the $1\frac{1}{4}$-mile long chairlift to the highest point reached by aerial lift in New England. From the 4,214′ summit, you can explore 50 miles of trails spread over five mountains.

Location, Hours, and Prices

General Location: Central Vermont, 16 miles east of Rutland and 19 miles west of Woodstock at the junction of US Route 4 and VT 100 in Sherburne

Getting There: Killington is about $2\frac{3}{4}$ hours from Boston. Take I-93 to just south of Concord, New Hampshire. Exit onto I-89 North and follow to US 4/Rutland, Exit 1, in Vermont. Follow US 4 West to Killington. From Hartford, Connecticut (about 3 hours), follow I-91 to north of Bellows Falls, Vermont. Take Exit 6 (Rutland) onto VT 103 and follow to VT 100. Take VT 100 North to US 4 West to the resort. From New York City it's $4\frac{3}{4}$ hours via the Connecticut Turnpike (I-95). Take the Turnpike to I-91 and then follow the directions from Hartford. From New York and New Jersey via the New York Thruway, take the Thruway to Exit 24 Albany. Take Northway (I-87) North to Fort Ann/Rutland Exit 20. Pick up NY 149 and follow east to US 4. Turn left and follow east to Killington. From Philadelphia, Washington, D.C., and points south, take feeder highways to New Jersey Turnpike. Exit onto Garden State Parkway and follow to the New York Thruway. Then follow directions for New York City and New Jersey areas. From Buffalo, Cleveland, Toronto, and the Midwest, take feeder highways to the New York Thruway (I-90). Exit at Albany onto Northway (I-87) and follow north to Fort Ann Exit. Pick up NY 149 and follow east to US 4. Turn left on US 4 and follow east to Killington. Airports are available in Boston, Hartford, New York, Newark, Albany, Rutland, Lebanon (NH), and Burlington.

JERRY LEBLOND PHOTO COURTESY KILLINGTON RESORT

Biking Season: Daily, June through mid-October; weekends only, late May to early June

Elevation: Snowshed Base Lodge 2,200′; summit of Killington Peak, the highest area in Vermont accessible by an aerial lift, 4,241′

Hours: Daily, 9–6; early and late season skiing may affect mountain biking operations, so please call ahead at 802/422-6232.

Prices: Trail pass \$8/adult, \$5/junior 12 and under; 1 ride on Killington Peak Chairlift and trail pass \$18/adult, \$10/junior; all-day Killington Peak Chairlift and trail pass \$25/adult, \$15/junior.

Regulations/Restrictions: Helmets are required when riding on the trail system. Riders must sign a mountain biking release at the Mountain Bike Rental Shop, open daily 9–6, before riding on the mountain.

The Rides

Trails are mostly ski trails and work roads with singletrack in the woods. About 75% of the terrain on ski trails is open terrain. The Mountain Roadway system is used daily during summer months for transportation of maintenance crews, equipment, and materials. On these roads, riders should be aware of traffic.

Terrain Description: Combination

Mileage/Number of Trails: 50 miles of trails spread across 5 of Killington's 6 mountains

Difficulty: Some trails may be generally easy but with areas of more difficulty. Killington does not rate trails by different levels, but trails are available for all abilities.

Trails Under Development: None

Recommended Trails: Easy Way (5.5 miles for beginners); Jon's Jaunt (2 miles for intermediate riders); Outback (2 miles for advanced riders)

Mountain Bike Lift: 1

Trails Accessible from Lift: 26, all interconnected

ROBERT BOSSI PHOTO COURTESY KILLINGTON RESORT

Biggest Vertical Drop: 3,150′

Longest Trail: 7.5 miles (Long Way)

Other Local Trails: None

Trail Map: Included in Killington's free mountain biking brochure

Local Services

Killington bills itself as a complete mountain bike center, and with rentals, guided tours, instruction, lift access, and races, no one would disagree. The surrounding area boasts lots of lodging options, restaurants, and other recreational opportunities.

Mountain Bike Services: Rental equipment, including bikes, accessories, and clothing available from the Mountain Bike Shop at Killington Base Lodge, open daily, 9–6. Riders can rent 24-speed front-suspension and full-suspension bikes. Classes and group or private lessons are available as well as guided tours. Staff members are constantly on the mountain to maintain the trails. Full facilities are available at the Killington Base Lodge, and there is a restaurant at Killington Peak Lodge.

Special Events: For 1996, Memorial Day Weekend Triathlon, May 25—ski Superstar trail, mountain bike 6.2 miles, and cross-country run 3 miles, advance registration required, call 802/422-6252.; Vertical Drop, in mid-June, is a NORBA-sanctioned mountain bike race featuring a challenging 2,000′ vertical drop and more than 6 miles of uninterrupted downhill cycling—open to all classes of racers, preregistration advised, call 802/422-6232. Thunder and Lightning-Pedros New England Mountain Bike Series

Race, July 28, is a singletrack course voted the "best mountain bike course ever to grace a ski area," $25 preregistration, cash and product prizes, open to all levels of racers, special lodging rates available.

Emergency Facilities: Phones located at various places on the mountain, and first aid rooms located in several areas. Refer to trail map.

Accommodations: 116 lodges, country inns, motels, and condominiums offer a variety of accommodations for every budget and lifestyle. Capacity for 4,500 at the base of the mountains in condominium suites and hotel rooms; 18,000 capacity in the region. Packages are available by calling the Killington Lodging Bureau, 800/621-6867, and the Killington Travel Service, 800/372-2007.

Dining: 62 restaurants and nightspots in the region, including the famous Wobbly Barn and the Pickle Barrel. Hemingway's, Vermont's only 4-star restaurant and rated in the top 25 in the nation, also resides in Killington.

Off-the-Bike Activities: Hundreds of activities in the Killington region: tennis, golf, camps, fishing, hiking, ethnic festival, rodeo, music festival, micro-brew and chili cook-off festival, food and wine festival, craft fair, air show, scenic chairlift rides, Vermont State Fair, Octoberfest, Sheep and Wool Festival

Other Services and Features: Road cyclists take note: Killington hosts the Tour De Cure, a cycling tour benefiting the American Diabetes Association, as well as the Killington Stage Race, a 5-day stage race for the best amateur and professional riders in the country.

Mount Snow Resort

Mount Snow, VT 05356

(800) 245-7669

(802) 464-3333

A truly world-class venue, Mount Snow frequently hosts international mountain bike competitions. It also offers cyclists over 140 miles of lift-served terrain along with a full array of other cycling services—not to mention the view of four states from the summit of Mount Snow at 3,600'.

Location, Hours, and Prices

General Location: Near West Dover and Wilmington

Getting There: Route 7E to Bennington. Route 7E becomes 9E. Follow 9E 21 miles to Wilmington. Take a left at the second light onto 100 North. Mount Snow is 9 miles up Route 100N.

Biking Season: May-October; call for confirmation, 800/245-7669.

Elevation: Base 1,900'; summit 3,600'

Hours: Daily, 9-4

Prices: $9/trail fee; $18/1 chairlift ride with bike, $28/all-day chairlift rides with bike, $9/foot passenger ride

Regulations/Restrictions: Helmets required

The Rides

You can find a bit of everything in Mount Snow's extensive trail network—technical singletrack, doubletrack jeep trails, moderate singletrack, and dirt roads. In general, beginners should stick to the bottom of the mountain, while expert riders should head for the summit.

ROBERT BOSSI PHOTO COURTESY KILLINGTON RESORT

Terrain Description: Cross-country

Mileage/Number of Trails: 140 miles

Difficulty: Not indicated

Trails Under Development: The Hardening trail from summit to base should open summer of 1996.

Recommended Trails: Crosstown area (beginner); Crosstown area and lower mountain (intermediate); top of Mount Snow (expert)

Mountain Bike Lift: 1

Trails Accessible from Lift: Not indicated

Biggest Vertical Drop: 1,700′

Longest Trail: 2.5 miles

Other Local Trails: Trails connect to valley trails and surrounding eastern ridge area.

Trail Map: Available at main Base Lodge at Mount Snow

Local Services

Theme weekends, instruction, rentals, tours, and top-notch races are among Mount Snow's cycling services. In recent years, the resort has also developed a strong dual slalom race series. Other visitor services can be found on-site or nearby, and can be booked through a central reservation number.

Mountain Bike Services: The Mount Snow Mountain Bike Center offers rentals, instruction, and tours. 2-hour rentals run $22/rigid frame, $30/suspended frame; 4-hour rentals cost $27/rigid frame, $38/suspended frame; 1-day rentals run $33/rigid frame, $47/suspended frame; 2-day rentals are $45/rigid frame, $89/suspended frame. Instructional tours cost $20/2 hours, $30/4 hours. 1-day school (Saturdays only) costs $90/without bike rental, $99/with bike rental. 2-day school runs $149/without bike rental, $165/with bike rental.

ROBERT BOSSI PHOTO COURTESY KILLINGTON RESORT

Special Events: Scheduled for 1996, Mountain Bike Demo Day, Memorial Day weekend; Grundig/UCI Mountain Bike World Cup and Jeep National Championship Series, June 20–23—dual slalom, downhill, cross-country, observed trials competitions for all classes, including the world's best international racers; Vermont Dual Slalom Series, July 6, 20, 27, August 10 and 17, with championship race on

Labor Day Weekend; Inn to Inn Tour, July 13–14, combines country inns and backcountry riding, repeated September 14–15; Wilderness Overnight Weekend, July 20–21, guided biking and camping tour, repeated September 7-8; Family Mountain Bike Weekend, July 27–28, designed to meet the needs of every family member, repeated August 17–18; Women's Weekend, August 3–4, has riding exercises, training tips, nutrition, equipment reviews, and riding for women, repeated August 10–11; Mountain Bike Extreme Tour, August 24, a true test of grit; Wicked Wild Mountain Bike Festival, August 31–September 1, with fun events like the mud bog, mountain bike limbo, obstacle course, and more. Events and dates are tentative; call to confirm, 800/245-7669.

Emergency Facilities: First aid at base

Accommodations: Call 800/245-SNOW

Dining: Call 800/245-SNOW

Off-the-Bike Activities: Summer events include Home and Garden Show, Celebrate Kids!, Art on the Mountain, Vermont's Green Mountain Irish Music Festival, Vermont State Chili Cookoff, Mount Snow Brewers Fest, and Harvest Craft Show.

Other Services and Features: Mt. Snow is a perennial stop on the World Cup and National Championship Series race circuits.

Stratton Mountain Resort

RR1 Box 145
Stratton Mountain, VT 05155-9406
(800) STRATTON (reservations)
(802) 297-2200

Stratton is an all-season resort with a complete village, four hotels, condos, skiing and snowboarding in winter, and biking, golf, tennis, hiking, and horseback riding in summer. In summer of 1996 as we went to press, Stratton was embarking upon major improvements to the trail network. During this construction, some services may not be available, so please check with the resort for the latest information.

Location, Hours, and Prices

General Location: Southern Vermont, 2½ hours from Boston, 4 hours from New York City

Getting There: 81 miles from Albany, New York. Take Route 7 to Vermont (becomes Route 9) and on to Bennington. Take US 7 North to Manchester. Then follow Route 30 South to Bondville and Stratton access road.

Biking Season: May–October, with lift access late June to mid-October

Elevation: Base/resort 1,872'; summit 3,875'

Hours: Daily, 10–4

Prices: TBD

Regulations/Restrictions: Helmet required for lift access. Must stay on marked trails.

The Rides

At Stratton, an eight-minute gondola rides deposits you at the summit, where you can tackle one of several downhill routes. Looking for something a little less challenging? Try the gently rolling, wooded trails in the Sun Bowl area. Note that the number and difficulty of trails, as well as access to trails, may change during the planned 1996 trail expansion.

Terrain Description: Varied

Mileage/Number of Trails: 15+ trails

Difficulty: Sun Bowl trails are suitable for beginner through advanced riders. Stratton Mountain trails are for advanced riders only.

Trails Under Development: $25,000 in capital improvements to the trail network during the summer of 1996

Recommended Trails: Main Line, Rabbit Run, Sprint (beginner); Buck's Run, Black Bear, Old Log Road (int.); Camel's Hump, Upper Kidder Brook, Lower Kidder Brook (advanced)

Mountain Bike Lift: 1

Trails Accessible from Lift: 15+

Biggest Vertical Drop: 2,003'

Longest Trail: 3 miles

Other Local Trails: Lots of road biking and mountain biking throughout Bennington County. A Recreation Map & Guide to the county that is available at outdoor stores.

SHARON MCNEILL PHOTO COURTESY SUNDAY RIVER

Trail Map: Available from the Recreational Activities Center in Stratton Village or the Gondola Station

Local Services

You can find everything you need for a mountain bike vacation at Stratton Mountain or in Stratton Village. The nearby communities of Manchester, Arlington, and Bennington provide additional lodging, dining, and recreational options.

Mountain Bike Services: Rentals (with helmets) and guided tours; junior, standard, and high-performance bikes can be rented for 2 hours, 4 hours, or all day. Contact Stratton Mountain Sports at 802/297-3001.

Special Events: TBD

Emergency Facilities: First aid in base lodge area

Accommodations: Mountain Villas on-site; wide variety of country inns, lodges, and motor inns on and around the mountain; call Stratton Central Reservations at 800/STRATTON

Dining: Stratton Village and in nearby Manchester; call 800/STRATTON

Off-the-Bike Activities: Stratton is very big on golf and tennis, and has lodging and camping packages for both activities. The new Resort Activities Center can arrange horseback riding, canoe trips, country fairs, summer theater, fishing, dance festivals, and more. Shopping is popular thanks to the boutiques in Stratton Village and the outlet shopping in Manchester. The resort also offers scenic gondola rides, concerts, a KidsKamp, and child care.

Other Services and Features: Stratton Mountain is southern Vermont's highest summit.

New Hampshire

Attitash Bear Peak Cranmore Resort

P.O. Box 308
Route 302
Bartlett, NH 03812
(800) 223-7669 (lodging)
(603) 374-2368
(603) 374-1960 (fax)

At Attitash Bear Peak Cranmore and the Fields of Attitash, you can take a ride on the alpine slide, cool off on the water slides, and, for kids ages 2 to 7, check out Buddy Bear's Playpool. Looking for a memorable outdoor experience? Try the mountain bike shuttle to the White Mountain National Forest or take a scenic chairlift ride to the White Mountain Observation Tower for the best views around. For the Valley's most exciting lift-served mountain biking, head to Cranmore in North Conway. Cranmore also offers tennis camps for all ages as well as AdventurKids camps. Check out the scenic dining at the Meister Hut mountaintop restaurant, where the food is as fabulous as the views.

Location, Hours, and Prices

General Location: Northern New Hampshire's Mt. Washington Valley

Getting There: From Boston ($2\frac{1}{2}$ hours), take I-95 North to Spaulding Turnpike (NH 16) to Route 302 West. From Portland, Maine ($1\frac{1}{2}$ hours), take Route 302 all the way.

Biking Season: Memorial Day to Columbus Day weekend

Elevation: Base 550'; summit 2,300'

Hours: Weekends, Memorial Day to mid-June and early September to mid-October; daily, mid-June to early September.

Prices: Single ride ticket covers 1 ride on alpine slide or scenic chair or a half-hour on water slides, $7/adults, $5.50/children, $5.50/seniors; the double ticket allows 2 rides on one of the above, $12/all ages; the value ticket entitles you to unlimited use of the alpine slide, water slides, scenic chair, Buddy Bear's Playpool, or lift-served mountain biking on Attitash Peak, $18/all ages

Regulations/Restrictions: Helmets required at all times for cycling

The Rides

At Attitash Bear Peak Cranmore, peaks known collectively as The Presidentials, there's riding for all ability levels, from a gentle tour along the Saco River to expert cruising down the slopes of Cranmore and in White Mountain National Forest. At press time, some details of the mountain biking program were not set. Call for the latest updates.

Terrain Description: Combination

Mileage/Number of Trails: TBD

Difficulty: TBD

Trails Under Development: TBD

Recommended Trails: Thorne Pond Interpretive Trail network (beginner)

Mountain Bike Lift: 1 (currently the Skimobile Express Superquad)

Trails Accessible from Lift: TBD

Biggest Vertical Drop: 1,200′

Longest Trail: TBD

Other Local Trails: Both Cranmore and Attitash Bear Peak connect to a variety of trail systems within the surrounding forest and to town trail networks such as Whittaker Woods in the village of North Conway.

Trail Map: Regional maps are available in the bike shop at Cranmore and sell for around $5.

Local Services

There's plenty of activities for children and families here, but serious cyclists won't be disappointed either—the resort has rentals, shuttles, and races, too.

Mountain Bike Services: Attitash Bear Peak Cranmore offers a full rental shop, light repair and tuning shop, bike patrol, and a shuttle to nearby trails. All-day rentals run $30/adult, $15/child; half-day rentals cost $20/adult, $7/child; hourly rentals run $7. Bike shuttle available for $5/person.

Special Events: Cranmore runs a weekly local race league called Cyclemeisters, which runs for 10 weeks throughout the summer. Another event hosted by local bike shops is the White Mountain Fat Tire Festival, September 17–20, 1996, which includes group rides. Tech Talk sessions and a series race take place on September 19. Call Red Jersey Cyclery at 603/383-4660.

Emergency Facilities: Full-time patrol

Accommodations: 16,000 beds available in the Mt. Washington Valley; call 800/223-7669

Dining: Available at the summit of Cranmore in the beautiful setting of the Meister Hut. In the surrounding area, over 100 restaurants, pubs, and bars can be found.

Off-the-Bike Activities: Alpine slide, water slides, kids' activities, scenic chairlift rides, horseback rides, swimming, golf, soccer camp and tournament, blueberry festival, equine festival, rodeo, Native American Intertribal Powwow, White Mountain Jazz and Blues Festival, fall festival

Other Services and Features: Reach Attitash Bear Peak online via American Online at bearpeak@aol.com. Visit their home page at http://www.nxi.com/WWW/attitash/homepage.html.

SHARON MCNEILL PHOTO COURTESY SUNDAY RIVER

Gunstock

P.O. Box 1307
Laconia, NH 03247-1307
Street Address: Route 11A
Gilford, NH 03246
(603) 293-4345

A year-round county recreation area, Gunstock houses New Hampshire's third largest ski resort in winter and a campground, a full events calendar, and activities in the summer.

Location, Hours, and Prices

General Location: Lakes region of New Hampshire

Getting There: Approximately 1 hour north on Route 93 from Manchester; 2 hours north on Route 93 from Boston

Biking Season: May–early November

Elevation: Base 900′; summit 2,300′

Hours: TBD

Prices: TBD

Regulations/Restrictions: TBD

The Rides

Gunstock is currently anticipating an expansion of their services to include rentals, repairs, a mountain bike trail map, and patrolled and maintained trails.

Terrain Description: Combination

Mileage/Number of Trails: Currently all trails are open to bikes.

Difficulty: TBD

Trails Under Development: TBD

Recommended Trails: TBD

Mountain Bike Lift: TBD

Trails Accessible from Lift: TBD

Biggest Vertical Drop: 1,400′

Longest Trail: 2.5 miles

Other Local Trails: Yes, throughout the Belknap Mountains

Trail Map: In development

Local Services

Most visitor services can be found in the area surrounding Gunstock. On-site there is a campground, and we should soon see bicycle services too.

Mountain Bike Services: Plans call for rentals, repairs, and patrolled trails.

Special Events: Race tentatively scheduled in September, to be sponsored by the Gunstock Ski Club

Emergency Facilities: Gunstock anticipates having a Safety Services presence in the near future.

Accommodations: Lodging nearby; call 800/531-2347 for the local Chamber of Commerce. There's also a full-service campground on-site.

Dining: Nearby; call the Chamber of Commerce at 800/531-2347

Off-the-Bike Activities: Motorcycle hill climb in June, Crafts Festival in July, Brewfest in July, La Celebration in August, and Country Jamboree in September

Other Services and Features: Within 10 minutes of Lake Winnipesaukee

Mt. Sunapee Ski Area and State Park

P.O. Box 2021
Route 103
Mt. Sunapee, NH 03256
(603) 763-2356

Owned and operated by the New Hampshire State Park system, Mt. Sunapee has chairlift rides, a public beach, special events, hiking, a picnic area, and lift-served mountain biking in the summer months.

Location, Hours, and Prices

General Location: Western central New Hampshire, close to I-89 and I-91

Getting There: From Boston, take I-93 to Concord. Then take I-89 from Concord to Exit 9. Take Route 103 West for 17 miles to the Mt. Sunapee traffic circle. The access road is one option from the circle. The ski area has a huge amount of free parking.

Biking Season: July 1–Columbus Day

Elevation: Base 1,230′; summit 2,740′

Hours: Daily, 10–5

Prices: $8/1 chairlift ride, $15/unlimited rides, $5.50/foot passengers

Regulations/Restrictions: Helmets required. No riding when trails are wet.

The Rides

Mt. Sunapee's lift service provides access to two summit trails. Although these trails are rated "easier," they are not recommended for beginners.

Terrain Description: Combination

Mileage/Number of Trails: 2

Difficulty: Intermediate

Trails Under Development: None

Recommended Trails: Trails are not named.

Mountain Bike Lift: 1

Trails Accessible from Lift: Both

Biggest Vertical Drop: 1,510′

Longest Trail: 3 miles

Other Local Trails: All trails open for downhill biking may also be climbed. Several miles of hilly cross-country terrain are also available.

SUKI COUGHLIN PHOTO COURTESY MT. SUNAPEE

Trail Map: Available free at the mountain, or by calling 603/763-2356

Local Services

Basic food and bike services are available at the ski area. Lodging and more dining choices are located nearby.

Mountain Bike Services: Rentals are available at Bob Skinner Ski and Bike Shop, $20/day or $25/suspension bike.

Special Events: Festival

Emergency Facilities: Mountain staff will respond to reported accidents with EMTs on 4WD vehicles.

Accommodations: Access to 400 nearby hotel, motel, and inn beds; call 800/258-3530

Dining: 2 cafeterias at the mountain; many restaurants within 5–10 miles

Off-the-Bike Activities: Scenic chairlift rides, beach, hiking, craft fair

Other Services and Features: Family ski area. Close to metropolitan areas, but not in a commercialized region.

Waterville Valley Ski Area Ltd./ Base Camp Adventure Center

Town Square, P.O. Box 525
Waterville Valley, NH 03215-0525

(603) 236-4666

Easy to get to from the Boston area, Waterville Valley Ski Area features about 30 miles of trails, lift service, and other cycling services for mountain bikers. The surrounding White Mountain National Forest offers miles of logging roads to explore as well.

Location, Hours, and Prices

General Location: Waterville Valley in the White Mountain National Forest

Getting There: Waterville Valley is 2 hours north of Boston's Logan Airport. Take I-93 North to Exit 28 in New Hampshire. Take Route 49 East for approximately 11 miles to the Valley.

Biking Season: Memorial Day through Columbus Day

Elevation: Base 1,500'; top of Snow's Mountain 2,090'; surrounded by 4,000' mountains

Hours: Daily, 9–6; lift operates Friday–Sunday, 9–3.

Prices: $5/1 lift ride; $6/trail pass only; $20/all-day lift and trail pass, $15/half-day lift and trail pass.

Regulations/Restrictions: Helmets mandatory; trail pass required for cross-country riding

The Rides

One paved road leads into the valley where you'll find singletracks, doubletracks, and forest roads climbing up into White Mountain National Forest. Waterville Valley's own trail network features weekend lift service. The area is working on several connector trails to help link the town, the mountain, and the forest.

Terrain Description: Combination

Mileage/Number of Trails: 30 miles

Difficulty: 30% easiest, 30% more difficult, 40% most difficult

PHOTO COURTESY WATERVILLE VALLEY SKI AREA/BASE CAMP ADVENTURE CENTER

Trails Under Development: Constantly expanding and maintaining trail system. Currently looking to improve some connector trails to better integrate the town to the mountain.

Recommended Trails: Snow's Mountain Trail to Livermore Road (off top of mountain for beginners); Roundabout (intermediate ski slope, but smooth); Monument Trail (gnarly singletrack for experts).

Mountain Bike Lift: 1

Trails Accessible from Lift: 3 main trails connect to other trails

Biggest Vertical Drop: 590′

Longest Trail: 3-mile loop (Snow's Mountain and Livermore Road—Forest Service doubletrack closed to vehicles)

Other Local Trails: 30-mile network of mountain bike friendly trails. For information on riding opportunities in White Mountain National Forest, write or call 719 N. Main, Laconia, NH 03246, 603/528-8721.

Trail Map: Free with trail pass; pick up at Base Camp Adventure Center

Local Services

With races, rentals, tours, and lessons, Waterville's Base Camp Adventure Center is a full-service bike facility. Several lodging and dining options make Waterville Valley a great destination for a mountain bike getaway.

Mountain Bike Services: Rentals, guided tours, and maps; group and private lessons available on weekends

Special Events: Scheduled for 1996, Memorial Day Kids Bike Festival with parade, obstacle course, free bike inspection; Waterville Valley Wilderbeast/Pedro's New England Point Series, July 21 (racing); Waterville Valley Off-Road Challenge, September 15.

Emergency Facilities: EMT on call, 4WD rescue vehicle with specially built evacuation trailer

Accommodations: Call Central Reservations at 800/468-2553 (800/GO VALLEY)

Dining: On-site, several options available

Off-the-Bike Activities: Boating, fishing, golfing, hiking, horseback riding, in-line skating, and swimming. Waterville Valley also has an indoor sports center.

Maine

Back Country Excursions

RFD 2, Box 365
Limerick, ME 04048
(207) 625-8189

Billing itself as a touring hostel and lodge, Back Country Excursions of Maine (BCE) offers two-day standard packages that include lodging, most meals, use of lodge facilities, and guided mountain bike tours. BCE sits on 12 acres of heavily forested hills in the middle of a 10,000-acre semi-wilderness preserve—perfect for cycling, hiking, skiing, and canoeing.

Location, Hours, and Prices

General Location: Foothills of the White Mountains just across the New Hampshire border in southern Maine

Getting There: 2½ hours from Boston, 6 hours from New York City, 45 minutes from North Conway, New Hampshire, and 1 hour from Portland, Maine. Directions mailed with reservations.

Biking Season: May to November

Elevation: 600′

Hours: 24 hours a day

Prices: Packages range from $115–$200 per person, depending on size of group and type of accommodation

Regulations/Restrictions: Helmets required; must sign a waiver

The Rides

BCE's varied terrain includes lots of hills and foothills, with both technical and wide trails for beginners to experts. (*Dirt Rag* magazine describes the more technical terrain as "not for the faint of living.") Be prepared for shallow water crossings, too. BCE also houses The Palace, a technical terrain garden.

Terrain Description: Combination

Mileage/Number of Trails: 70 miles

Difficulty: 15% easiest, 60% more difficult, 15% most difficult

Trails Under Development: Rock-n-Log Palace Technical Terrain Garden always being expanded

Recommended Trails: Cedar and Wiggen Mountain Cross-Country Loop (5 loops possible for different riding levels)

Mountain Bike Lift: No

Biggest Vertical Drop: Not indicated

Longest Trail: 22 miles

Other Local Trails: None indicated

Trail Map: Free, but most rides are guided.

ROBERT BOSSI PHOTO COURTESY WATERVILLE

Local Services

BCE offers most bicycling services, with an emphasis on guided tours and instruction. Casual lodging and dining are on-site at the self-contained center. BCE's standard package includes meals and snacks, but not dinner.

Mountain Bike Services: Rentals, instructional clinics, teen adventure camps

Special Events: Scheduled for 1996 are the Season Kick-off Tour, May 17–19; Memorial Weekend Group Tour, May 24–17; Diamondback/Dirt Rag Tour featuring pro rider Gunner Shogren and trials rider Annie Brown, June 14–16; Pre-4th of July Group Tour, June 28–July 1; July 4th Weekend Group Tour; Maine Fat Tire Festival, July 12–14; Teen Mt. Bike Adventure Weeks, July 27–August 9 (2 sessions); Labor Day Weekend Group Tour, August 30–September 2; Fall Foliage Tours throughout September and October, starting September 6–9; Columbus Weekend Group Tour with bicycle framebuilder Ted Wojcik and family, October 11–13.

Emergency Facilities: Rescue squads

Accommodations: On-site, private rooms, a yurt, and campsites.

Dining: Breakfast, lunch, and snacks included in package. Guests have access to a kitchen for cooking their own dinners, or they can eat at nearby restaurants.

Off-the-Bike Activities: Combination tours include biking/canoeing or tubing/hiking. Lots of wildlife viewing and swimming holes, too. Facilities include hot tub and sweat lodge.

Other Services and Features: Located in one of Maine's least visited regions, BCE is quiet, rustic, and magical. Owner Cliff Krolick will customize tours and packages to meet individual, group, or family needs and preferences.

Lost Valley Mountain Bike Center

P.O. Box 260
Auburn, ME 04212-0260
(207) 784-1561

A four-season recreation center, Lost Valley opens its trail network to mountain bikers on a daily basis during the summer.

Location, Hours, and Prices

General Location: 40 miles north of Portland, 30 miles south of Augusta

Getting There: From Portland, take the Maine Turnpike north to Exit 12 (Auburn). Take the first right (Route 202 South), then right again on Kitty Hawk Avenue and right again on Hotel Road. Continue 8 miles on Hotel Road, bearing left at the fork and going straight at the light. Then turn left at the blinking yellow light, and you'll see the Lost Valley Sign after a sharp bend in the road. Call for directions from points north.

SHARON MCNEILL PHOTO COURTESY SUNDAY RIVER

Biking Season: Mid-April to mid-November

Elevation: 250′ vertical

Hours: Daily, 9–5

Prices: $5/all-day trail use fee, $60/season pass

Regulations/Restrictions: Helmets are mandatory

The Rides

The Lost Valley trail network combines singletrack and doubletrack with some ski slopes for a total of 10 miles of mostly intermediate terrain.

Terrain Description: Combination

Mileage/Number of Trails: 10 miles

Difficulty: 20% easiest, 60% more difficult, 20% most difficult

Trails Under Development: New singletrack for 1996

Recommended Trails: All

Mountain Bike Lift: No

Biggest Vertical Drop: 250′

Longest Trail: Not indicated

Other Local Trails: No

Trail Map: Free with trail fee

Local Services

You can find most day services at Lost Valley, including mountain bike classes and on-site dining. Other amenities can be found in the surrounding area.

Mountain Bike Services: Classes

Special Events: 1996 Maine Mountain Bike Championship Series Race, September 15; Fall Festival Race in September

Emergency Facilities: First aid building, local hospital

Accommodations: Coast Line Inn, 207/784-1331

Dining: Yes

Off-the-Bike Activities: None indicated

Other Services and Features: None indicated

Sunday River Mountain Bike Park

Box 450
Sunday River Road
Bethel, ME 04217

(207) 824-3000

(207) 824-2111 (fax)

America's fastest growing ski resort, Sunday River sprawls over eight interconnected mountains and hosted over 546,000 skier/rider visits in 1994-95. Truly a full-service resort, Sunday River offers the mountain bike vacationer a choice of lodging and dining on the mountain and in town, and serves up a full array of bicycling services and events.

Location, Hours, and Prices

General Location: Western Maine between Rumford and Auburn

Getting There: A 3½-hour drive from Boston. Take Route 95 North to the Maine Turnpike. Take Exit 11 (Gray). Pick up Route 26 North toward Norway/South Paris. Take Route 26 to Bethel, and then follow the signs for Route 2 and Sunday River.

Biking Season: Late May to mid-October

Elevation: Base 830'; summit 3,150'

Hours: Open weekends from late May to the third week of June. Open daily from third week of June to early September. From September to October, park is open daily with lift service on weekends only. Park is open 9–4, and lifts operate 9–3.

Prices: $22/all-day midweek park pass, $24/all-day weekend park pass; $17/single lift ride and trail access pass; $8/single lift ride for hikers; $150/season pass

Regulations/Restrictions: Mandatory helmets; must have ticket to use trail network

SHARON MCNEILL PHOTO COURTESY SUNDAY RIVER

The Rides

Sunday River added to its reputation as a premier year-round destination when it became the first eastern ski resort to offer lift-served mountain biking. In addition, its park features 60 miles of scenic trails spread across eight interconnected mountain peaks, and the surrounding area has mile after mile of back roads and logging tracks to explore. The park offers an enjoyable mix of challenging and relaxing terrain. Bikers can ride up one of two lifts (South Ridge quad, North Peak triple), or test themselves with grueling uphill climbs and singletrack descents. Along the way, there are panoramic views, sparkling mountain streams, and a hundred different types of wildflowers. Hawks, ravens, grouse, deer, fox, and moose frequent the area.

Terrain Description: Combination

Mileage/Number of Trails: Over 35 trails comprising 60+ miles on the trail map (but over 100 miles available)

Difficulty: 30% easiest, 40% more difficult, 30% most difficult

Trails Under Development: Constant development each summer, usually adding 5-10 miles each summer.

SHARON MCNEILL PHOTO COURTESY SUNDAY RIVER

Recommended Trails: Green Acres to Sensation (beginner); Flat'n 'Em (intermediate); Grab 'Em! (advanced)

Mountain Bike Lifts: 2

Trails Accessible from Lifts: All (35+)

Biggest Vertical Drop: Over 3,000'

Longest Trail: Over 7 miles (Catch 'Em Trail)

Other Local Trails: Well over 100 miles available between Sunday River trail network and the logging roads on resort property

Trail Map: Available free at the South Ridge Base Lodge

Local Services

You can find everything you need for a mountain bike vacation at Sunday River, from rentals to a dual slalom course. For a weekend getaway, check out their special two-day package, which includes rentals, lessons, guided tours, trail and lift pass, and even lunch.

Mountain Bike Services: Rentals with helmets, clinics, kid's camp, bike patrol, terrain garden, dual slalom course. $45/all-day bike rental and park access pass, $50/all-day high-performance bike rental and park access pass, $34/half-day bike rental and park access pass, $39/half-day high-performance bike rental and park access pass (half-day is defined as 9-12 or 12-3); $5/all-day helmet rental; $30/2-hour coaching (each additional rider $10); $20/guided tours (3 hours in the afternoon). Sunday River offers Learn to Mountain Bike programs (prices TBD): the 1-day program includes 2 hours of personalized instruction in the terrain garden, bike and helmet rental, and all-day lift and trail access pass; the

2-day package features 2 hours of instruction on Saturday, a 2-hour tour Saturday afternoon, a 3-hour tour on Sunday morning, 2 days of bike rentals, a 2-day lift and trail access pass, and 2 lunches. Ticket Concourse has on-site repairs, rentals, and sales of bikes and related equipment.

Special Events: River Rage Mountain Bike Festival, August 24–25, 1996, with dual slalom, cross-country, Kamikaze downhill—part of the Maine Point Series; tentative Pro-Flex/L.L. Bean Mountain Bike Festival. Road riders may want to check out the Trek Across Maine, Sunday River to the Sea, June 14–16, 1996, a fund-raising tour for ,the American Lung Association (call 800/458-6472 for details)

Emergency Facilities: Patrol on-site with available paramedic services; Bethel Community Hospital and Stevens Memorial Hospital nearby

Accommodations: 5,000 beds at resort, call 800/543-2SKI; 5,000 beds in town, call 207/824-BARS; 2 local campgrounds

Dining: 5 restaurants on the mountain; many in town

Off-the-Bike Activities: Hiking (Appalachian Trail is nearby at Grafton Notch), swimming, shopping, moose watching, golf, tennis, canoeing

Other Services and Features: Half the town is on the National Historic Register.

Troll Valley Cross-Country Ski and Fitness Center

RR4, Box 5215
Farmington, ME 04938
(207) 778-3656

Originally established as a cross-country ski center in 1985, Troll Valley added a fitness center in 1989, and then a mountain bike program in 1993.

Location, Hours, and Prices

General Location: Western mountains of Maine

Getting There: From the Portland Jetport, go north on the Maine Turnpike to Route 4 at Exit 12, and then on to Route 2 in Wilton. Then go 5 miles on Routes 2 and 4 to Red Schoolhouse Road. Take a left and continue 1 mile to Troll Valley.

Biking Season: Memorial Day to end of October

Elevation: 400′ to 980′

Hours: Wednesday–Sunday, 9–6

Prices: $3/per rider per day

Regulations/Restrictions: Helmets required; riding alone not recommended

The Rides

Troll Valley offers 10 miles of forest-lined trails in the cross-country ski network. Terrain varies from open fields to ledge cliffs, with rolling hillsides as well as steep ups and downs. From the trails, you get views of the Longfellow Mountains, the Western Maine foothills, and the flatlands of the Sandy River Basin.

From Troll Valley, you can also access 20 miles of rail trail, an easy ride through several of the villages and towns of Franklin County. In the surrounding area, you can find paved and dirt backroads through the Longfellow Mountains foothills for all ability levels.

Terrain Description: Cross-country

Mileage/Number of Trails: 10 miles of trail, 20 miles of rail trail, many more miles of paved and dirt roads

Difficulty: 50% easiest, 30% more difficult, 20% most difficult

Trails Under Development: Continuous development

Recommended Trails: Rail Trail or Easyway Maze (beginner); Goat Path, Well and Middle Hill, Seth's Run (intermediate); Tom's Challenge and Lori's Trail (advanced).

Mountain Bike Lift: No

Biggest Vertical Drop: 580′

Longest Trail: Rail Trail (17 miles one way)

Other Local Trails: Yes, in the Longfellow Mountains

Trail Map: Available free at ticket counter with trail pass, or request by mail

Local Services

At present, bicycle services at Troll Valley are limited to classes and minor repairs, but the area plans to add more services in the near future. A full bike shop with rentals and repairs is nearby. Other services you'll find on-site include camping, a cafeteria, and a fitness center with showers, changing rooms, and hot tubs.

Mountain Bike Services: Rentals available nearby. Classes by appointment ($5/rider), camps in planning stage. Bike patrons monitored via sign-in/sign-out box. Children's riding and indoor play area. Minor bike repairs done in the Bull Pen. Bike sales and major repairs best done at Northern Lights, LTD, 3½ miles from Troll Valley in West Farmington.

Special Events: Tom Sayward Memorial Fat Tire Festival, first Sunday in August, a NORBA cross-country event

Emergency Facilities: Evacuation plan, hospital 1 mile away

Accommodations: Several motels and bed and breakfasts within 5 miles, call Greater Farmington Chamber of Commerce at 207/778-4215. Camping is available on-site.

Dining: Cafeteria on-site, other restaurants within 5 miles

Off-the-Bike Activities: High school mountain bike competition, league events during fall; hiking and jogging facility

Other Services and Features: Fitness center has universal gym, stationary bike, hot tub, sauna, changing rooms, and showers.

CHAPTER 9

CANADA

British Columbia

Silver Star Mountain Resort

Box 2
Silver Star Mountain, BC V1B 3M1
(800) 663-4431 (reservations)
(604) 542-0224
(604) 542-1236

Located in the Okanagan Valley, Silver Star features an 1890s western theme village in a picturesque alpine setting. In addition to lift-served mountain biking, the resort offers hotels, bars, restaurants, and other facilities.

Location, Hours, and Prices

General Location: 20K east of Vernon in the Okanagan Valley in south-central British Columbia

Getting There: From Vancouver take the Coquihalla Connector and Highway 97 to Vernon. From Calgary, travel west on the TransCanada Highway to Sicamous and south to Vernon on Highway 97. By air, flights arrive at the Kelowna airport.

Biking Season: Mid-June to mid-October

Elevation: Base/village 5,200′; 6,200′ summit

Hours: Mid-June to early September, daily, 10–5; then weekends only until mid-October

Prices: $7.50/single chairlift ride, $15/day pass; $5/adult trail fee, $2/child trail fee

Regulations/Restrictions: Stay on designated mountain bike routes

The Rides

Lift service provides access to over 40 kilometers of dedicated mountain bike trails. The trails combine roads, doubletrack, and singletrack over mostly beginning and intermediate terrain. A highlight is the World Cup Bike Route, which was used for the 1994 World Cup finals.

Terrain Description: Combination

Length/Number of Trails: 40K

Difficulty: 30% easiest, 60% more difficult, 10% most difficult

Trails Under Development: None

Recommended Trails: Paradise Trail (beginner); Repeater Road-Gold Mountain (intermediate); World Cup downhill route (advanced)

Mountain Bike Lift: 1

Trails Accessible from Lift: All but 2

Biggest Vertical Drop: 1,000′

Longest Trail: 10K

Other Local Trails: Good downhill route to the town of Vernon, a 5,000′ vertical over 30K

Trail Map: Free at Ski and Sport Shop in the Village Centre

Local Services

A family-oriented resort, Silver Star offers full meal and accommodation services for overnight or multi-night visitors. All on-mountain guests enjoy complimentary mountain bike rentals, pool privileges, and reduced summer rates. Ask about their special lodging packages, such as the Family Mini-Vacation. Kids under 16 stay free.

Mountain Bike Services: Rentals, including helmet and trail pass, run $9.50/hour for adults, $7.25/hour for children; $15.50/2 hours for adults, $11.50/2 hours for children; $27/4 hours for adults, $17.50/4 hours for children. Guided tours range from $49–$135. Two-day technical camps cost $199, including accommodations and meals. Dates for 1996 are June 22-23, June 29-30, July 20–21, August 3–4, August 14–15, and August 31–September 1. CallSkedaddle Tours at 800/663-4431 or 604/764–0990 for information.

Special Events: (1996) Canada Cup Mountain Bike competition with cross-country and downhill racing, August 17–18.

Emergency Facilities: Bike patrol and first aid on duty daily

Accommodations: 6 hotels with many room types; call 800/663-4431

Dining: 2 restaurants and a deli open daily throughout summer

Off-the-Bike Activities: Scenic chairlift rides, hiking, horseback riding, in-line skating, indoor pool, and hot tubs

Other Services and Features: Silver Star hosted the World Cup finals in 1994.

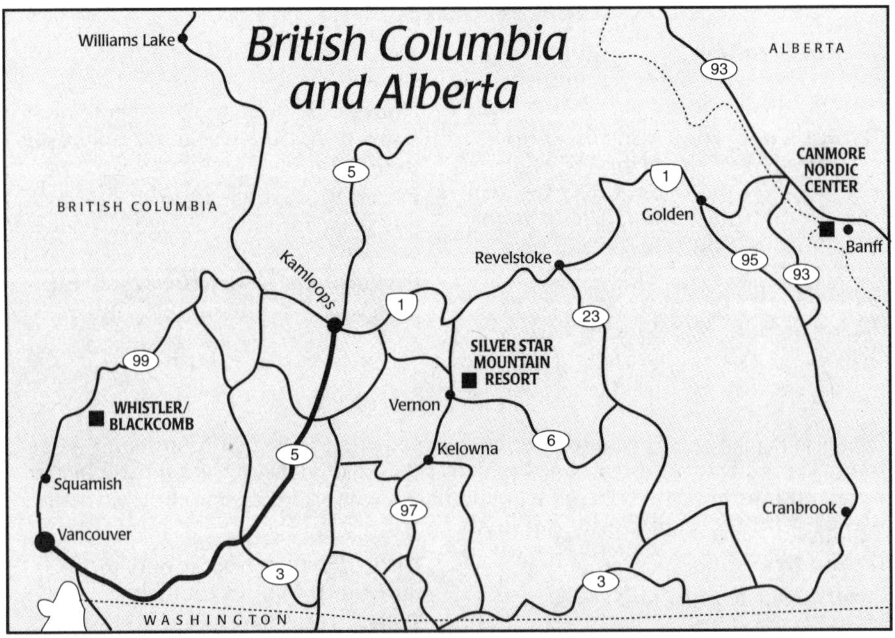

Whistler Resort

P.O. Box 67
Whistler, BC V0N 1B0
(604) 932-3434

Blackcomb Ski Resort

4245 Blackcomb Way
Whistler, BC V0N 1B4
(604) 932-3141

These two side-by-side resorts are among Canada's best-known skiing/mountain biking venues. The site of several top national and international competitions—the Cactus Cup, the Canadian National Mountain Bike Championships, and the Cheakamus Challenge)—the area has been profiled extensively by Mountain Biking magazine, which holds an annual bike industry symposium there.

Biking on the two mountains is limited to guided descents. From mid-June to early September, you can take a 2-hour guided descent of Blackcomb through Whistler Outdoor Experience (604/932-3389). Expect to pay about $40, which includes a lift ticket. At Whistler, you can ride up or down the mountain (with a 4,000′ vertical drop possible), but you will need a guide. Whistler Backroads Mountain Bike Adventures (604/932-3111) offers a $40 Mountain Bike Descent package, which includes a lift ticket and guide.

The company also offers several multi-day heli-biking trips to more remote areas, something you may not find elsewhere. Area shops and outfitters also rent bikes and guide tours.

Off the mountains, Whistler has plenty of bike paths and trails in the valley. Novice riders should stick to the paths, while skilled technical riders can enjoy the challenges of trails like Cut Yer Bars, Shit Happens, and A River Runs Through It.

Whistler Village, shared by Whistler and Blackcomb, has a variety of accommodations, restaurants, and shops. Off-the-bike activities include hiking, mountaineering, backcountry tours, children's programs, fishing, golfing, horseback riding, in-line skating, rafting, paragliding, paintball, racquet sports, and summer skiing on Blackcomb.

TOM STILLO PHOTO COURTESY CRESTED BUTTE MOUNTAIN RESORT

Alberta

Canmore Nordic Centre

Box 1979
Canmore, AB T0L 0M0
(403) 678-2400
(403) 678-5696 (fax)

A four-season multi-recreational facility, Canmore Nordic Centre has a full-service cafe and sport shop that offers lessons and rentals. Surrounded by the panoramic Kananaskis Country and Alberta's Rocky Mountains, 70 kilometers of trails wind through alpine forest terrain.

Location, Hours, and Prices

General Location: 2 miles south of the town of Canmore on Spray Lakes Road in Kananaskis Country

Getting There: Canmore is a 1½-hour drive due west of Calgary International Airport, and just east of the Banff National Park gate.

Biking Season: May–October

Elevation: 1,425 meters (4,675')

Hours: Day lodge open daily, 9–5

Prices: No charge for summer use

Regulations/Restrictions: Helmets and bells recommended

The Rides

Canmore opens about 45 miles (70K) of cross-country skiing trails for biking, hiking, and orienteering, and provides easy access to nearby Banff National Park.

Terrain Description: Combination

Length/Number of Trails: 70K

Difficulty: 20% easiest, 40% more difficult, 40% most difficult

Trails Under Development: None

Recommended Trails: Banff Trail (beginner); 5K, 2.5K (intermediate); 10K, 15K (advanced)

Mountain Bike Lift: No

Biggest Vertical Drop: Not indicated

Longest Trail: 15K loop

Other Local Trails: Trail access to the town of Banff via Banff golf course

Trail Map: Available free at day lodge

Local Services

Best known for its world-class cross-country skiing and biathlon trial systems, the centre has plenty of day-use services for mountain bikers, including rentals and races. Accommodations and more dining options can be found in the town of Canmore.

Mountain Bike Services: Trails Sports Inc. has bike and in-line skate rentals, site tours by bike, and group bike excursions. The day lodge has a lounge, washrooms, showers, and information. Bill Warren Training Centre has a weight room and sauna.

Special Events: 1996 events include a 24-Hour Adrenaline Mountain Bike Race, July 20–21; Alberta Mountain Bike Championships Rocky Mountain Rage, August 3–4; and the Canada Cup Mountain Bike Race Hobies Howler, August 10–11.

Emergency Facilities: First aid room located in day lodge; emergency phone numbers on pay phone at day lodge for after-hours emergencies

Accommodations: In the town of Canmore; see the Alberta Accommodation Guide

Dining: Nordic Centre Cafe provides cafeteria service (limited days and hours) and catering for special functions. Numerous restaurants are 10-minutes away in Canmore.

Off-the-Bike Activities: On-site hiking, disc golf, orienteering, sightseeing, bird watching; nearby you'll find canoeing, kayaking, mountain climbing, golfing, camping, July 1st parade and festivities, Heritage Day Folk Festival, and Scottish Highland Games

Other Services and Features: The centre was the host site for the 1988 Winter Olympics Nordic events. International and national cross-country, biathlon, and Nordic combined events are hosted every year.

Ontario

Searchmont Resort

P.O. Box 1029
Sault Ste. Marie, Ontario P6A 5N5
(800) 663-ALGOMA
(705) 781-2340
(705) 781-2483 (fax)
Searchmont@age.net (e-mail)

A Midwest skiing destination located just over the border of northern Michigan, Searchmont offers mountain biking and other outdoor activities in a beautiful wilderness area known as the "Mountains of the Midwest."

Location, Hours, and Prices

General Location: 25 miles northeast of Sault Ste. Marie, Ontario, and 90 minutes north of the Mackinaw Bridge. Please see the Wisconsin/Michigan map in Chapter 6.

Getting There: From Michigan, take I-75 to Sault Ste. Marie. Then take 17 North to 556 to 532.

Biking Season: May–October

Elevation: Base 800′; summit 1,500′

Hours: Open daily

Prices: Daily trail fee is $7.50/Canadian, $6/U.S.

Regulations/Restrictions: Helmets strongly recommended for adults and mandatory for children

The Rides

Searchmont's trails total some 150 miles. All routes—from backwoods roads and trails to challenging singletrack—feature lakes, wetlands, waterfalls, and scenic views. You share these trails with hikers, horseback riders, and OHV users.

Terrain Description: Combination

Length/Number of Trails: 150 miles

Difficulty: 22% easiest, 50% more difficult, 28% most difficult

Trails Under Development: None

Recommended Trails: Mountainview Trails, Goulais Flats, Goulais River System (beg.); Criterium Trail, Goulais River System, Perry Brook Loop (int.); Achigan Cannonball (adv.)

Mountain Bike Lift: No

Biggest Vertical Drop: Not indicated

Longest Trail: 42K

Other Local Trails: No

Trail Map: Issued with daily trail pass; interpretive trail guide costs $3

Local Services

You can find just about anything you're looking for at Searchmont. Those on a budget should look into the resort's very affordable, inclusive biking packages.

Mountain Bike Services: Rentals cost $25/day, $15/half day.

Special Events: (1996) Goulais River Freedom Float Weekend, May 24–17 and Red Maple, September 13–15.

Emergency Facilities: None

Accommodations: Lodging at resort, including trailside villas and chalets. Biking packages start at $55/U.S., and include trailside accommodations, 3 meals, trail pass, tax, and gratuities.

Dining: Meals provided at the main lodge to in-house guests. Numerous restaurants are located 25 miles away in Sault Ste. Marie.

Off-the-Bike Activities: Searchmont Circus has a flying or single trapeze, trampoline, clowning, and acrobatics. Other activities: hiking, canoeing, camping, fishing, and swimming.

Other Services and Features: Agawa Canyon Train Tour—take the local train to beautiful Achigan and ride back to the resort.

PHOTO COURTESY MONT-SAINTE-ANNE

Quebec

Mont-Sainte-Anne

P.O. Box 400
Beaupre, Quebec G0A 4P0
(800) 463-1568 (reservations)
(418) 827-4561
(418) 827-3121 (fax)

Only 30 miles from beautiful Quebec City on 30 unspoiled square miles in the Laurentian Forest, Mont-Sainte-Anne offers a unique North American French atmosphere with a wide choice of outdoor activities. In summer, the resort features 200 kilometers of mountain biking trails, including three lift-served downhill runs. In winter, Mont-Sainte-Anne is renowned for its top notch facilities for alpine skiing and snowboarding with a vertical of 2,050 feet, cross-country skiing on 215 kilometers of trails, ice skating, dogsledding, snowshoeing, paragliding, and, nearby, snowmobiling.

Location, Hours, and Prices

General Location: 25 miles east of Quebec City, Mont-Sainte-Anne is one of the major attractions of the Cote-de-Beaupre region. From the highlands facing the St. Lawrence River, the resort offers breathtaking views from its trail network or from the summit of the mountain.

Getting There: From Quebec City, take Route 138 East via Montmorency Highway to Beaupre, then Route 360 to Mont-Sainte-Anne. From Montreal via Highways 20 or 40, take the Henri IV Highway to the Sainte-Anne de Beaupre exit (Highway 40 East), then Route 138 East to Beaupre and Route 360 to Mont-Sainte-Anne.

Biking Season: The mountain is usually open for biking from the end of May to mid-October. For 1996, the mountain is open daily for individuals from June 1 to September 2, and on weekends from September 2 to October 14. For groups it is open from May 25 to October 14.

Elevation: Base 175 meters (575'); summit 800 meters (2,625'); vertical 626 meters (2,050')

Hours: Weekdays, 9–5; weekends, 8:30–5; gondola hours, 11–5

Prices: Daily rate for trail access is $5/person (free for 6 years and under and 70 years and older); full-day gondola ticket (includes trail access) is $18/person. Access to trails is free with full-day gondola ticket or with a bike rental from Sports Experts (on-site).

Regulations/Restrictions: Helmets are highly recommended for all trails and mandatory for downhill trails. Mont-Sainte-Anne publishes a list of 15 additional regulations and safety measures.

The Rides

Mont-Sainte-Anne's trails are mostly technical singletrack, making it a popular venue with racers and advanced riders. The area's new downhill race course is considered one of the most technical on the World Cup circuit. Less-skilled riders can find gentle, scenic terrain near the Jean-Larose River, while the aerobically challenged can take a gondola to the top of the mountain.

PHOTO COURTESY MONT-SAINTE-ANNE

Terrain Description: Combination

Length/Number of Trails: 33 trails totaling 200K

Difficulty: 10% easiest, 36% more difficult, 52% most difficult, 2% extreme

Trails Under Development: None

Recommended Trails: Le Circuit Jean-Larose, by the Jean-Larose River, is a gentle trail with beautiful scenery (beginner); Endoro Sud (intermediate); Amazone Haute and Basse (advanced)

Mountain Bike Lift: 1 (8-passenger gondola fitted with hooks for bikes)

Trails Accessible from Lift: 5

Biggest Vertical Drop: 625 meters (2,050')

Longest Trail: Longest downhill is L'Echappee, 18K; the longest cross-country routes are Circuit Jean-Larose, 7.5K, and the Circuit Jean-Larose/ Chemin du Ruisseau Rouge/Boucle Saint-Nicolas loop, 19.3K.

Other Local Trails: No

Trail Map: Available free at the ticket booth, the information counter, or the rental shops

Local Services

World-class Mont-Sainte-Anne has hosted the Grundig Mountain Bike World Cup since 1991. The area has been selected as the site of the 1998 Mountain Bike World Championships. Besides bike races and rentals, on-site activities include two 18-hole golf courses at the base of the mountain, panoramic rides in an eight-passenger gondola, hiking, in-line skating, and paragliding. A 166-site campground welcomes tents and all types of vehicles. Accommodations (nearby or in downtown Quebec City) can be booked through a single toll-free number.

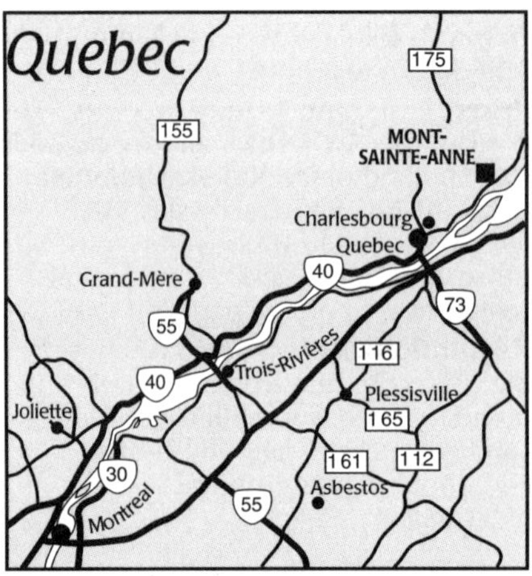

Mountain Bike Services: On-site equipment rental of regular or front-suspended bikes (including helmet and trail access): 1 hour costs $12/ regular, $20/suspension; 2 hours is $20/regular, $32/suspension; 3 hours is $22/regular, $35/suspension; 4 hours is $24/regular, $40/suspension; 5–8 hours is $33/regular, $50/suspension. There's a daily bike patrol and on-site showers and bike showers. Guided tours are available on request for groups.

Special Events: Grundig Mountain Bike World Cup, June 14–16, 1996; Mountain Bike World Championships, September 1998

PHOTO COURTESY MONT-SAINTE-ANNE

Emergency Facilities: A patrol station is located at the base of the mountain. A medical clinic and hospital are within 5 minutes of the resort.

Accommodations: 166-site campground for tents and all types of vehicles with direct access to mountain bike trails. Central reservation bureau offers a wide choice of lodging facilities (hotels, motels, condos, chalets, inns, B&Bs) at the base of the mountain, nearby, or in downtown Quebec City. Call toll-free from the U.S. or Canada, 800/463-1568; local number 418/827-5281.

Dining: There are snack bars at the base and at the summit of the mountain. Nearby, there's a wide choice of restaurants, from fast food to fine dining. In Quebec City, only 30 minutes away, you can find an infinite variety of restaurants.

Off-the-Bike Activities: Hiking, in-line skating, paragliding, golfing (two 18-hole courses); rental service for hiking and in-line skating; instruction and tandem flights for paragliding; rentals and instruction for golfing; day camps for kids

Other Services and Features: Nearby and in Quebec City, you can find a bundle of activities, museums, and attractions all summer long. Among the special events are an International Jazz & Blues Festival, Quebec Horse Show, International Children's Folklore Festival, Quebec International Summer Festival, Cirque du Soleil, Loto-Quebec Fireworks Festival, Plein Art outdoor arts and crafts exhibition and sale, Expo-Quebec, and the Mont-Sainte-Anne Autumn Festival.

Appendix

IMBA Rules of the Trail©

The International Mountain Bicycling Association's Rules of the Trail have been recognized by the U.S. Forest Service, Bureau of Land Management, the Sierra Club, and the International Cycling Union—the world governing body of bicycle racing. These rules apply wherever you ride, including ski areas.

1. **Ride on open trails only**. Respect trail and road closures (ask if not sure), avoid possible trespass on private land, obtain permits and authorization as may be required. Federal and State wilderness areas are closed to cycling. Additional trails may be closed because of sensitive environmental concerns or conflicts with other users. Your riding example will determine what is closed to all cyclists!

2. **Leave no trace**. Be sensitive to the dirt beneath you. Even on open trails, you should not ride under conditions where you will leave evidence of your passing, such as on certain soils shortly after a rain. Observe the different types of soils and trail construction; practice low-impact cycling. This also means staying on the trail and not creating any new ones. Be sure to pack out at least as much as you pack in.

3. **Control your bicycle!** Inattention for even a second can cause disaster. Excessive speed maims and threatens people; there is no excuse for it!

4. **Always yield trail.** Make known your approach well in advance. A friendly greeting (or bell) is considerate and works well; startling someone may cause loss of trail access. Show your respect when passing others by slowing or even stopping. Anticipate that other trail users may be around corners or in blind spots.

5. **Never spook animals.** All animals are startled by an unannounced approach, a sudden movement, or a loud noise. This can be dangerous for you, others, and the animals. Give animals extra room and time to adjust to you. In passing, use special care and follow the directions of horseback riders (ask if uncertain). Running cattle and disturbing wild animals is a serious offense. Leave gates as you found them or as marked.

6. **Plan ahead.** Know your equipment, your ability, and the area in which you are riding, and prepare accordingly. Be self-sufficient at all times, keep your machine in good repair, and carry necessary supplies for changes in weather or other conditions. A well-executed trip is a satisfaction to you and not a burden or offense to others. Keep trails open by setting an example of responsible cycling for all mountain bicyclists.

 "Dedicated to the appreciation of and access to recreational lands, non-profit IMBA welcomes your support. IMBA is a non-profit advocacy organization that promotes mountain biking that is environmentally sound and socially responsible. IMBA educates mountain bikers, helps government officials promote the sport through innovative management techniques, sets a positive image for off-road cycling, promotes volunteer trail work, and keeps trails open and in good condition for everyone. To join IMBA or receive additional information, call 303/545-9011 or write IMBA, P.O. Box 7578, Boulder, CO 80306.

Resorts Offering Lift-Served Mountain Biking

As of spring, 1996, the following resorts planned lift service for their mountain biking guests.

Angel Fire Resort (NM)

Attitash Bear Peak Cranmore (NH)

Beaver Creek (CO)

The Big Mountain Ski and Summer Resort (MT)

Breckenridge Ski Resort (CO)

Brian Head Resort (UT)

Brundage Mountain (ID)

Copper Mountain Resort (CO)

Crystal Mountain (WA)

Deer Valley Resort (UT)

Donner Ski Ranch (CA)

Grand Targhee Ski and Summer Resort (WY)

Keystone Resort (CO)

Killington Resort (VT)

Lutsen Mountain (MN)

Mammoth Mountain (CA)

Maverick Mountain (MT)

Mount Sunapee (NH)

Mt. Hood Ski Bowl Winter and Summer Resort (OR)

Mt. Shasta (CA)

Mt. Snow Resort (VT)

Mt. Waterman Ski Area (CA)

Northstar-At-Tahoe (CA)

Purgatory Resort (CO)

Sandia Peak Ski Company (NM)

Schweitzer Mountain Resort (ID)

Shanty Creek (MI)

Silver Star (BC)

Silver Mountain (ID)

Ski Acres Mountain Bike and Hiking Center (WA)

Ski Plattekill (NY)

Ski Rio (NM)

Snow Summit (CA)

Snowbird Ski and Summer Resort (UT)

Snowmass (CO)

Solitude Ski Resort (UT)

Squaw Valley, USA (CA)

Steamboat Ski and Resort Corporation (CO)

Stratton Mountain Resort (VT)

Sunday River Mountain Bike Park (ME)

Sunrise Park Resort (AZ)

Vail (CO)

Waterville Valley Ski Area (NH)

Whitetail Ski Resort and Mountain Bike Center (PA)

Winter Park Resort (CO)

Wisp Four Season Resort (MD)

Unconfirmed Programs

The following resorts are known or reported to have mountain biking programs, but did not respond to our questionnaire. The symbol ❖ indicates possible lift-served biking.

CALIFORNIA

❖ Mt. Baldy, P.O. Box 459, Mt. Baldy, CA 91759, 909/981-3344. A Southern California resort just one hour's drive from Los Angeles, Mt. Baldy has offered weekend lift-serviced mountain biking in the past. Other facilities include a snack bar and restrooms. The ski area hosted the Mt. Baldy Cup Mountain Bike Race Series in 1994 and 1995. For information on the race series, contact race promoter Blue Sky Events, 1718 Bonita Avenue, LaVerne, CA 91750, 909/593-3277.

Sierra Valley Lodge, P.O. Box 115, Calpine, CA 96124, 800/858-0322. Located 60 miles northwest of Reno, Nevada, this historic lodge provides access to over 130 miles of service roads and trails. Facilities and other activities include a restaurant, live music, horseback riding, hiking, fishing, golf, shopping, and a nearby railway museum.

❖ Snow Valley, P.O. Box 2337, Running Springs, CA 92382, 909/867-2751. Phone coversations with resort personnel indicated that the area would offer mountain biking services in the summer of 1996; it has offered lift service and rentals in the past. Snow Valley has also served as a race venue for several years, most notably as a stop on the Bud Light California Mountain Bike Challenge series. Contact race promoter MESP at 818/707-8867.

IDAHO

❖ Bogus Basin Ski Resort, 2405 Bogus Basin Road, Boise, ID 83702, 208/332-5100, 208/332-5102. The resort operates two chairlifts on select weekends for mountain biking, with access to beginner, intermediate, and advanced terrain. Lifts run from 10-4, and tickets cost $12. Food, lodging, and rentals available on-site.

Lookout Pass Ski Area, Box 108, Wallace, ID 83873, 208/744-1392. Lookout Pass Recreation Area offers tours and rentals. The area has also hosted a Washington-Idaho-Montana point series race for the past five years. Call 208/556-7211.

Soldier Mountain Ski Area, P.O. Box 465, Fairfield, ID 83327, 208/764-2526. Mountain bikers are free to ride the trails at Soldier Mountain since it is located on Forest Service land, but the resort does not operate any facilities for cyclists in the summer months. If you're interested in riding in the area, contact the Fairfield District of Sawtooth National Forest at 208-764-2202.

ILLINOIS

❖ Chestnut Mountain, Galena, IL, 800/397-1320. Chestnut offers no-charge lift service and rentals with rates of $10/hour, $18/day. In addition to other events, Chestnut has hosted a Specialized Cactus Cup race. Lodging, dining, and other activities can be found on-site.

MAINE

Big Rock, Mars Hill, ME, 207/425-6711. *Bicycling* magazine reports that Big Rock has lift-served mountain biking and rentals.

Black Mountain of Maine, Rumford, ME, 207/364-8977. *Bicycling* magazine reports that Black Mountain charges $3/day to use its trail system. The resort hosts races, but apparently has no other bike-related services.

Carter's Farm Market and Cross-Country Ski Center, Route 26, RR1, Box 710, Oxford, ME 04270, 207/539-4848. Dirt roads and cross-country ski trails are open to guests of this lodge. Dining is available on-site.

Saddleback Ski Area, Box 490, Rangeley, ME 04970, 207/864-5671. Miles of logging roads, ski trails, and snowmobile routes are open to cyclists, but the upper mountain is not. You can find lodging, dining, and a bike shop in the town of Rangeley.

Sugarloaf/USA, Carrabassett Valley, Kingfield, ME 04947, 207/237-2000. IMBA reports that Sugarloaf has lodging, dining, and a bike shop on-site. The area has its own mountain biking trails, tours, maps, rentals and races, and accesses hundreds of miles of additional roads and trails.

MASSACHUSETTS

❖ Jiminy Peak, Hancock, MA, 413/738-5500. Jiminy Peak charges $4/ride for lift-served downhill riding on its 8 miles of trail.

MICHIGAN

❖ Boyne Resort, P.O. Box 19, Boyne Falls, MI, 49713, 800/GO BOYNE, 616/549-6000. Boyne has 18 miles of lift-served downhill trails and cross-country ski trails. Lodging, dining, bike rentals, golf, and tennis can be found on-site.

Cannonsburg, Cannonsburg, MI, 616/874-6711. There is no fee to use the resort's 200 miles of trails. In the past, the resort has hosted bike races.

Crystal Mountain, 12500 Crystal Mountain Drive, Thompsonville, MI 49683, 616/378-2000, 800/968-7686. Crystal Mountain has 11 miles of marked and mapped trails (including a mountain bike only trail), rentals, and tours. There's a $3 trail fee. Lodging, dining, and other outdoor activities area available on-site.

Indianhead Mountain, 500 Indianhead Road, Wakefield, MI 49968, 906/229-5181. Indianhead has bike rentals and 200 miles of trails.

Sugarloaf USA, 4500 Sugarloaf Mountain Road, Cedar, MI 49621-9755, 800/968-0576, 616/228-5461. Sugarloaf has trails for mountain biking (including a loop around Sugarloaf Mountain), rentals, and races/events. Dining and lodging on-site; Sleeping Bear Dunes National Lakeshore is nearby.

MINNESOTA

Hidden Valley/Trezona Mountain, 141 E. Chapman, Ely, MN, 55731, 218/365-4512. These two areas offer 16.5 miles of cross-country trails to bicyclists at no charge. Rentals available.

Welch Village, P.O. Box 146, Welch, MN, 55089, 800/421-0699, 612/222-7079. Welch Village has rentals and 5 miles of trails open to cycling, but it is primarily a race site.

MONTANA

❖ Big Sky Ski and Summer Resort, 1 Lone Mountain Trail, P.O. Box 160001, Big Sky, MT 59716, 800/548-4486, 406/995-4211. Big Sky has 68 miles of combina tion terrain with lift service and rentals available. Latest known rates were $18/half day, $25/day for lift/trail access. There is lodging on-site and great fly fishing and whitewater rafting nearby.

Marshall, Missoula, MT, 406/258-6000. Marshall does not charge mountain bikers to use its 10 miles of trails. No lift service, no rentals, or other services are available.

❖ Montana Snowbowl, P.O. Box 8226, Missoula, MT 59807, 406/549-9777, 406/329-7562 (fax). Snowbowl has a mountain bike park with lift service ($7.50/day), NORBA races, and special events. Call for brochure and trail map.

NEW HAMPSHIRE

❖ Bretton Woods Summer Park, P.O. Box 351, Twin Mountain, NH 03595, 603/278-5000. Bretton Woods offers lift-served cycling, 29 trails and loops, a Base Area Garden with obstacles for technical training, an Advanced Terrain Garden, rentals, and races.

❖ Loon Mountain Park, Route #112, RR1, Box 41, Lincoln, NH 03251, 603/745-8111 (ext. 5566). Loon Mountain has 25 miles of mountain bike trails (most of which are closed to horses), gondola service, a self-guided tour from Loon Mountain through Franconia Notch State Park, maps, a bike shop, and lodging and dining on-site.

NEW MEXICO

❖ Red River, P.O. Box 900, Red River, NM 87558, 505/754-2223. Red River offers lift-served riding for $12/day (May-October). There are plentiful riding opportunities in the surrounding Carson National Forest; for a map and more information, contact the Red River Chamber of Commerce, Box 870, Red River, NM 87558, 800/348-6444, 505/754-2366.

The Lodge at Snow Canyon, One Corona Place, P.O. Box 497, Cloudcroft, NM 88317, 800/395-6343, 505/682-2333. Snow Canyon has rentals and combination riding terrain, and hosts the Lizard Rally.

NEW YORK

❖ Scotch Valley Ski Area, P.O. Box 339, Stamford, NY 12167, 607/652-3132, 607/652-7337 (fax). Scotch Valley has 35 kilometers of mountain biking terrain, a downhill course, dual slalom course, kids' BMX park, weekend lift service ($12/day), rentals, and organized races/events.

NORTH CAROLINA

Cataloochee Ski Area, Route 1, Box 502, Maggie Valley, NC 28751, 704/926-0285, 800/768-0285, 800/768-3588 (24-hour race information). Just 35 miles west of Asheville, Cataloochee has sponsored a race series for five years, including events in the Western North Carolina Points Series and the Jamis Eliminator Mid-Atlantic Dual Slalom Championships. For more information on the Maggie Valley, call Visitor Information at 800/334-9036.

Fairfield/Sapphire Valley Resort, 4000 Highway 64, West Sapphire, NC 28774, 704/743-3441. This family-oriented resort in the Appalachian mountains offers mountain biking and a host of other outdoor activities.

NORTH DAKOTA

Bottineau Winter Park, Bottineau, ND, 701/263-4556. Bottineau has 25 miles of trails open to mountain bikers at no charge from May to September.

Frostfire Mountain, Walhalla, ND, 701/549-3600. Frostfire has 4 miles of trails open to riders.

PENNSYLVANIA

Crystal Mountain, Hughesville, PA, 717/584-2698. Crystal Mountain allows access to its 30 miles of trails for $5/day. It also has rentals.

Sawmill Mountain, P.O. Box 5, Morris, PA 16938, 800/532-7669. Sawmill is surrounded by 500 miles of trails. It offers rentals and tours and hosts organized events. A country inn and restaurant are located at the resort.

Tussey Mountain, Boalsburg, PA, 814/466-6266. There is no charge to use Tussey's 200 miles of trails. The area also offers rentals.

UTAH

❖ Sundance Ski Area, RR#3, Box A-1, Sundance, UT 84604, 801/225-4107. IMBA reports that Sundance has mountain bike terrain with lift service.

VERMONT

Ascutney Mountain, P.O. Box 699, Brownsville, VT 05037, 802/484-7711. Ascutney has rentals 15 miles of biking trails.

❖ Jay Peak Resort, Route 242, Jay, VT 05859-9621, 802/988-2611, 800/451-4449. Jay Peak has lift-served mountain biking ($5/day), rentals, and competitions.

❖ Pico Ski Resort, 2 Sherburne Pass, Rutland, VT 05701, 802/775-4346. Pico has a trail network divided into sections according to skill level. Lift service costs $5/day, and rentals are available.

Smugglers' Notch Resort, Route 108, Smugglers' Notch, VT 05464, 802/644-8851. Smugglers' Notch has dirt roads and cross-country ski trails for mountain bikers, trail maps, bike rentals, and lodging and dining on-site.

❖ Stowe Mountain, Stowe, VT, 802/253-7311. Stowe has some 75 miles of trails, lift service ($10/day), rentals, and races.

Sugarbush Resort, RR1, Box 350, Warren, VT 05674, 802/583-2381. Sugarbush has backcountry roads and trails open to cyclists (you must pay a fee and check in before riding), and provides a trail map. Lodging and dining are available on-site.

VIRGINIA

Bryce Resort, P.O. Box 3, Basye, VA 22810, 540/856-2121. Located in the Shenandoah Valley, Bryce offers rentals for $15/half day, $35/day. The resort's trails are open to bikes as are nearby National Forest trails. You'll find lodging, dining, and other activities at the resort.

Massanutten Resort, P.O. Box 1227, Harrisonburg, VA 22801, 703/289-9441. Massanutten, located on 5,300 acres in the Shenandoah Valley, has trails for mountain biking, a bike map, rentals, lodging, dining, and other activities on-site. It has hosted races in the past.

WEST VIRGINIA

Alpine Lake, Route 2, Box 99D2, Terra Alta, WV 26764, 800/752-7179, 304/789-2481. Alpine offers trails, rentals, and several organized events.

❖ Timberline Four Seasons Resort, Box 488, Timberline Road, Davis, WV 26260, 800/633-6682, 304/866-4801. Best known for the 24 Hours of Canaan endurance race, Timberline has over 16 miles of trails, weekend chairlift service ($10), free maps, rentals, and accessories. Lodging is available on-site. Call for dates and information on the 24 Hour race. The whole Canaan Valley is well known for its excellent mountain bike terrain.

WISCONSIN

Devil's Head Resort, S6330 Bluff Road, Merrimac, WI 53561, 800/472-6670. Devil's Head has 28 kilometers of mountain bike trails, 22 ski trails, and over 800 acres of woods and prairie. An on-site mountain bike center provides service and sales.

WYOMING

Snow King Resort, P.O. Box SKI, Jackson Hole, WY 83001, 800/522-KING, 307/733-5200. Snow King Resort opens its trails to mountain bikers, but limits lift use to riders on organized mountain bike tours. The resort's trails open onto the Bridger-Teton National Forest, where you can find many more miles of riding. Lodging, dining, and other outdoor activities are also available.

Togwotee Mountain Lodge, Box 91, Moran, WY 83013, 800/827-4433, 307/353-2300. Located near the Continental Divide on the Bridger-Teton National Forest in northwestern Wyoming, this Lodge sits just 16 miles outside the Grand Teton National Park entrance. Although biking possibilities in the National Park are limited, you can access 150 miles of Forest Service roads that lead to vistas of the Absaroka and Teton mountain ranges. Summer season runs from mid-June to early October. Besides lodging and dining on-site, you can find fishing, float trips, hiking, and horseback riding in the area. The nearest bike shop with rentals and maps is in the town of Moose. Contact Mountain Bike Outfitters at 10 Moose Lane, Moose, WY, 307/733-3314.

Upcoming Programs

The following resorts are working toward opening their trails to mountain bikes. Please call individual resorts for current information.

CALIFORNIA

Sierra Summit, P.O. Box 236, Lakeshore, CA 93634, 209/233-2500. Conversations with area personnel revealed that Sierra Summit has plans for mountain biking services beginning in 1996. The nature of those services remains unknown at press time.

Ski Sunrise, P.O. Box 645, Wrightwood, CA 92397, 619/249-6150. Located in the Angeles National Forest in Southern California, Ski Sunrise will not have any mountain biking in 1996, but has long-term plans to develop mountain biking services.

Snowcrest, 2505 Foothill Blvd., Suite B, La Crescenta, CA 91214, 818/248-3539, fax 818/248-3620. (Formerly Kratka Ridge) Snowcrest reports that it may attempt to offer some mountain biking services in the summer of 1996. The ski area is located on the Angeles National Forest in the San Gabriel Mountains, a popular spot for Los Angeles-area mountain bikers.

Sugar Bowl, P.O. Box 5, Norden, CA, 916/426-3651. Legendary for its great snow, Sugar Bowl will not have mountain biking in 1996, but has plans to develop a program. Call for latest update.

MONTANA

Red Lodge Mountain Resort, Box 750, Red Lodge, MT 59068, 406/446-2610. Located 6 miles west of the quaint town of Red Lodge and 60 miles from Billings, Red Lodge Mountain Resort is just 60 miles from Yellowstone National Park via the Beartooth Highway, the "most beautiful highway in America," according to Charles Kuralt. To get there from Billings, take Interstate 90 to Laurel, and then take U.S. 212 to Red Lodge. The resort has just started a 10-year, $20-million expansion. As of spring 1996, it does not have mountain biking, but anticipates that it will in two to three years. Call for the latest information before visiting.

NEVADA

Heavenly Ski Area, P.O. Box 2180, Stateline, NV, 89449-9919, 800/243-2836, 916/541-1330. Heavenly does not currently offer mountain biking in an organized manner. The mountain is open to cyclists if they want to venture out on their own (most of the mountain is on U.S. Forest Service land), but they do not offer lift service or any specially cleared trails. Heavenly is in the process of revising its Master Plan and will reassess mountain biking after the plan is approved.

Mt. Rose Ski Area, 22222 Mt. Rose Highway, Reno, NV 89511, 702/849-0704. Mt. Rose does not currently offer summer mountain biking, but has tentative plans for the future.

WYOMING

Jackson Hole, P.O. Box 290, Teton Village, WY 83001, 307/739-2753. Wyoming's best-known resort does not currently offer mountain biking, although its Master Plan calls for adding bike services when the resort builds out in four to five years. A spokeswoman for the resort cited the area's unsuitably steep, rugged terrain as the primary reason for not having mountain biking. The resort does host the yearly Rendezvous Hill Climb, in which cyclists ride up the mountain and take the tram down. If you're interested in this organized brutality, call Guest Services at the above number.

Discontinued Programs

ALASKA

Hilltop Ski Area, 7015 Abbott Road, Anchorage, AK, 907/346-1446, 907/346-3391. Hilltop found that mountain biking "was not profitable" so discontinued its program and liquidated its mountain bike inventory.

CALIFORNIA

Mountain High, P.O. Box 428, Wrightwood, CA 92397, 619/249-5477. This Southern California resort has offered mountain bike services in the past, including bike rentals, lift-served riding, and special events such as the "Insane" Wayne Croasdale Classic Race (Croasdale is a local resident). However, ski area personnel report that they may not offering any mountain biking in 1996 unless they can find an outside operator.

MAINE

Camden Snow Bowl, Camden, ME, 207/236-3438. While Camden has offered lift service to its bike trails and hosted races in the past, the resort reported that it had no plans for mountain biking in 1996.

PENNSYLVANIA

Camelback Ski Area, P.O. Box 168, Tannersville, PA 18372, 717/629-1661, 717/620-0942 (fax). Discontinued mountain biking in the summer of 1995.

The Care and Feeding of a Mountain Bike

BY R. W. MISKIMINS

ROUTINE CHECKUPS FOR YOUR BICYCLE

The key to years of fun and fitness from your mountain bike is giving it checkups on a regular basis. You need to know how to clean it, lubricate a few places, make simple adjustments, and recognize when something needs expert attention. For the average rider, most bike shops recommend tuneups once a year and complete overhauls every two to three years. All of the maintenance in between your trips to the bike shop you can do yourself. Given below is a nine-step checkup procedure—a list to run through after every extensive ride—before you head back out into the hills again.

1. CLEANUP

Unless the frame is really filthy, use a soft rag and a non-corrosive wax/ polish such as Pledge to wipe off the grime and bring the old shine back. If you need to use water or soap and water prior to the polish, don't high-pressure spray directly at any of the bearing areas (pedals, hubs, bottom bracket or head set). You should clean all your components, too (including the chain and the rear cogs), but use a different rag and a lubricant such as Tri-Flow or Finish Line for wiping them down. Do not use polish or lubricants to clean your rims—an oily film will reduce your braking ability. Instead, wipe off the rims with a clean dry rag. If you need to remove rubber deposits from the sidewalls of the rims use acetone as a solvent.

2. INSPECTION

After you get the grit and grime off, check out the frame very carefully, looking for bulges or cracks. If there are chips or scratches that expose bare metal (especially when the metal is steel), use automotive or bicycle touch-up paint to cover them up. Your inspection should also include the components. Look for broken, bent or otherwise visibly damaged parts. Pay special attention to the wheels. When you spin them, watch the rim where it passes the brake pads. Look for wobbles and hops, and if there is a lot of movement, the wheel needs to be trued at home (or take it to a bike shop) before using it. Look for loose or broken spokes. And finally, carefully check your tires for sidewall damage, heavy tread wear, cuts and bulges, glass and nails, thorns, or whatever.

3. BRAKES

Grab the brakes and make sure they don't feel mushy and that the pads are contacting the rim firmly (be certain the brake pads do not rub against the tires!). If the brakes don't feel firm, there are barrel adjusters at one or both ends of the wire cables that control the brakes—turn them counterclockwise to take up some of the slack. If you are unsure as to the dependability of your brakes, for safety's sake let a bike shop check them.

4. BEARING AREAS

Most cyclists depend upon professional mechanics to fix any problems in the pedals, hubs, bottom bracket or head set, but they should be able to recognize when something is wrong. Spin the wheels, spin the crankarms (and the pedals) and move the handlebars from side to side. If you feel notches or grittiness, or if you hear snapping, grating or clicking noises, you have a problem. Check to make sure each of the four areas is properly tightened. To check for looseness, try to wiggle a crankarm side to side or try to move a wheel side to side. Check your headset adjustment by holding the front brake, rocking the bike forward and backward, and listening for clunking sounds.

5. SHIFTING

Presuming your bike has gears, check to make sure you can use all of them. The most common problem is the stretching of the inner wire that operates the rear derailleur. If your bike is not shifting properly, try turning the barrel adjuster, located where the cable comes out of the derailleur. Turn it just a little; usually a counterclockwise direction is what you need. Unless you know what you are doing, avoid turning the little adjustment screws on the derailleurs.

6. NUTS AND BOLTS

Make sure the nuts and bolts which hold everything together are tight. The handlebars and stem should not move around under pressure, and neither should your saddle. And make certain that the axle nuts or quick-releases that hold your wheels are fully secure—when a wheel falls off, the result is almost always crashtime. If you have quick-release hubs, they operate as follows: Mostly tighten them by holding the nut and winding the lever, but finish the job by swinging the lever over like a clamp (it's spring-loaded). Do not wind them up super tight as you would with a wingnut—for safe operation they must be clamped, and clamped very securely, with considerable spring tension! If you are at all uncertain regarding the use of quick-releases, go by a bike shop and ask for a demonstration.

7. ACCESSORIES

Make sure all your accessories, from water bottles to bags to pumps to lights, are operational and secure. Systematically check them all out and if you carry flat-fixing or other on-the-road repair materials or tools, make sure you've got what you need and you know how to use what you carry. Statistics show that over 90% of all bicycle breakdowns are the result of flat tires, so it is recommended that you carry a pump, a spare tube, a patch kit, and a couple of tire levers with you whenever you ride.

8. LUBRICATION

The key to long-term mechanical happiness for you and your bike is proper and frequent lubrication. The most important area of lubrication is the chain—spray it with a Teflon-based or other synthetic oil (WD-40, household oil, and motor oil are not recommended), then wipe off all the excess. You can use the same lubricant for very sparsely coating the moving parts of your brakes and derailleurs.

9. INFLATION

You now are ready for the last step. Improper inflation can lead to blowouts or pinch flats. Read the side of your tires to see what the recommended pressure is and fill them up. If there is a range of pressures given, use the high figure for street cycling, the low figure or near it for off-road riding.

After going through these nine steps of getting your bike ready you've earned another good long ride!

Basic Skills for Mountain Biking

BY R. W. MISKIMINS

Everybody knows how to ride a bike—at least almost everybody can ride around the neighborhood. But with the advent of the mountain bike, riding a two-wheel pedal-powered machine has gotten more complicated. Watch a pro-level mountain bike race and the need for "technical skills" will become obvious. Can you handle steep hills, big rocks, creeks, muddy bogs, loose sand, big tree roots, deep gravel, or radical washboards? These are the kinds of factors that differentiate mountain biking from road riding and that demand skills and balance above and beyond those required to ride around the neighborhood. The key to acquiring these abilities is practice—start easy and work diligently until you achieve high-level control of your bike.

1. BICYCLE

All mountain bikes are not created equal. Some are better suited to staying on pavement. They have too much weight, too long a wheelbase, ineffective braking systems, sloppy shifting, too smooth tread on the tires, poorly welded frames, and so on. As a general rule, the mountain bicycles marketed by the discount store chains, department stores, and sporting goods stores are only suited to on-road, non-abusive use. Bicycles from bike stores, excepting their least expensive models, are generally suited to heavy duty, skilled off-road use. They should be relatively light (under 30 pounds), and have a fairly short wheelbase and chainstay (for agility), moderately steep head angle (again for agility), strong and dependable braking and shifting systems, well-made frames, and knobby/aggressive tires.

For details on choosing the right bike for you, consult the experts at your local bike shop. They can help you not only with selecting a bicycle, but also with various accessory decisions, in such areas as suspension forks, bar ends, and gear ratio changes. And of extreme importance, whatever bike you decide on, get the right size for you. If a bike is too big for your height and weight, no matter how hard you try, you will never be able to properly handle it. If you are in doubt or in between sizes, for serious off-road riding opt for the smaller bike.

2. FUNDAMENTAL PRINCIPLES

There are some very general rules for off-road riding that apply all the time. The first, "ride in control," is fundamental to everything else. Balance is the key to keeping a bike upright—when you get out of control you will lose your ability to balance the bike (that is, you'll crash). Control is directly related to speed, and excessive speed for the conditions you are facing is the precursor to loss of control. When in doubt, slow down!

The second principle for off-road riding is "read the trail ahead." In order to have time to react to changes in the trail surface and to obstacles, you should be looking ahead 10 to 15 feet. Especially as your speed increases, you want to avoid being surprised by hazardous trail features (rocks, logs, roots, ruts, and so on)—if you see them well ahead, you can pick a line to miss them, slow down to negotiate them, or even stop to walk over or around them.

The third principle is to "stay easy on the grips." One of the most common reactions by novices in tough terrain is to severely tense up, most noticeably in a "death grip" on the handlebars. This level of tightness not only leads to hand, arm and shoulder discomfort but interferes with fluid, supple handling of the bike. Grip loosely and bend at the elbows a bit—don't fight the bicycle, work with it!

The last general principle to be presented here is "plan your shifting." If you are looking ahead on the trail, there should be no shifting surprises. Anticipate hills, especially steep ascents, and shift before your drive-train comes under a strong load. Mountain bikes have a lot of gears and their proper use will make any excursion more enjoyable.

3. CLIMBING

Mountain bikes were originally single-speed, balloon-tire cruisers taken by truck or car to the top of a hill and then used for exciting and rapid descent. After a few years, they were given gears to eliminate the shuttle. Today's off-road bikes have 18 to 24 speeds, with a few extremely low gears so they can climb very steep hills. One of the keys to long or difficult climbs is attitude; it's a mental thing. You need to be able to accept an extended, aerobic challenge with the thoughts "I can do it" and "this is fun."

Your bike is made with hill-climbing in mind. Find a gear and a pace that is tolerable (not anaerobic) and try to maintain it. Pick a line ahead, stay relaxed, and anticipate shifting, as noted earlier. In addition, be alert to problems in weight distribution that occur when climbing. It is best to stay seated, keeping your weight solidly over the traction (rear) wheel if possible. However, if the slope is so steep that the front wheel lifts off of the ground, you will have to lean forward and slide toward the front of the saddle. Constant attention to weight distribution will give you optimum traction and balance for a climb. And make sure your saddle height is positioned so when your foot is at the bottom of a pedal stroke, your knee is very slightly bent—a saddle too low or too high will significantly reduce both power and control on a steep and difficult climb.

4. DESCENDING

This is where most serious accidents occur, primarily because a downhill lends itself to high speed. It is unquestionably the most exciting part of mountain bike riding—expert riders reach speeds up to 60 mph! For descents, the "stay in control" and "read the trail ahead" principles can be injury-saving. Know your ability and don't exceed it. And be certain your brakes are in good working order—don't believe the slogan "brakes are for sissies." On steep and difficult downhills everyone has to use them. Regarding braking, always apply the rear brake before the front (to avoid an "endo"—that is, flying over the handlebars), and if possible, brake in spurts rather than "dragging" them. On easy hills, practice using your brakes to get comfortable with them.

As was the case for steep uphills, steep descents require attention to weight distribution. Many riders lower their saddle an inch or two prior to descending (to get a lower center of gravity). All cyclists quickly learn to lift their weight slightly off the saddle and shift it back a few inches to keep traction and to avoid the feeling of being on the verge of catapulting over the handlebars. Practice this weight transfer on smooth but steep downhills so you can do it comfortably later on obstacle-laden terrain. Finally, it is possible to go too slow on a difficult downhill, so slow you can't "blast" over obstacles. Instead, because of lack of momentum, hazards can bring you to an abrupt stop or twist your front wheel, and both of these results can cause loss of control.

5. TURNING

A particularly treacherous time for mountain bikers is high speed or obstacle-laden turns. The first principle is: don't enter a curve too fast. Turns often contain loose dirt and debris created by all the mountain bikes that preceded you. Slow down before you get there; you can always accelerate during the turn if you choose. Lean around the turn as smoothly as possible, always keeping an eye out for obstacles. It is common for the rear wheel to skid in turns. To take the fright out of that phenomenon, go find a gentle turn with soft dirt and practice skidding to learn how you and your bike will respond.

6. OBSTACLES

If you get into the real spirit of off-road cycling, you will not ride just on smooth, groomed trails. You will encounter rocks, roots, limbs, logs, trenches, ruts, washboards, loose sand (or dirt or gravel), and water in a variety of forms from snow and ice to mud bogs to free-flowing springs and creeks. Obviously, the easiest means for handling an obstacle is to go around it; however, you can't always do that. For raised obstacles, those you need to get up and over, riders need to learn to "pop the front wheel." To practice this, find a low curb or set out a 4x4 piece of lumber. Approach it, and just before the front wheel impacts it, rapidly push down then pull up the front wheel. The wheel lift is enhanced if you simultaneously lower and raise your torso and apply a hard pedal stroke. After your front wheel clears the obstacle, shift your weight up and forward a little so the rear wheel can bounce over it lightly.

If you encounter "washboards," the key to relatively painless negotiating is to maintain a moderate speed and get into a shock absorbing posture—slightly up and off the saddle, knees slightly bent, elbows slightly bent, loose grip on the handlebars, and relaxed. Soft spots in the trail can make your bike difficult to control and create an instant slowdown. If you have to deal with loose, deep sand, dirt or gravel, the key is to go slower but "power through." Shift your weight back a little (for better traction), then keep your bike straight and keep pedaling. Maintaining momentum and a straight line is also important in mud holes; be certain to do any shifting prior to soft spots or muddy bogs (otherwise you will lose momentum). Sharp turns can present a particular problem in these conditions—you will be much more prone to losing the rear wheel to a slide out, so be extra cautious in sandy or muddy curves.

Going through water can be a lot of fun, or it can be a rude awakening if you find yourself upsidedown on a cold February afternoon. Before any attempt to cross a waterway, stop and examine it first. Make sure it isn't so deep that it will abruptly stop you, then find the route that has the fewest obstacles (look for deep holes, big rocks, and deep sand). Approach the crossing at a fairly low speed and plan on pedaling through it (rather than coasting) for maximum traction and control. Be aware of the potential for harmful effects that riding through water can have on your bearings (if they are not sealed) and exposed moving parts. Plan on lubricating your chain, derailleurs, inner wires, and so on, when you return home. Finally, regarding snow and ice, stay away from it as much as possible. Snow riding can be fun but if it's deep, it can be very laborious. Maintaining momentum and avoiding buried obstacles are the two major tasks for snow riders. Also, the difficulty of steep ascents and descents are significantly magnified by a few inches of snow. Most mountain bikers riding on snow prefer flat or nearly flat terrain.

R. W. Miskimins is the owner of Great Basin Bicycles in Reno, Nevada. He is the author of Lake Tahoe's 20 Best Pavement and Dirt Rides, Guide 13—Reno/Carson Valley, and coauthor of several other mountain bike guidebooks by Fine Edge Productions (see page 208).

Resources

In addition to the brochures, maps, and questionnaire responses we received, the following resrouces were consulted in compiling the listings in this book.

Bicycle Utah Vacation Guide, Bicycle Utah, 1996.

"Cycling Peaks," *Bicycling,* May 1995, pp. 62–70.

Cyclists' Yellow Pages, 17th edition, Adventure Cycling Association, 1996.

Mountain Bikers Almanac, Grant Wolf, Inc., 1995.

"Mountain Biking At Ski Resorts," *Mountain Bike Action,* July 1991.

"Peak Experiences," three-part series appearing in *Mountain Biker,* May–July 1996.

"Summer Fun," *Mountain Biking,* June 1993, pp. 34–45 and ff.

"A Summer Surge to the Slopes," *Los Angeles Times,* July 1995.

"Sunshine State Surprise," *BIKE,* February 1996, pp. 84–85.

Trailfinder '96 1,000 Great Places You Can Ride This Year, International Mountain Bike Association and *Mountain Bike,* 1995.

"Up, Up and Away," *Shape,* May 1996, pg. 133.

Resort Index

Alpine Lake ... 196
Alyeska Resort ... 17
Angel Fire Resort ... 108
Ascutney Mountain ... 195
Aspen ... 65
Attitash Bear Peak Cranmore Resort ... 166

Back Country Excursions ... 172
Bark Eater Inn ... 148
Base Camp Adventure Center ... 170
Bear Valley Cross-Country Ski and Adventure Company ... 39
Beaver Creek ... 67
Big Mountain Ski and Summer Resort ... 59
Big Rock ... 193
Big Sky Ski and Summer Resort ... 194
Black Mountain of Maine ... 193
Blackcomb Ski Resort ... 181
Bogus Basin Ski Resort ... 192
Bolton Valley Resort/Mountain Bike and Adventure Center ... 155
Bottineau Winter Park ... 195
Boyne Resort ... 193
Breckenridge Ski Resort ... 69
Bretton Woods Summer Park ... 194
Brian Head Resort ... 95
Brundage Mountain ... 31
Bryce Resort ... 196
Buck Hill Ski Area ... 125

CAMBA Trail System ... 131
Camden Snow Bowl ... 199
Camelback Ski Area ... 199
Canmore Nordic Center ... 182
Cannonsburg ... 193
Carter's Farm Market ... 193
Cataloochee Ski Area ... 195
Catamount Family Center ... 157
Chequamegon Area Mountain Bike Association Trail System ... 131
Chestnut Mountain ... 192
Copper Mountain Resort ... 71
Craftsbury Nordic Ski Center ... 158
Crested Butte Mountain Resort ... 72
Crystal Mountain (Michigan) ... 193
Crystal Mountain (Washington) ... 18
Crystal Mountain (Pennsylvania) ... 195

Deer Valley Resort ... 98
Devil's Head Resort ... 196
Diamond Peak Ski Resort at Incline Village/Crystal Bay ... 57
Donner Ski Ranch ... 40

Elk Meadows Ski and Summer Resort ... 99

Fairfield/Sapphire Valley Resort ... 195
Flagstaff Nordic Center ... 105
Frostfire Mountain ... 195

Galena Lodge ... 33
Garnet Hill Lodge and Cross-Country Ski Center ... 148
Giants Ridge Resort ... 126
Golden Eagle Lodge, Inc. ... 128
Gone Riding! ... 123
Grand Targhee Ski and Summer Resort ... 63
Gunstock ... 168

Hardrock Mountain Bike Park/Gone Riding! ... 123
Heavenly Ski Area ... 197
Hidden Valley (Pennsylvania) ... 141
Hidden Valley/Trezona Mountain ... 193
Hill's Resort ... 35
Hilltop Ski Area ... 199
Holiday Valley Resort ... 150
Homestead ... 100

Indianhead Mountain ... 193
Inn at Starlight Lake ... 143

Jackson Hole ... 198
Jay Peak Resort ... 195
Jiminy Peak ... 193

Keystone Resort ... 74
Killington Resort ... 160

Latigo Ranch ... 77
Levis Mounds/Bruce Mound ... 133
Lodge at Snow Canyon ... 194
Lookout Pass Ski Area ... 192
Loon Mountain Park ... 194
Lost Valley Mountain Bike Center ... 173
Lutsen Mountain Bike Park ... 129

Mammoth Mountain Bike Park ... 41
Marshall ... 194
Massanutten Resort ... 196
Maverick Mountain ... 61
Methow Valley Sport Trails Assoc. ... 24
Monarch Ski Resort ... 77
Mont-Sainte-Anne ... 185
Montana Snowbowl ... 194
Mt. Bachelor Ski and Summer Resort ... 27
Mt. Baldy ... 192
Mt. Hood Ski Bowl Winter and Summer Resort ... 28
Mt. Rose Ski Area ... 197
Mt. Shasta Ski Park ... 46
Mount Snow Resort ... 162

Mt. Spokane State Park ... 21
Mt. Sunapee Ski Area and State Park ... 169
Mt. Waterman Ski Resort ... 47
Mountain High ... 199
Mountain Home Lodge ... 20

North Tahoe Regional Park Trail System ... 51
Northstar-At-Tahoe ... 49

Outdoor Experience at Catamount Family Center ... 157

Park City Ski Area ... 101
Paust's Woods Lake Resort, Inc. ... 134
Pico Ski Resort ... 195
Pines and Mines Mountain Bike Trail System ... 135
Purgatory Resort ... 79

Red Lodge Mountain Resort ... 198
Red River ... 194

Saddleback Ski Area ... 193
San Juan Hut System ... 87
Sandia Peak Ski Company ... 110
Sawmill Mountain ... 195
Schweitzer Mountain Resort ... 36
Scotch Valley Ski Area ... 194
Searchmont Resort ... 183
Shanty Creek ... 136
Sierra Summit ... 197
Sierra Valley Lodge ... 192
Silver Mountain Ski and Summer Resort ... 38
Silver Star Mountain Resort ... 179
SilverCreek Ski Area ... 81
Sipapu Lodge and Ski Area ... 112
Ski Acres Mountain Bike and Hiking Center ... 23
Ski Butler/Bike Butler ... 121
Ski Homewood ... 51
Ski Plattekill Mountain Biking Ctr ... 152
Ski Rio ... 113
Ski Sunrise ... 197
Smugglers' Notch Resort ... 195
Snow King Resort ... 196
Snow Summit Mountain Resort ... 53
Snow Valley ... 192
Snowbird Ski and Summer Resort ... 102
Snowcrest ... 197
Snowmass ... 83
Snowshoe Mountain Resort ... 119
Soldier Mountain Ski Area ... 192
Solitude Ski Resort ... 103
Squaw Valley, USA ... 55
Steamboat ... 84
Stowe Mountain ... 195
Stratton Mountain Resort ... 164
Sugar Bowl ... 197
Sugar Mountain Resort ... 115
Sugarbush Resort ... 196
Sugarloaf USA (Michigan) ... 193
Sugarloaf/USA (Maine) ... 193
Sun Mountain Lodge ... 24
Sun Valley Resort ... 38
Sundance Ski Area ... 195
Sunday River Mountain Bike Park ... 175
Sunrise Park Resort ... 106

Telluride ... 87
10th Mountain Division Hut Assoc. ... 90
Timberline Four Seasons Resort ... 196
Togwotee Mountain Lodge ... 196
Trezona Mountain ... 193
Troll Valley Cross-Country Ski and Fitness Center ... 177
Tussey Mountain ... 195

Vail ... 90
Vasa Trail ... 138
Vista Verde ... 92

Waterville Valley Ski Area Ltd./ Base Camp Adventure Center ... 170
Welch Village ... 194
Whistler Resort ... 181
Whitetail Ski Resort and Mountain Bike Center ... 144
Winter Park Resort ... 93
Wintergreen Resort ... 117
Wisp Four Seasons Resort ... 146
Woodbury Ski and Racquet ... 154

Map Index

Arizona ... 106
British Columbia and Alberta ... 180
California and Western Nevada ... 44
Colorado ... 68
Idaho ... 32
Mid-Atlantic States ... 142
Minnesota ... 127
Montana and Wyoming ... 60
New Mexico ... 110
Northeastern Florida ... 123
Oregon ... 26
Quebec ... 186
The Northeast ... 156
The South ... 116
Utah ... 100
Washington ... 19
Wisconsin, Michigan, and Ontario ... 132

OUTDOOR PUBLICATIONS FROM FINE EDGE PRODUCTIONS

RECREATION TOPO MAPS

(with Mountain Biking, Hiking and Ski Touring Trails. 6-color, double-sided, includes trail profiles & route descriptions)

Eastern High Sierra-Mammoth, June, Mono, 2nd Ed., ISBN 0-938665-21-9	$9.95
Santa Monica Mountains, ISBN 0-938665-23-5	$9.95
San Bernardino Mountains, ISBN 0-938665-32-4	$9.95
San Gabriel Mountains–West, ISBN 0-938665-13-8	$8.95
North Lake Tahoe Basin, 2nd Ed., ISBN 0-938665-34-0	$8.95
South Lake Tahoe Basin, 3rd Ed., ISBN 0-938665-35-9	$8.95

Laminated copies – $5 surcharge.

MOUNTAIN BIKING GUIDEBOOKS

Mountain Biking North America's Best 100 Ski Resorts, ISBN 0-938665-46-4	$16.95
Mountain Biking Northern California's Best 100 Trails by Fragnoli & Stuart, ISBN 0-938665-31-6 (classic routes, 80 detailed maps, 300 pages)	$16.95
Mountain Biking Southern California's Best 100 Trails, Douglass & Fragnoli, eds., ISBN 0-938665-20-0 (classic routes, 80 detailed maps, 300 pages)	$14.95
Lake Tahoe's 20 Best Pavement & Dirt Rides, by Miskimins, ISBN 0-938665-36-7	$6.95
Guide 1, Owens Valley and Inyo County, 2nd Ed. by Douglass, ISBN 0-938665-01-4	$9.95
Guide 2, Mammoth Lakes and Mono County, 3rd Ed. by Douglass, ISBN 0-938665-15-4	$9.95
Guide 3A, Lake Tahoe South, 3rd Ed. by Bonser & Miskimins – 128 pp., ISBN 0-938665-27-8	$10.95
Guide 3B, Lake Tahoe North, 2nd Ed. by Bonser, ISBN 0-938665-07-3	$9.95
Guide 4, Ventura County and the Sespe, 3rd Ed.,by McTigue, ISBN 0-938665-18-9	$9.95
Guide 7, Santa Monica Mountains, 3rd Ed. by Hasenauer & Langton, ISBN 0-938665-38-3	$11.95
Guide 10, San Bernardino Mountains by Shipley, ISBN 0-938665-16-2	$10.95
Guide 11, Orange County and Cleveland N.F. 2nd Ed. by Rasmussen, ISBN 0-938665-37-5	$11.95
Guide 13, Reno/Carson Valley by Miskimins, ISBN 0-938665-22-7	$10.95

NAUTICAL BOOKS

Exploring the South Coast of British Columbia, ISBN 0-938665-44-8 Gulf Islands and Desolation Sound to Port Hardy and Blunden Harbour	$39.95
Exploring the North Coast of British Columbia, ISBN 0-938665-45-6 Allison Harbour to Dixon Entrance, including the Queen Charlotte Islands	$39.95
Cape Horn–One Man's Dream, One Woman's Nightmare, by Hemingway-Douglass, ISBN 0-938665-29-4	$22.50
Exploring the Inside Passage to Alaska–a Cruising Guide, ISBN 0-938665-33-2	$49.95
Exploring Vancouver Island's West Coast–a Cruising Guide, ISBN 0-938665-26-X	$36.95
Exploring California's Channel Islands, an Artist's View, by Gates, ISBN 0-938665-00-6	$6.95

OTHER GUIDEBOOKS & MAPS

What Shall We Do Tomorrow–Mammoth Lakes Sierra, by Douglass & Huggins, ISBN 0-938665-30-8	$10.95
Favorite Pedal Tours of Northern California, by Bloom, ISBN 0-938665-12-X	$12.95
Ski Touring the Eastern High Sierra, by Douglass & Lombardo, ISBN 0-938665-08-1	$8.95
The Adventurer's Guide to the Sierra Nevada Mountains – full-color, 2-sided map, ISBN 0-9619827-3-X	$9.95
The Adventurer's Guide to the Sierra Nevada Mountains – laminated wall, ISBN 0-9619827-4-8	$19.95

COMING IN 1996

Mountain Biking the Eastern Sierra's Best 100 Trails, ISBN 0-938665-42-1

Guide 9, San Gabriel Mountains: Angeles National Forest and North to Mt. Pinos, ISBN 0-938665-43-X

To order any of these items, see your local dealer or order direct from Fine Edge Productions. Please include $2.50 for shipping with check or money order. California residents add 7.25% tax.

Fine Edge Productions, Route 2, Box 303, Bishop, California 93514
PHone: 619-387-2412 / Fax: 619-387-2286